T0248025

The
Maurice
Burton
Way

The
Maurice
Burton
Way

Britain's
First Black
Cycling Champion

MAURICE BURTON & PAUL JONES

BLOOMSBURY SPORT

LONDON · OXFORD · NEW YORK · NEW DELHI · SYDNEY

BLOOMSBURY SPORT
Bloomsbury Publishing Plc
50 Bedford Square, London, WC1B 3DP, UK
29 Earlsfort Terrace, Dublin 2, Ireland

BLOOMSBURY, BLOOMSBURY SPORT and the Diana logo are trademarks of
Bloomsbury Publishing Plc

First published in Great Britain 2024

This edition published 2024

A catalogue record for this book is available from the British Library

Library of Congress Cataloguing-in-Publication data has been applied for

ISBN: HB: 978-1-3994-0739-7; ePUB: 978-1-3994-0738-0; ePDF: 978-1-3994-0737-3

2 4 6 8 10 9 7 5 3 1

Typeset in Minion Pro by Deanta Global Publishing Services, Chennai, India
Printed and bound in Great Britain by CPI Group (UK) Ltd, Croydon, CR0 4YY

To find out more about our authors and books visit www.bloomsbury.com
and sign up for our newsletters

For Bill Dodds

CONTENTS

1

De Ver Cycles

I pull out a photo. Maurice Burton is on his courier bike at Hyde Park corner. The year is 1986. There is snow on the ground and he's riding with panniers, full mudguards, and a Belgian winter hat. Just eighteen months earlier he had been at the Buenos Aires Six-Day race, tearing around the indoor track at 55kph.

He glances at the image with an easy familiarity, the kind of look that suggests there aren't any photos he hasn't seen, but then stops, his head moves back, a jerk of recognition – perhaps he doesn't recognise this photo after all. Maurice Burton reaches across, holds it in finger and thumb and looks afresh at this new artefact, unearthed in the evening sun of a South London beer garden, where we are surrounded by braying people watching rugby on a very big television. A fragment of time from forty years ago rolls on to the table, breaking against the present; everything about it says something. The bike sparks a story: the courier bag, the shiny overshoes, everything. We talk.

We spend the evening immersed in conversations about bike racing, looking at faded and creased photographs, monochrome pictures of Eddy Merckx – the 'cannibal', the greatest cyclist of them all – in among others, like Antipodean folk hero Danny Clark, known to those 'who know'. Famous names emerge alongside those that have long since disappeared into memory, only to reappear momentarily because of a question, a name, a place; suddenly here in the present again; the cast list in the story of Maurice Burton's life. The story moves around, from person to place and back again, this time across to Belgium.

The deceptively respectable Belgian town of Ghent becomes the centre of a radial wheel of place and memory, around which other places fall out of the fog of time and acquire solid shape through reminiscence: Paddington Recreation Ground, Antwerp, Herne Hill Velodrome, Saffron Lane, Aarhus, Milan, Meadowbank, Trinidad. We talk about the ramshackle wooden temporary cabins at the track, home for the riders during a six-day cycling event. Photos of riders on the big outdoor tracks sit on the table between us, I can hear the zip of tyres across concrete hitting the seam with a repetitive thwup; the surface glaring, a binary brightness when compared to photos of the dark, dense interior of the velodrome at Ghent – 't Kuipke, or 'little bowl' – a sensory overload of Siberian pine, cigarette smoke, greasy chips, Belgian drinking songs, the rolling Rs and harsh consonants of Flemish commentary, and the whirr of a fixed chain. In each photo, I can feel the formation of words that I know will land on the page.

Our meeting feels like a Madison, the demented, impenetrable track race where two riders circle, one racing while the other rests, only to switch places at a moment's notice. We are circling the track. Maurice hurtles around, stories flying off with centrifugal force, and then I'm thrown in, gathering them up, writing notes, trying to catch up, trying not to crash, to grab a hand-sling and get back into the fray.

We arrange to meet at 10 a.m. at his bike shop, De Ver Cycles. I ride across from Paddington, pleased to take in a short section of Cycleway 7, or 'The Maurice Burton Way', which has been informally named in his honour. I've never met anyone who has a cycleway named after them before. It is a belated recognition for this extraordinary pioneer of British cycling. I have written stories, biographical stuff, many times, but each has been within the linear scope of my existence. This is different. The opportunity to collaborate is exciting. There are challenges, there is diligence, all of that is to come. A sense of possibility hangs in the heavy London air as I ride south through the ceaseless chatter of the city.

De Ver Cycles is huge, independent, slightly chaotic. A yellow Victorian-fronted block with a grey-brick fascia, three shops wide and surrounded by newbuilds. It is on a busy street, a classic London combination of old and new, with the enormous frontage of De Ver standing incongruously on the main road. We are south of the river. From De Ver, the city sprawls southwards, on and on, rolling down until at some point it gives up, apologetically, and becomes the Surrey countryside. I used to ride this way on Sunday mornings, heading out with the Dulwich Paragon for lazy loops of Biggin Hill and Westerham. South London is the beating heart of metropolitan cycling culture, full of traditional clubs like the De Laune, Addiscombe and Norwood Paragon, alongside historic locations:

3

Herne Hill, Crystal Palace and now De Ver. South London is where Maurice's dad, Rennal Burton, ended up in 1950, travelling from Jamaica, via Avonmouth and a short stay in Bristol.

The shop is closed on Wednesdays. It is time to catch up, do some admin and ride bikes in the afternoon. His phone is ringing but Maurice ignores it. The late-summer sun is languid. Maurice unlocks the shop so we can go inside and talk. Bike shops are anachronistic, analogue places. They are places for browsing, lifting stuff off shelves, trying things on and not sending them back in a carefully pre-cut plastic envelope. This one has all the tactile warmth of the bike shop, but somehow feels different. On the wall are framed jerseys with the national colours striped across the middle. Magazine covers, articles, press clippings compete for space amid the familiar logos of the bike trade. An archive of material sits in the back office; more magazines, faded and yellowing, next to logbooks marked with ribbons, some with pages open, handwritten notes, a sketch of a flattened oval with distance, time and speed marked out around the edge.

The workshop space is huge, but the tools of the trade are becoming obsolete. The wheel truing stand, state of the art in its day, sits silently on the floor, not called upon anymore because wheels come from the factory and when they wear out, new wheels are bought. This is in keeping with both our disposable habits and the constant imperative of the bike industry to sell you new stuff that is better than the old stuff. Lots of gleaming bikes are crowded into the front of the shop, even though there is a national shortage of bikes. This is because Maurice is canny and he buys his stock far in advance from manufacturers he has known for decades; thirty-five years of contacts come in handy. Gun-metal grey and shark grey, matt grey, these are the current colours, the colours you see on shiny new cars, colours that absorb colour: more matt than matt. A sultry Colnago sulks in the corner and I wish it were mine.

Maurice Burton's phone rings again. Out the back lurks an additional space, another large shop floor, more storage. We inhabit a corner, perch on a sofa and talk. He hasn't eaten yet today. This makes me nervous; I know that when I haven't eaten, I can go from zero to angry in around three seconds. Last night, Maurice was at a book launch in central London, catching up with old friends and rivals over a pint at the pub next door, sharing stories from championships and meetings from long ago. Races were analysed again, forty years later but it feels like yesterday, who beat who, who did the dirty, why the win wasn't a win, or why it was. Scores can never be settled but they are laughed about, bonded over, for the most part; the glue that joins competitors together, they are no longer racing but the race remains everything, life the metaphor.

Maurice drinks camomile tea. I am surprised by this. He makes me a camomile tea. I shuffle my notes, find the questions, set out the recorder. He looks around the room, pauses, sips his tea. His movements are steady, deliberate, possessed by a preternatural calm. He looks across the table, makes eye contact and says, 'With other people it was constant, a steady thing. With me, everything I've had I had to fight for.'

2

Peckham

'Have you heard of the Maroons?' asks Maurice.

I *have* heard of the Maroons, because of a John Agard poem called 'Checking Out Me History', which I teach to Year 11 students. In the poem, Agard lists the people he was never told about at school: Toussaint Louverture, Mary Seacole and Nanny Maroon. He is one of the few non-White British writers to escape the government's curriculum purge of 2010. John Agard's poem says something to me, but much more to many others in search of a past that they are not told about.

I read a bit deeper. Nanny Maroon is perhaps the most famous of the Maroons. They were autonomous communities of free Black people, hence the etymology; the word 'Maroon' derives from the Spanish *cimarrón*, meaning 'fierce' or 'unruly'. The origins of the Jamaican Maroon community can be traced to the English invasion of 1655. When the Spanish colonists fled, slaves, free Blacks and former slaves, along with some native Taíno, banded together into ethnically diverse groups in the mountainous interior. The Maroon population grew over time and fought a campaign of insurgence and several wars against the English colonisers. Maurice's father, Rennal, and uncle, Egerton, were Maroon (they grew up in Portland, Jamaica), and Maurice Burton is proud of his heritage, the deep and intense spirit of resistance. 'It's Moore Town, home of the Nanny of the Maroons. My grandmother was called Crawford and they were Maroon. They originally came from Ashanti, from Ghana.' The surname 'Crawford' resonates; Crawford's Town was a key Maroon settlement after the First Maroon War, named after rebel leader, Edward Crawford.

For Rennal and Egerton, things were difficult. Their mother died when Rennal was four years old; their father 'was off doing other things, they didn't have a strong relationship with him.' In the absence of close family ties, the pull of elsewhere proved strong. By the time both were able to work, the prospect of employment in Jamaica was remote. So, they enlisted in the US Farm Worker Program. Seventy thousand Jamaicans, Barbadians and Bermudians were recruited from 1943 to 1947 as a result of the wartime labour shortage. Neither of the brothers had left the island before. It was an entirely new experience, compounded by the social context of the Southern states, as Maurice explains:

> Being Jamaican, their mentality was different from the Black Americans. For example, they went into a bar and when they came out there was a Black American outside, full of surprise. 'Man you went in *that* bar?' They didn't care. The White people had to be careful because these guys were there with the government, it was a different situation. Eddie [Egerton] told about this time they needed cigarettes, and so he walked a couple of miles down to this kiosk. The guy wouldn't handle the money from a Black man, he gave him the cigarettes but then just closed it down, so Eddie didn't have to pay. Of course, he told everyone how he went to the place and got given cigarettes, so they all went down there. The guy saw them coming and just closed the whole place down. It was quite an experience, they got away with things the locals couldn't, but it was an experience they hadn't had before. Living in Jamaica, they hadn't come across that kind of thing.

His phone rings again. It rings even when not ringing. I can see the screen light up, seeking attention, the needy 'vrrrrr' sound as it shakes on the sofa. Maurice Burton is a very busy man. The shop is not open today but the phone still rings.

With the end of the war, the brothers returned to Jamaica. Once they'd been away, Jamaica seemed smaller, more parochial. With the end of the Farm Worker Program, Egerton headed to the UK, with Rennal following shortly after, on the SS *Bayano*, an Elders & Fyffes banana boat carrying seventy passengers and 1750 tonnes of bananas on each run. He disembarked at Avonmouth on 3 August 1948, five weeks after the arrival of the HMT *Empire Windrush*. While the *Windrush* is seen as the symbolic starting point for contemporary multicultural Britain, at least in the popular imagination, the ship also serves as a metonym for arrival into the UK at that time, via Bristol and elsewhere, and the starting point for the contemporary West Indian community in the UK. The immediate effects in the late 1940s were profound, with families upended as parents moved 4000 miles away in a rapid displacement. This rippled outwards, down through the generations, with children and grandchildren experiencing the echoes of seismic change. As second-generation 'Windrush', Maurice's life and story is shaped by the effects of migration, time and geography.

Rennal disembarked from tropical sun on the other side of the ocean to a UK 'summer', lurching seamlessly into the asphalt grey of winter and constant dark. Maurice remembers a lingering antipathy towards the UK weather: 'Dad hated the cold and everything that went with it,' a feeling echoed by writer Jools Walker, recalling her mother's account of arriving in London: 'She came over in British summer and to her it was absolutely freezing. Add to that the black smoke and smog, everything just felt like it was covered in thick nasty fog. It's a culture-shock, literally the shock of the cold.'[1]

Rennal got a job in Bristol as a carpenter with his younger brother, Egerton. They did not stay long. Within a year, Egerton moved to London, and again Rennal followed, this time settling in Brixton where 'at that time, there were only about two Black people living

---

[1] Jools Walker's book, *Back in the Frame* (Sphere, 2020), is a lovely memoir about cycling, but also much more than that: 'an alternative to all that noise that tells us what cycling is and isn't.'

there.' Maurice identifies with Uncle Eddie, with whom he shares a temperament.

> He didn't suffer fools gladly. I remember a funeral once, he was looking for a family friend, Stella. He asked this bloke, who didn't know where she was, so he just went off on the guy outside the church, looking at him, saying, 'WELL WHERE IS SHE?' and the guy said nothing. He says, 'I'm asking you a QUESTION. Well what kind of a fuckin' IDIOT are you?' Eddie was like that, he just didn't give a fuck. He wasn't big, you just didn't mess with him.

Eddie was a skilled tailor, and before long Rennal joined him in the garment industry, becoming a presser. It's a physical and highly skilled trade. He would press new suits and fashion wear, preparing for sale, but also for big events. He worked 'up west':

> The last job he did was for Jean Muir [a fashion designer]. He used to come home and there'd be a picture of Princess Diana or Margaret Thatcher in the newspaper and it was him who actually prepared the dress, he'd been the one, sorting what they were wearing. He was good at his job and that's what he did all his life, always in high fashion places.

In Farringdon, Rennal met Gracie Spires, a seamstress and machinist at the same company. Gracie was born in Camberwell. Her father, Edgar, was born in Camberwell and her mother was born in Walworth; a longstanding lineage in South East London. The wedding photo has the two branches of the families together on the steps of the church, with Rennal and Eddie at the centre; the pressing immaculate; trouser length absolutely perfect, just the kick at the bottom; lapels big and sharp. On the far right, Eddie's wife, Renee, with Rennal and then Gracie alongside her mother (also, confusingly, called Gracie). Gracie and her mother moved in with Rennal, who by that point had bought his first house. Financial discrimination was a defining feature of the colour bar in the 1950s and 1960s,

9

and many 'Windrush' arrivals used the pardner system (a pooled savings scheme) as a means to circumvent racist financial lenders. It was a way of raising money for a deposit to buy a house or other expensive items in a world where bank managers routinely refused mortgages or advised the applicant to go back to Jamaica.

In simple terms, everyone in the pardner hands over a set amount each week or month. This is the 'hand' and the organiser is 'the banker'. At the end of the week or month, the banker hands over all the contributions, 'the draw', to the member whose turn it is. It continues in this way until everyone is paid. It provided the means to raise a deposit for a house, to escape the real dangers of tenanted accommodation or the challenges in finding somewhere to rent – or someone to rent *to* you – in the first place

Rennal Burton was one of the few who managed to obtain a high-interest mortgage for his first house in Denman Road, Peckham.

'Dad's first house was about £900. It was a three-storey building, we'd live on the ground floor and he'd rent out all the rooms above, which helped towards the mortgage. Dad helped people with the pardner system, in that situation, when they were unable to get money from the bank.' It equates to £21,000 in today's money, but this makes no sense in terms of contemporary London prices. A terrace on Denman Road in 2022 sold for £1.1 million.

The family, with Maurice born in 1955, were happy in Peckham, even if Rennal was not entirely comfortable living with his mother-in-law.

He [Rennal] wasn't a bad guy, but now and again, he didn't come home from work straight away, maybe went to the pub. He wasn't what they expected a British husband might have been. Dad told me how it used to be among English people, in those days – the brown envelopes with the wages in, a lot of men had to give them to the wife unopened. Well, my dad wasn't into that sort of thing, you know, hehehe, his money was his money. So he bought another house two roads along, he moved into that one, said to Mum, 'You can stay with your mother in that one or come with me,' and she decided to go with him. We moved to Bushey Hill Road, opposite the Art College, and we lived there until 1964.

Wider experiences of mixed-race marriages were traumatic, for both Black and White people, who faced social ostracism, exclusion from the family and a severing of ties. *Picture Post*, a popular weekly magazine, ran a cover story in 1954 with the heading: 'Would you let your daughter marry a negro?' The writer Trevor Philpott goes on to somehow critique racism *and* fan the flames by pandering to contemporary anxieties, chiefly around mixed-race marriages. First-hand accounts of weddings with no family members attending, mixed-race couples being stared at on buses, or worse, appear throughout Colin Grant's *Homecoming*, an oral history of the Windrush generation and their experiences in the UK.

The contemporary rhetoric within communities and in the press, on the airwaves, on television, was deeply troubling and harmful, apocalyptic fears of infiltration and miscegenation appeared in the popular press and on the radio. Those brave enough to speak out faced intense, racist, populist retaliation, including hate mail, racist graffiti on doors. Language fomented in the pages of the *Daily Mail* spoke of the 'flood' and the 'door still open', some of it horribly similar to contemporary comments, citing 'the invasion on our southern coast', undermining our claims to live in a more enlightened, welcoming society.

Maurice's parents' experience was typical of the time. He speaks with characteristic understatement: 'It was difficult, they didn't find it easy. I can tell you that there were very few relatives in contact from Gracie's side. They didn't approve. It wasn't easy for my mum at all. Most of the relatives that I know are from my father's side.'

12

Within the immediate family context, a close network was centred around Rennal and Eddie, with an extended group including Dexter, Maurice's close family friend, and Uncle Joe. Their names crop up throughout the conversations – lodestars, influences on Maurice, the source of stories and family myth. They became a tight-knit group. Dexter's family were in North London. They spent time together, went away on holidays to Clacton-on-Sea.

When we grew up, it was me and Dexter, we were like brothers more than anything else. We didn't really know people, not as family, friends, anyone who had both parents who were White, we didn't know them, no. We never really saw anything of my mum's side of the family. All the people I grew up around were Black people.

There was an additional layer of complexity within the burgeoning West Indian community and diaspora, as it expanded rapidly within a space of fifteen years. Families were separated by migration, with mostly men travelling across for work. On occasion this led to a reshaping of family identities in surprising ways. As was the case for many others, Rennal Burton's past in Jamaica appeared in Bushey Hill Road in 1957.

> I was about two years old when I got a brother who was not from my mum. Norbert was born and grew up in Jamaica. His mum wrote to my dad and said he was out of control, so dad sent for him and brought him over here. I don't remember how much news my dad had given my mum that he was even coming.
>
> My dad came down heavy on him as well. I remember my brother borrowed somebody's bike and he had an accident and Dad had to pay for it and he wasn't too happy. My brother was down Choumert Road in Peckham, had a bike with him, saw my dad in the distance and he just dropped the bike, left it there and RAN.

The image of Norbert legging it from Dad provokes a full-bodied laugh from Maurice. The memories are startling, vivid, funny, the sight of Rennal, a glimpse, then every teenage boy's utter terror at the wrath of an angry father, running away to escape a beating. But you can't run forever, you have to go home at some point.

Our conversation circles around his childhood, and Maurice's experiences at primary school, where he was singled out:

> My voice was a bit deeper than the others. When we used to sing hymns in the morning, the headmistress made me stand by the piano. She said, 'You're a groaner,' they didn't find it acceptable, my voice, the way I sang. From an early age, I was made to feel different from other people. They did a school play and my part was a piece of coal. They got a thing and they covered me and I was a piece of coal. Can you imagine? My mum went to watch me in the school play and I was a piece of coal.

The experience was repeated in the immediate neighbourhood. Most of the kids Maurice played with were White.

It was always a problem for me to knock on their doors. The parents didn't like it. I was six, maybe seven years old. My friends had to come out to the street and meet me there. It was just what we did. On one occasion I went up the end of the road where we lived, it was slightly uphill, there were adults sitting there, and three kids playing. They came over and started beating me up. They were hitting me on the floor. While they were doing this to me, I saw the parents, the men, just sitting there. I thought, don't they know that it's wrong, that they can't do that? But they just let 'em do it. I looked at them and I thought, Why don't you stop them from doing it? But they watched and they did nothing. That's the point when I realised the difference between me and them; when I was seven years old. I knew then that things weren't the same for me as they were for other people. Things were going to be different for me in life.

3

Burbage Road

In 1969, cycling in Britain was pretty much a Masonic sect. Clubs were invisible, parochial organisations that had significant importance to their members, but were effectively closed to the wider community. It is a paradox of sorts. Cycling clubs (CCs) celebrate fellowship, often explicitly, via mottos, embossed trophies and crests, the trinkets of the cycling movement. They are rooted in working-class traditions and the leisure movement. Historically, they provide solace, escapism and inclusivity to particular people at a particular time. And yet membership requires a degree of esoteric knowledge, being 'put up', seconded, agreed at the committee meeting. A part of the attraction was the sense of being within, speaking a coded language of componentry, shared knowledge of cyclist-friendly cafes known to cater to the club run, of cycling 'special' rail services with whole carriages dedicated to touring cyclists heading out into the countryside from the city, or even weekend visits to 'the huts', a collection of bungalows and lean-tos on Northall Road in Essex owned by East London clubs. Groups would ride out to the club's designated hut for a weekend of racing and riding, sharing the cooking duties or heading to the local pub. The Crest CC hut was known as Stag Hall, and regulars recall fondly how it 'smelt like a youth hostel and was full of mice.' Ultimately, the social, cultural and demographic change brought about by mass-ownership of the motor car did for the special train services, the huts and, to some extent, the altruistic idea of club-life.

Outside of the familial, closeted membership of cycling clubs, there were occasional glimpses of a different representation of cycling. Olympian Clyde Rimple from Trinidad made the front cover of popular cycling magazine *Coureur* in 1955 and was a regular at the Reading track. The Trinidadian track team came over in the late 1960s and early 1970s; they rode regularly at Herne Hill and Paddington. Similarly, Xavier Mirander and others from the Jamaican Olympic team were brought over by Welsh coach Ted Gray to ride in the UK in the early 1970s, but there were very few, if any, visible Black riders.

For most people, cycling was a utility activity, a means of getting to work, or leisure insofar as children like to ride around the neighbourhood on clunkers. Maurice did just that, pelting around the streets with friends.

> I used to ride with Dexter [and] Tony Fife and Alphonse Nicholas, two Black guys we knew quite well who were older than us, we were friends, a group. We'd ride out, go to places on the bike, meet up on Blackfriars. I had a bike I got from a boy who did a paper round. It cost 2 shillings and sixpence, this Dawes with Cyclo Benelux gears which didn't work that well. Then I saw a Young's bike in a garden. The forks were bent but I managed to sort it all out. I'm quite mechanically minded, I can look at it and figure out how it works, then fix it.
>
> We used to go to Herne Hill. I'd been there with them and seen the track, we just looked at it, rode around the site, didn't ride on the track or anything like that. They had done it though and told me how they gave you the proper track bikes and all that, it was a glimpse of what went on there.

They would have glimpsed a 450m oval with banked concrete turns, seen riders accelerating down off the banking, reckless, death-defying overtakes, the horrid metallic noise of crashes, elbows-out sprint finishes and endurance efforts with everything in between; an exhilarating sight. Herne Hill at the time was the home of track cycling in Britain, the host venue for cycling at the 1948 Olympics and a centre point for cycling culture across the capital. Every year the Good

Friday Meeting brought together elite riders from across the country and further afield.

While track cycling, and racing at Herne Hill specifically, has broadened its appeal over the years and is striving for greater diversity, it is also clear that like most cycling clubs, historically it served a small subsection of the wider community, and that subsection was predominantly White and male. Once you're in, it feels joyous to become a part of, but it can be an exclusive and difficult world to break into. In the absence of any kind of outreach, it is almost impossible to get into cycling unless someone else shows you the way. Many people have stories of clubs they didn't join because they turned up and no one spoke to them. I didn't join the Severn Road Club because they didn't wait for me on the way back into Bristol and I got lost and bonked. Rewind fifty years and it was even more challenging for a young Black cyclist with no connections.

> I knew I wanted to go to Herne Hill, I'd even been to Young's Cycles in Lewisham and bought some cycling shoes. But it wasn't a case of 'Let's see what happens,' because I didn't know *how* to. I joined the Cycle Touring Club[1] because that was the only thing I knew. I didn't know about the De Laune, any of the clubs, how to join these clubs, there was no information. How would you know? Right enough maybe you could look it up in a phone book or something, but, unless you knew someone or actually turned up at a race and spoke to people then you wouldn't know. I didn't know.

For Maurice, it wasn't the track or clubs that made it accessible, or even the efforts by a committed bunch of cycling-evangelists. It was the Inner London Education Authority (ILEA). Someone at the ILEA headquarters in the mid-1960s decided to put cycling on the sports curriculum for South London secondary schools. I wonder if it was a calculated effort, maybe someone at City Hall *really* cared about cycling, or perhaps it was just an awareness that there was a nearby

---

[1] A national organisation with a high profile, focused on touring, long rides, youth hostels and camping stoves.

velodrome and a Wednesday afternoon-sized gap in the timetable that needed filling. Either way, it was a prescient decision that demonstrates the life-changing potential and importance of community facilities.

I was at Roger Manwood school. We'd do sports one afternoon a week – football, rugby or hockey – and then in the summer you could choose athletics, cricket, tennis maybe. You had to be fourteen or over to do the cycling, so it wasn't until late September 1970 when I first went to Herne Hill.

The first time, we didn't ride on the track, we had to go up into the grandstand and Bill Dodds went through everything with us first, told us how it worked, what to do, the rules, everything else. But one thing stood out in my mind. He said, 'From here, you can go to the Olympic Games.' When I heard that, I thought, This is the place that I need to be. The next week for the very first time, we had a little race. I came second, I went too early, with a whole lap to go, and somebody just got past me. It was a whole lap, over 400m, sprinting flat out for all that time. I didn't know it was too early. That was the last time I lost a race with the school.

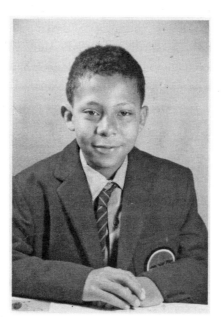

Bill Dodds and Sean Purcell had established Velo Club Londres at Herne Hill in 1964 with the aim of encouraging young riders into cycling. Timing is everything, and it aligned perfectly with the ILEA Cycling Education Centre. Purcell and Dodds became full-time coaches to the programme. Later they were joined by Bob Addy, John Clarey and Mike Armstrong. It was Dodds in particular who became an important figure for the young Maurice Burton.

> He was like a second father to me. He wasn't just a cycling coach, he was approachable. I didn't really have that deep relationship with my dad, not at that stage in my life; if I said the wrong thing it wasn't good.
>
> Bill was from a different environment and different people. I could sit down and talk and ask him anything I wanted, tell him anything, if there was ever a problem I could go and talk to Bill. Sometimes, in the school holidays I'd ride to where he lived and I'd spend the whole day there talking to him about things, I was quite close to him in that respect.

There was also a more pragmatic reason why track cycling appealed, compared with the road. Schoolboys couldn't race on the open road at that point, and the closed traffic-free circuits – old airfields mostly – were dotted all over the place, creating a practical obstacle.

> First, you have to get to the race. How am I going to get to the race? I couldn't imagine my dad taking me to a race, *hahahah*, and even if he did it definitely wouldn't be something he'd want to do every weekend. It wasn't going to happen.
>
> I remember riding [an open road race] once when I was a junior, it was in Hoo, near Medway. It pissed down with rain the whole day. Two guys got away in a break, I came third, and I won a cigarette lighter. I thought, Well, this is a lot of work for a cigarette lighter!

Compare that with the last race I did at Paddington track in 1976. I rode three races; won two and was second in the other one. I won £56 – that was more than a week's work for a lot of people. There's a big difference between £56 and a cigarette lighter.

In 1971, Maurice went along to see the Good Friday Meeting at Herne Hill. Outside of the nationals, it was the biggest event in the track calendar, a packed programme of racing with international stars competing. It kick-started the season, the classic curtain-raiser for the track leagues, featuring any number of different disciplines, from the *you-blink-you-lose* madness of the match sprint to the simplicity of the 20km scratch race where first across the line wins.

While walking around and watching the racing, Maurice picked up a copy of *International Cycle Sport*[2] from one of the stalls. The same magazine sits on his office desk at De Ver, fifty-two years later. He grabs it and brandishes it at me, a totem, a mythical item of real significance. It is full of images of the European track scene: vivid, startling stuff with all the emotive power of memory and the past. But in 1971, it had the force of the present.

> This was the first magazine I bought and it is so important to me. There is a picture of Roger De Vlaeminck on the front. There is Eddy Merckx. Then this is the Antwerp Six, with Peter Post, and this is Gust Naessens, and the title 'Sercu and Son', that was the first time I came across Patrick Sercu and his father Albert. These were people who I would later meet and work with. But at that time I didn't know what this was or who they were. All I knew was I wanted to be in *that* cabin, riding *that* circuit. It was my first real awareness of this bigger world of track cycling. I just looked at the magazine and I thought, *This* is where I'm going.

A universe expanded outwards from the pages of the magazine – consisting of indoor tracks, Belgian cycling dynasties, trackside cabins and soigneurs, deafening music and beer and vertiginous banked tracks, races that lasted for six days, riders competing until 3 a.m., sometimes later, every night for a week, a cascading and intoxicating world, fully formed. Everything changed in a moment; there was track cycling, there was Herne Hill, but suddenly here, now, was the Continent, the six-day circuit, Ghent, Antwerp, Rotterdam, Berlin, Munich, Milan, a tantalising prospect, a projected future, an aspiration.

---

[2] An influential and very lovely cycling magazine led by Jock Wadley that ran from 1968 to 1984, emerging from the ashes of *Coureur*.

From 1972 onwards, Maurice raced regularly as a junior at Herne Hill, with occasional visits to the Paddington track, riding across the city on a geared bike, pushing a borrowed VC Londres track bike alongside. He became a fixture in the junior track league and moved up the rankings rapidly. Herne Hill was an important track, but for a brief period of time the 'national' velodrome was Saffron Lane in Leicester. It opened in 1968 and hosted the World Championships in 1970. At 333m, it was shorter than Herne Hill, and tighter, with steep bankings that plunged abruptly down into the compressed straights, their concrete surface painted white. It was 'awkward, anachronistic and open to the vagaries of the weather',[3] and while imperfect, it was as close to a world-class track as you could get in Britain in 1968. There is glorious footage of races dotted around the internet from throughout the thirty-year lifespan. My favourite is a tandem sprint event featuring a track stand, followed by aggressive racing, a collision and a desperate struggle to bring in a wobbling, mortally wounded tandem without serious injury to the pilot or stoker. It feels like a scene from a war film, a stricken bomber jet coming in to land at an unseemly angle, the crowd hushed in nervous terror, bodies flying everywhere.

Saffron Lane was the location for the National Championships each year, including the juniors, which was the next step in Maurice's cycling development. The idea that young riders would be supported, perhaps through some nascent development pathway, was a long way off in 1972. Maurice didn't even have a track bike of his own, so borrowed one of the council bikes from Herne Hill. They were old frames made by Young's of Lewisham, with cotter pins hammered into the crank arm to keep it in place. Having got the train to Leicester, Maurice rode the junior sprint heats and came fourth, missing out on the final, before winning the junior

---

[3] www.cyclingweekly.com/news/latest-news/icons-of-cycling-leicester-velodrome-194716

devil-takes-the-hindmost, a race where the last rider in the bunch is eliminated each lap. He featured for the first time in the magazine *Cycling Weekly*, a brief report on his first national title. The 'Devil' format has seen a resurgence since featuring in the rejigged Olympic omnium and is great to watch. It bunches up like a ragged accordion as everyone scrambles to avoid the cut. The experience was Damascene: his first time riding outside of London, the intense crowd of the nationals, an overwhelming sense of spectacle. It made a lasting impact: 'I was determined that I was coming back next year.'

Away from Herne Hill, Maurice would sometimes head to the other big London track at the Paddington Recreation Ground, riding the senior races and track leagues. One of the dominant young riders at Paddington was Steve Heffernan. He raced against Maurice regularly, and the two formed a slightly uneasy friendship, forged through rivalry and a shared sense of being outsiders. They sometimes travelled together to Leicester and beyond in order to compete. At Paddington, both riders came across Danny Clark for the first time. Clark was one of a group of Antipodeans who had moved to Europe and were hoping to turn professional and ride the six-day circuit.

It was a distance race and me and Heff were sprinting for the win, side by side, and it was me or him, we knew one of us was going to win. All of a sudden, somebody just went *whooooosshh* past us, and Heff looked at me and I looked at Heff, and I thought, *What the...?* Because *nobody* could do that, I mean they might have beaten us, but nobody from round our way could do that to *us*. We just thought, Well who the bloody hell was that? And it was Danny Clark, with his silver medal in his pocket from the kilo at the Munich Olympics, and I'll tell you the truth, and I'll say it in front of Danny, he's the only guy I've never got the better of. I met this guy in Lanzarote last year who was in the same race, he remembered it like it was yesterday as well. This guy was behind us, ahead of Danny when he started to wind it up. Danny needed to get through and said something but this guy didn't really hear him. The next thing he heard Danny shout out, 'For fuck's sake mate, will you get out of the *fucking* way!' and he came through, then over the top of all of us like a motorbike.

The next milestone was a track weekend at Calshot, run by the English Schools Cycling Association (ESCA), consisting of a series of coached sessions for the next wave of potential elite riders. Maurice persuaded Joe Clovis, another young Black rider from the Herne Hill group and VC Londres, to come along. Calshot is a tiny track, at 142m long with 45-degree bankings, 300m shorter than Herne Hill. It is an indoor track, with a superficial resemblance to the covered Continental six-day tracks, including 't Kuipke in Ghent. It sits at the end of a narrow finger of land near Southampton, reaching out into the Solent (which makes sense in terms of the building's original function as an aircraft hangar for enormous flying boats). Maurice was motivated by a burgeoning sense of determination and desire, to make it as a bike rider, to visit the indoor tracks and to chalk up experience, but the issue was getting to Calshot in the first place.

We had to get down there with a track bike *and* a road bike *and* you needed spare wheels, all of your stuff. On the Friday I got together with Joe, we said to our parents, 'We're going somewhere.' How they just let us go I don't know, but that was how it was. It was raining and I had on my suit, because that was how professionals turned up at races, so that's how I did it. I don't know if Joe had his suit on, but we both had our track bikes. I was riding the road bike while pushing the track bike, with a bag strapped to the track bike and two spare wheels on the outside of that.

We rode from Forest Hill in the rain, past the Horniman Museum, down into Victoria to get the train. When we got to Southampton it was dark and we only had one set of lights between us, I had the front and Joe had the back. How in the hell we found the place I don't know. The next day, we started on the track with the novices and one of the instructors saw us straight away and we got put into the elite group.

Along with the track drills, there were talks and film screenings. One cine reel featured the 1965 Russian World Sprint Champion, Omar Pkhakadze. It struck a chord with both Maurice and Joe Clovis; not because of his riding, but because of what happened when he crashed:

> He got up as if it was nothing. And the truth is, I fell off that day. The film was in my mind. I didn't care, I got back up, carried on riding, I didn't have the fear. Joe was the same. Sometimes people looked at me as though I was a bit dangerous. When you think about it, I just did whatever it takes: this is what I'm going to do, I'm going from here to there, and no matter what I have to do, I'm going to get there. That's what we did that weekend, and it worked out.

4

Saffron Lane

Over the winter of 1972 and into 1973, Maurice worked closely with Bill Dodds, drawing up a comprehensive training programme based around the track dimensions and demands of Herne Hill. He drew a diagram of the circuit with sections marked off to correspond to pyramid efforts; start with a short sprint, rest, go into a longer sprint, rest, then build up until you're sprinting for the whole lap, then reverse the process. It's simple, savage and effective. There were three targets in 1973: the Good Friday Meeting, the European Junior Championships, and the National Championships back at Saffron Lane in Leicester.

The Good Friday Meeting at Herne Hill kicked things off. It attracted the biggest stars of the day, certainly in terms of track racing. None came bigger than Frenchman Daniel Morelon, the reigning (multiple) Olympic sprint champion. He won the World Championship sprint five times and would go on to win later that year in San Sebastián. There was quite a bit of hero worship from Maurice. Also lining up was the Australian John Nicholson, the silver medallist in Munich.

The prestige event for newer riders on Good Friday was the White Hope Sprint and it was Maurice's first time in the race. The name of the race seems to stem from the idea of an up-and-coming challenger, a new rider taking on the establishment. 'The Great White Hope' was a phrase coined by Jack London, writing about the 'hope' that a White boxer might defeat Jack Johnson, thus reasserting a form of racial supremacy at the turn of the century. In the race, Maurice made an error:

> My chainrings were a bit worn, the label for the number of teeth had worn away. I thought I had 48:15 on there – an 88in,[1] but my legs were spinning like hell, and I made the final and I lost it by half a wheel, we were all in a line. A few days later when I was looking for the 46in and I couldn't find it I realised I had the wrong chainring, it was an 82in. If I had the right gear on, I think I would have won it, I mean I had the wrong gear on and I still made the final!

The next step was selection for the European Junior Championships in June 1973, which meant riding at Leicester under the eye of the national coaches, including British Cycling Federation (BCF) boss Norman Sheil.[2] Along with Bill Dodds, Sheil became a formative influence on Maurice. Getting to Saffron Lane involved another schlep across London, getting the train with a track bike, spare wheels and kit, before walking from the station to the velodrome.

> I got on the track, got going, and Norman Sheil was watching. His eyes popped out of his head. Norman could see I was good. He was behind me from that point onwards. He even gave me my first pair of trainers. I always remember him saying, 'Let your legs do the talking.' That was the point when things started to happen. Norman sent me on to Lilleshall, the national training centre. The School

---

[1]Primer: the bigger the gear, the harder it is to pedal. It's measured in inches and equates to the distance the bike travels for one complete turn of the pedals. The front chainring and rear cog is in a ratio, with the chainring being much bigger and the cog smaller, hence 48:15. However, the smaller the chainring, the lighter the gear, whereas the smaller the rear cog, the heavier the gear. Finding the right gear for the right race is part of the fun.

[2]Norman Sheil was an early pioneer in British Cycling, winning two Commonwealth golds on the track and two World Championships. He also rode the Tour de France in 1960. He was head coach at British Cycling and established the ESCA.

PTA gave me £10 towards the trip, bearing in mind my first job was £9.50 a week. They were proud that I was on the national team.

The Irish team were there as well, including Sean Kelly, he was a character, even back then. I always remember, even though we were track riders, we had to ride on the road up there. We did this thing on the Wrekin, a 60-mile route. On the way back I jumped on to a truck as it came past,[3] followed it up to Lilleshall and when we got back, I was on my own, I'd left the whole damn lot of 'em behind.

It augured well for the European Championships at the Munich Radstadion Velodrome,[4] but like the White Hope Sprint before, expectation failed to marry up with reality. Maurice puts it down to wider issues. For instance, he had a bigger chainring for the event, which he had bought himself; there was still no support from the Federation for equipment. The new chainring made a horrible noise. Changing the chain would have solved the issue, but the mechanics instead tried filing the teeth on the chainring, which didn't work.

In the sprint, I came up against a Russian and he didn't look like a boy, he looked like a man. It didn't go well either. I was also riding in the points race, the distance was more my thing anyway, I made it into the final, using some wheels from Mike Armstrong, one of the coaches at Herne Hill who had ridden the amateur sixes [six-day events] in West Germany, he was an accomplished rider. When I got out of the saddle the tyres came off both wheels.

[3] Not literally; he got very close and drafted the lorry, catching the slipstream. Finding a lorry or bus travelling at 35–40mph on a long stretch of flat road is about the most exhilarating thing you can do on a bike. Just don't tell anyone about it afterwards.

[4] The Radstadion was one of the first of the newer indoor velodromes; purpose-built for the 1972 Olympics and a part of the spectacular Olympic Park on the edge of the city, built (literally) from the ruins of the Second World War. The 56m-high Olympiaberg overlooking the city is a *Trümmerberg* or rubble-hill. The velodrome was razed in 2015.

Afterwards they asked me if I was using shellac.[5] They said the wheels weren't prepared properly. How can you tell a seventeen-year-old boy to get those wheels ready? It's the mechanic's job. All I know is that the bloody tyres came off, and that was the end of my experience. I can't say I would have won but I made it to the final and that's what happened.

Sprint tyres used on the track are glued on. It's a messy business. If not secured properly, a tubular tyre can unseat, just roll off the rim, typically when cornering. It isn't a very nice experience, putting it mildly. Maurice gets a bit cross when I ask if this is what happened. We have been chatting for quite a while now and I remember he hasn't eaten. He might be hungry, or he might still be annoyed at the tyres. I don't ask a follow-up question. His experience with the technical side of things, the support from the Federation and the mechanics was thrown into sharp relief when looking around at the other teams, especially the Belgians.

Jean-Luc Vandenbroucke was the star of the championships, he won the pursuit, but I was watching the grey-haired man who carried his bike for him, Germain Martens. The way the Belgians did things compared with our lot was a different thing altogether. Some of these guys had a camera round their neck. Don't forget, they weren't paid, it was like a flippin' holiday. What happened to me could *never* have happened to the Belgian team. I saw all of this and I thought, these people know what they are doing. Germain never went to the six-days, he was the Belgian national mechanic,

[5]Using shellac to glue tyres is seriously old school. First, you order de-waxed shellac flakes. You then need to mix these with denatured alcohol to make a thick mixture. Next, create a separate thin mixture with a bit more of the alcohol. Paint a layer on to the rim with the thick stuff, allowing two days' drying time between each layer. Sometime later, when it is built up and dry, add the thin stuff on top and mount the tyre. Wait forty-eight hours minimum, then you can race. Theoretically, if you need to change a tyre, the thin 'bed' of shellac is all that needs re-coating. Easy.

he used to work in Dossche Sport[6] along with Marcel Rijkards, the Molteni mechanic, for Eddy Merckx, in Ghent. I named my son after him. Years later, I'd go into the shop and ask him how it was in the World Championships, and he couldn't tell me because he was working. They paid him the same money he got when working at Dossche, they just paid him to do the job and he did it. Years later, when I didn't have a full-time mechanic in the sixes, Germain prepared my wheels. He became the one that looked after my bikes.

Maurice Burton wasn't the first person to experience issues with the British Cycling Federation, and he won't be the last; this is the nature of professional sport. The question is whether white riders were experiencing similar, persistent problems. The evidence suggests they weren't.

Throughout 1973, Burton was committed to being a sprinter, he wanted to emulate his idol, Frenchman Daniel Morelon. The National Track Championships took place at the end of July at Saffron Lane. True to his word, Maurice returned, with his main target being the junior sprint title, but he also entered the senior events for experience. He backed himself to win the junior championship, and he did. A short article in *Cycling Weekly* covered the event: '[carrying] the leftover form of the European Championships in Munich, coloured VC Londres rider Maurice Burton won the junior sprint after "warming up" in the seniors championship'. Race is the defining characteristic for Maurice, but also for 'Burton's coloured clubmate Joe Clovis', who came fourth in the sprint. The difference is highlighted in every report.

For Maurice, away from the track, things were changing. He'd left school in the summer and was looking for work. In a contemporary interview with the cycling press, Maurice was clear about his ambition: 'what I need now are the rides abroad, international experience,

---

[6]Dossche Sport is still open in Ghent and is an integral part of Belgian cycling culture and history.

it's completely different over there … even though I'm the national champion, I've got a lot to learn.' The heading is peculiar: 'They've Gone for a Burton!' A quick Google suggests it is wartime RAF slang, meaning 'gone missing, died'. I remain confused.

The off-season meant more miles, more training, often long hours behind a motorbike ridden by Bill Dodds, aimed at both speed and endurance. The Commonwealth Games were in New Zealand in early January 1974, and Maurice's selection came 'out of the blue' but was a statement of belief from Norman Sheil. The minor issue was full-time work, the challenge of choosing a career that wasn't cycling.

> My parents didn't expect me to just be riding a bike, so I found a job as a silkscreen printer. I thought it was a good trade, it was £9.50 a week. I met up with Joe; his dad was a technician, one above a standard electrician, and Joe mentioned that an apprentice electrician was getting £22 a week! I thought you know what, maybe I'll change my job. He was working for Phoenix Electrical in Marshalsea Road, Borough. I went there, Bill Dodds came with me. I already had selection for the Commonwealth Games, and they thought it was a nice thing for them to have an apprentice representing England. I got the job, I did it for a year on and off, and to be honest with you I did take the piss a little bit, really, most of the time I was away racing or whatever.

The Commonwealth Games should have been a watershed moment for the eighteen-year-old Maurice, by some distance the youngest member of the squad. It turned out to be anything but.

> It was around the Commonwealth Games that I noticed things were different. For example, I had an invitation to meet with the Duke of Edinburgh, it was my name on the ticket, but they arranged it so that somebody else went instead of me. I'd just turned eighteen, and at that point I didn't feel confident enough in myself to stand up and say, 'Well hold on a minute, why is somebody else going?'

Commonwealth Games, 1974

It seemed to solidify earlier suspicions that somehow whatever he did he would struggle to gain recognition and support. By the start of the games, Norman Sheil had left the set-up. People like Sheil, and John Nicholson, the Australian sprinter, were supportive: 'they didn't worry too much about the colour of your skin. If you had the ability then they were happy to help you'.[7] Maurice had met John Nicholson at Paddington, 'ridden him all over the track' even if he did get beaten, but they formed a friendship. After the Games, Nicholson returned to London and mentored Maurice: 'He helped me, guided me, later on he even taught me how to drive.' The Commonwealth Games were a success for Nicholson but not for Maurice; he lost in the first round. In the team photo he is the only one without a medal. I wonder who thought it was a good idea to get a picture of everyone with their medals and have the only Black guy standing awkwardly at the side without one. One thing was certain, with the warmth of Sheil

[7]www.eurosport.co.uk/cycling/britain-s-first-black-cycling-champion-maurice-burton-on-his-experiences-in-cycling_sto7969451/story.shtml

replaced by the froideur of new coach Tom Pinnington, Maurice had one less ally in the team.

Nicholson had invitations to race in Europe after the Games and he suggested Maurice came along. It was an opportunity to train, to see the European tracks and maybe to get into some races. Before leaving for Milan, Burton and Nicholson headed to the Good Friday Meeting in April 1974, where one of the biggest crowds for years filed in expectantly to see a strong field, including Morelon, Dutchman Herman Ponsteen and rebel roadman and English folk hero Alf Engers, who 'slaughtered the field' in the Roadman's Pursuit. Burton lined up in the White Hope Sprint, aiming to go one better than the year before, and also entered the Three-Mile race. He won both comfortably and featured on the cover of *Cycling Weekly* magazine a week later, along with a race report. From there, it was on to Milan, and then Copenhagen.

> We started with the GP Milan Sprint at the Vigorelli, a prestigious race back then, taking place at the finish of the Giro d'Italia. That year, Eddy Merckx won the Giro with Fuentes in second. De Vlaeminck won the green jersey. At the finish, the Italian national coach Guido Costa recognised me because he was watching at Herne Hill when I won the White Hope Sprint. He was impressed with that ride, so he put me up in the rider's hotel and got me a ride in the GP. I didn't do much, rode against Morelon in the first round, and didn't win, but it was a good experience.

John Nicholson had contracts for some more races in Copenhagen and suggested Maurice might want to come along. Nicholson was sponsored by Geoffrey Butler Cycles and used the shop van, a small two-seater with everything in the back, including a derny motorbike[8] for training along the way and a mattress for sleeping. On the way to Milan, they stopped at Hanover and did some training on the track.

---

[8] A 'derny' is a small motorbike used for paced races or in training. The term 'Derny' is the brand name of the original manufacturer in the 1930s.

They only had track bikes so took turns to train behind the derny, stopping here and there along the way.

John Nicholson taught me how to drive on the way to Copenhagen. We'd be driving into town and he'd steer and then tell me when to change gear. Then on the motorway, I'd drive. To be honest, you just indicate, you don't have to change gear or do the more complicated stuff. Those were my driving lessons, with Nico, from Milan to Copenhagen. I didn't drive again for a little while.

White Hope Sprint, 1974

I'm unnerved by the distances involved. Maurice says 'we drove to Copenhagen' like it's a short hop from Streatham to Norwood, or like the journey I've done this morning, from Bristol to London, rather than a 1400km trek north through the entirety of Europe. I'm also slightly unnerved by his learning-to-drive technique, but not surprised. My gran once told me she never took a driving test. The past is a different place. Costa's recognition at Milan was a symptom of Maurice's growing profile, internationally at least. However, alongside his development as a rider, came the sense that things weren't the same for him as they were for others. A string of incidents solidified latent suspicions. In June, he won the London Divisional Championships at Herne Hill. Maurice mentions a photo of him on the podium, with the commissaires in attendance. One of them was spectacularly glum. Suddenly the tone changes; Maurice is defiant, but also embittered, and funny.

It's a great, lovely pic, *hehehehe*. I liked it, *HAHAHAH* you should have seen the commissaire's face! He was a big man. *Hehehe* he wasn't too happy about that. I remember winning a race at Crystal Palace, the second-placed rider congratulated me, it was at least a wheel, half a bike length, no doubt. A few minutes later, suddenly *I* was second. It would have been the same commissaire who decided I hadn't won. That same guy tried to get Russell Williams and Joe Clovis stopped from riding at Herne Hill. The scrutineers would check the tyres, usually at a glance. With Joe, they forced the tyres off his rims, saying they weren't safe, so he couldn't ride. Joe Clovis felt it wasn't right, so he devised a test. He told Paul Furnell that his wheels kept getting 'failed' at the scrutiny, pre-race. Paul didn't believe it, so Joe gave his wheels to Paul, and they passed the scrutiny without a second look. Joe then took the very same wheels up to be scrutinised, and they pushed them off the rim, saying they weren't safe. They just didn't want him to ride.

It happened a lot. I had a nasty accident at Herne Hill as a junior, I went straight over the bars, smashed my teeth, face, everything. They heard about it and thought they wouldn't see me again, but it didn't go that way. Even going back to when I was fifteen, I won the last race at Crystal Palace that year. Afterwards, everyone had gone, just me and the official were left. He looked at me and he said, 'You won't win these races next year.' The official was still alive when my son Germain was riding, he rode at Crystal Palace, he lapped 'em, with a single gear, he only had one gear, he was restricted. I just gave him the biggest gear he was allowed and just said, 'Ride that,' and when the hill came, he just kicked and lapped 'em all.

I said to the official, 'This is my son Germain.' He hadn't seen the last of me! There were a few people like that around there. They held the sport back. There were a lot of people, commissaires, it was a bit of power, and these people had … *a different mindset* y'know? You only have to look at their faces, the way they were looking at me, it was anger, contempt. They didn't want me there.

Things came to a head at the National Championships in Leicester in June 1974. In the run-up to the event, Maurice showed his form, beating an elite field at Nottingham track by several bike lengths. The report was full of praise: 'If anyone has any qualms about the future of British sprinting, then let him watch junior sprint champion Maurice Burton, VC Londres, power his way past the present establishment … he left Steve Heffernan, Ian Hallam, Geoff Cooke, Gary Wiggins[9] and other stars well behind…'

At this point, Maurice still wanted to be Daniel Morelon; his training was based around specific sprint work. The sprint is an elbows-out affair. Riders start side-by-side and the first to cross the line three laps later wins. It sounds simple, but it's a complex tactical battle, three parts intimidation and mind games, one part sheer strength and power. In recent years, Chris Hoy, Grégory Baugé and Jason Kenny have been the marquee riders in the men's event. Maurice travelled up the day before. He did a few laps of Herne Hill in the afternoon, before riding across London with spare wheels and kit, and getting the train. He didn't have anywhere to stay, so slept on rearranged seat cushions in a table tennis room at the track.

At the National Championships, Maurice was up against Dave Le Grys, a huge, scary-looking but well-respected rider with a reputation for hard riding. 'He won partly on intimidation.' It was enough for Maurice to sit up: 'I didn't want to fall off because I had a good

---

[9]Gary Wiggins became an accomplished six-day professional. He lived in Ghent, where son (Sir) Bradley was born, and reappears later in this book.

chance in the 20km, so I let the sprint go.' *Cycling Weekly* reported it as a 'dismal showing'.

It left the 20km scratch race as a last chance of glory in Maurice's hunt for a first senior national title. It's a straightforward race: 20km, first across the line wins. Burton was fresh from the London Championships where he had beaten the whip-fast Australian, Murray Hall. He had beaten Olympic hopefuls Heffernan, Cooke and Hallam. He had ridden the Commonwealths, but was also a reigning junior champion, making the step up to the full senior ranks. He had the potential to win. Getting ready in the track centre, he was very much on his own until a surprise intervention:

> Obviously, I knew other riders but I didn't have anyone with me as such. I was eighteen years old, I just turned up and did it. I was struggling with my number when Beryl Burton came over and pinned it on for me. I'd seen Denise Burton – we're the same age – at training sessions at Leicester. When you are young, you can be a bit shy when it comes to women, so I don't think I ever had a conversation with her, but then here was Beryl helping me out, she could see I was struggling and she mothered me.

The race report in *Cycling Weekly* is less than complimentary. The headline seems begrudging: 'Chaotic "20" falls to Burton', with a caustic comment in the first paragraph: 'the final was turned into a travesty of a championship'. It then lists the reasons why other riders didn't win. Mick Bennett didn't win because he crashed on the first lap, and when the race restarted, punctured on the last banking. Willi Moore didn't win because he was blocked by Mick Bennett. Chris Cooke didn't win because he broke his collarbone in the same crash. Steve Heffernan didn't win because he 'had been involved in a gruelling club team pursuit final earlier the same afternoon' and 'sold out in the sprint'. Afterwards, 'the dressing room was filled with broken men, while "Mo" jubilantly relived the last few laps that gave him the title on a plate'. There is some kind of grudging recognition – 'all credit to Burton for a capable finishing effort' – but then the article revisits the earlier litany with the acerbic conclusion: 'if Hallam, Moore and Bennett hadn't run into trouble, Burton would never have been allowed to walk away with it'. The word 'capable' is mealy-mouthed, demeaning Maurice's[10] hard work, talent and finishing speed. The event was televised. At the time, Joe Clovis rang Rennal and Gracie to let them know it was on, but Rennal was watching the wrestling; Mick McManus[11] was a big draw, and Maurice is still not sure if they saw him win. He is glad they probably didn't. When he stood on the podium to receive his jersey, boos rang out around the velodrome. 'They didn't like the colour of my skin. That's what I think.'

National Title, 1974, L-R Murray Hall, Maurice Burton, Steve Heffernan

Throughout the 1970s, racism was endemic at sporting grounds across the UK. West Brom Footballer Brendon Batson recalled being

---

[10]'Chaotic "20" falls to Burton!', *Cycling Weekly*, 1 August 1974.
[11]McManus was from Camberwell and a notorious cheat, bending the rules as far as he could. His *noms de guerre* included 'The Dulwich Destroyer' and 'The Rugged South London Tough Guy'. He was wellknown for his black wrestling trunks and not liking having his ears grabbed by opponents; hence his catchphrase: 'Not the ears, not the ears'.

shouted and screamed at, bananas thrown on the pitch, visceral, toxic racism. For Batson, as for Maurice, it started much earlier, with a poverty of expectation, a crushing expectation of failure; the paradox of visibility; his headteacher telling him, 'You'll never make a footballer because there's nobody like you.'

> 'What shocked me was the volume; the noise and level of the abuse was incredible. In the compact grounds of the Fourth Division you could hear every word, people shouting foul racist stuff, the monkey noises.'[12]

The reality of exclusion is clearly defined, a thread that starts at the end of Bushey Hill Road in 1962, then spools through time. Just a mile up the road at Filbert Street, Winston White was the first Black player for Leicester City, at the same time, in the same city. He struggled to block out the abuse from the crowd; he would mentor younger Black players coming through the ranks at Leicester, help them cope with the hostility coming from the terraces. 'If I said it never got to me, then I wouldn't be human. It was really bad in the 1970s. I became incredibly protective of young black players.'[13]

National Title, 1974, L-R Tommy Godwin, Maurice Burton, Steve Heffernan

[12]www.birminghammail.co.uk/sport/football/football-news/west-brom-hero-set-lift-21517991
[13]theathletic.com/2151569/2020/10/22/winston-white-leicester-city-burnley-black-history-month/#

Maurice saw the title as a consolation; perhaps not the one he wanted, but a first national title. As the first senior Black British Champion, at eighteen years old, it was a spectacular achievement and it should have been a catalyst for wider change in cycling and society, a shift in identity and attitudes. The opportunity was missed; the experience pushed Maurice away from the UK entirely, towards mainland Europe and a career as a professional bike racer.

I'd beaten the best riders, the likes of Bennett and Hallam, and I was eighteen years old. Alright, they might have their reasons why, but that's neither here nor there. I was a British champion at eighteen. I knew that Belgium was on a whole different level, and I didn't know if I'd be able to manage at that level, so I took a two-week holiday over Christmas and just thought, I'm going to go to Belgium and I'm going to find out if I'm any good at this or not. If I can do it and make something out of it then I'm going to do it, or otherwise I'm going to be an electrician.

It had to be one or the other.

5

A Primer

The concept of a six-day race began as a simple one: riders compete on bikes for six days, doing as many laps of a wooden indoor track as possible. The criteria for victory: ride further than everybody else in the allotted time. The Sabbath was the only thing that stopped the riders, hence six days, not seven, or more, endless days featuring moustachioed men powered by patent medicine and raw meat, riding in slower and slower circles until at some point there would be only one left. The six-day measured up to Victorian ideals of extreme endurance and physical strength, starting at midnight on a Sunday, and was ridden on penny-farthings (or 'ordinaries'). Between 1878 and 1881 there were thirty-three distinct six-day events in the UK, with two promoters running rival promotions. Super-quick (or 'crack', to use the contemporary term) cyclist George Waller was the marquee name but also the promoter. His team set up a board track in a large hall, or used a marquee if there was no suitable space available and then, once done, the circus rolled on around the UK. But then, in the early 1900s, it stopped, almost overnight. The formation of the Union Cycliste Internationale in 1900 didn't help. It became the governing body for the sport around the world. Britain opted out and cycling in the UK retreated into the straight-jacket of amateurism, with no payments, rewards or even fraternising with professionals and a peculiar, lasting obsession with time trials.

The extreme athletic theatre of the six-day concept instead found a happy home in the USA. The first Six Days of New York event was held at Madison Square Garden in 1891. Riders could sleep and start when they wanted, but the clock was always ticking. The desire to maximise time available led to the role of 'seconds', or a soigneur, an assistant there to support, provide food and so on. Typical features of sleep deprivation, hallucination, delusion, rage and falls were the norm and an important selling point for a ghoulish crowd. Spectators were drawn sadistically to the latter stages, watching as riders slipped into a ghostly state of mental and physical collapse, yet somehow still pedalling, eyes deep-set into the skull.

'An athletic contest in which participants "go queer" in their heads, and strain their powers until their faces become hideous with the tortures that rack them, is not sport. It is brutality. Days and weeks of recuperation will be needed to put the Garden racers in condition, and it is likely that some of them will never recover from the strain.'[1]

Major Taylor and Leon Hourier at Paris Velodrome Buffalo, 1909

[1] *New York Times*, 1897.

Riders would race for eight hours with one hour of sleep. Food was handed up in pots as the riders circled, with up to 12,000 spectators watching. One of the first superstars of the six-day was Major Taylor, a Black cyclist, who first rode in New York at Madison Square Garden in 1896, aged eighteen years old. His skill and speed were a headline draw wherever he raced. The US authorities tried to stop him racing, so he raced in Europe, and although he was allowed to race, he experienced pernicious, everyday racism. The parallels with Maurice Burton, seventy years later, are clear. Woody Headspeth followed Major Taylor to Europe after struggling to get a racing licence from the authorities in the USA; as did Germain Ibron. Competing in Amsterdam in 1905, Headspeth was not given a country of origin in the programme, instead labelled with the word 'negro'. Both riders were scheduled to appear at the big outdoor tracks in Carmarthen and Pontypridd:

'Ibron Germain (N____No. 2) At the present time there are five n_____s racing in Europe, but whether a new Major Taylor will be produced it is hard to say. Ibron Germain has been re-christened by the racing boys in Paris 'N_____ No. 2,' for the simple reason that he ranks as second to Major Taylor. 'N_____ No. 2' will make his first trip to Great Britain during the Whitsuntide holidays.'

By 1898, state authorities in Illinois and New York limited the six-day races to twelve hours per day. Promoters circumvented this with a simple but effective innovation: two-man teams. By having one rider on the track at all times, promoters ensured racing could continue for the full twenty-four hours, leading to an immediate increase in speed, distance and spectators, drawn to the renewed sense of spectacle. It signalled the emergence of the Madison – where both riders in the pair circle the track at the same time, one riding, usually higher up on the boards, while the other races, before switching in and out of the fray with a handsling. It was at first just a strategy, before becoming an established format in the six.

The popularity of the six-day event in the USA continued up to the 1930s, acquiring a celebrity following. Ernest Hemingway is an almost clichéd reference point, but with good reason: he writes brilliantly about European racing in *A Moveable Feast* in a scene describing how he was overwhelmed by the speed and atmosphere of the Vel' d'Hiver velodrome in Paris.

Two factors rang the last-lap bell for six-day racing in the USA. First, the Great Depression at the end of the 1920s changed everything – not just cycling, but leisure pursuits, livelihoods and disposable income. Second, the rise of the motor car and motor-racing redefined the spectacle of speed and acceleration. The kings and queens of the track were no longer the fastest people on the planet. The six-days of New York staggered into the post-war era, the last one held in 1950. Nowadays, it seems inconceivable that Madison Square Garden could ever host a bike race again, or that it ever did in the past, let alone give its name to the defining event of the six-day.

Ghent Six

After a tentative post-war restart, the European circuit grew in intensity and popularity, offering compelling entertainment during the winter months. The sixes became a part of the fabric and nightlife of European cities throughout the endless darkness of the winter, offering a heady mix of rousing music, hot-dogs and club singers, with bars open around the clock. They became a kinetic nightclub for the local community where the working populace mingled freely with local celebrities and the stars of the cycling firmament.

By 1974, the six-day circuit was well established, and the format was secure. Cycling royalty like Eddy Merckx or Patrick Sercu mixed with the artisans and the professionals, riders like Danny Clark or Gary Wiggins. In 1975, Eddy Merckx had won the Tour, Giro and Worlds in the same year, while Sercu had bagged the green jersey. They also rode together at Grenoble, Ghent, Rotterdam and Antwerp; riding the six-day circuit was a key part of their racing diet. In 1975, as Maurice Burton made his way across the Channel, the sixes were an essential part of European cycling culture and metropolitan nightlife, a relentless nocturnal cavalcade hurtling across the Continent, with Ghent at the centre of it all.

6

Arima

The Ghent velodrome is small, at 166m, a wooden, salad bowl-shaped circuit with 53-degree bankings. The name *kuipke* makes sense, being a Flemish diminutive meaning 'little dish' or 'cup'. The track creates significant physical pressure on the rider, hitting the transition from curve to straight and back again in under ten seconds, lap after lap, day after day. Each transition forces the rider down into the boards under the weight of gravity. The radius of the entire track is 11m, making it exceptionally tight, with eight- to nine-second laps creating havoc and considerable strain; centrifugal forces upwards of 270kg are mentioned by those in the know.[1] Ghent is the compressed, savage sibling of the long outdoor velodromes. In comparison, Herne Hill is a parish fete with a wobbly PA fading in and out across the windswept in-field, wide, sweeping curves and long straights, polite noise, raffle tickets; a summation of English cycling where time triallists and track riders compete somewhere in the middle of the two disciplines. People go to Herne Hill for the cycling, or the cycling stalls, or the cycling chat. A beer is a possibility if someone has set up a tent, but by no means a certainty.

Ghent is different. It's a claustrophobic *Truman Show* of a track, a low ceiling, a wall of death, the crowd stacked on top and filling out the middle, swaying to the sound of Belgian brass bands or, latterly, incessant, aggressive, terrible Euro-techno that somehow

[1] www.rouleur.cc/editorial/patrick-sercu-phenomenon

makes perfect sense, in the same way the 'Macarena' makes sense in a beachside bar in Magaluf, a combination of irresistible rhythm and pace filtered through an alcoholic gauze. It is a whirlpool of noise and movement, a fug of smoke and a cloying stench of chips and grease and mayonnaise, the senses assailed by intense heat – for the hotter it is, the more beer is drunk. In Ghent, or in Bremen, where 100,000 attend over the course of the week, spectators are there for the beer, the carnival and the celebration, the kitsch interval singer, crooning in the spotlight, the acrobats, marching bands and sleepless hedonism. Ghent is the template for all six-day events, the zenith, the Glastonbury of track races. It remains the headline event in the six-day circus, track racing in its purest, most intoxicating form. Maybe we're too genteel, or maybe we just don't do cycling like this in the UK, with all the hedonistic, sensory metropolitan frisson of a Fitzgerald novel. I ask Maurice what it's like, why it occupies such a space in the cultural imagination of cyclists, why it features on every bucket list. He comes alive, the excitement palpable: 'It's just unique. It's so compressed, so intense. And it's Belgium, that's the thing, Belgian cycling. What did you think of it the times you've been?'

Medhurst and Burton

I look at the floor, nervously. I haven't been. I wanted to go last year, but it didn't happen because of Covid-19; all of the remaining sixes were cancelled. This year, 2021, I was working, having recently changed jobs and wasn't really in a position to ask for time off. That's the trouble with teaching, everyone loves the holidays but if something comes up outside of those parameters, you're stuck. I keep an eye out for next year, I plan to ask my boss super early for 'family' leave, then get the tickets.

'Oh. You haven't been?'

'Er. No. I am going to go – 2022. I will.'

I am determined. I can't write a book about the six, focused on Ghent, the most important six, and not go to Ghent.

He looks away. There is a pause. We carry on.

Ghent has occupied a space in his imagination ever since it leapt out of the pages of *International Cycling Sport* at the 1971 Good Friday Meeting. It was inevitable that 't Kuipke would sooner or later pull Maurice Burton across to East Flanders. Others had gone before and it was nearby, a convenient base and a stepping-stone to the Continental scene. The plan was simple: get a ride in the track league, get seen, get a ride in the amateur six, get seen, get a contract for another amateur six, get seen, turn professional. The historic city of Ghent is the heartland of Belgian cycling, the capital of East Flanders, home to several one-day classics and a regiment of pro riders, including Patrick Sercu, the most successful six-day rider ever, with 88 wins out of 223 events. That's 1338 days of six-day racing, or three and a half years spent riding around the track.

Bill Dodds came up with the initial suggestion that Maurice should consider riding the boards in Ghent through the winter; it would be a way to get fit, hold his form, mix it up on the short tracks nearby – Antwerp, Rotterdam – then come back stronger, ready for the outdoor season and championships. It was an idea, something to consider, but nothing more. Then, an unsolicited airmail letter from the Trinidad and Barbados Track Federation arrived in December 1974. Inside the blue-and-red chevronned envelope was an invitation for 'Maurice Burton, National Track Champion' to ride in the Caribbean in February of 1975, all expenses paid. For Maurice, it was a dream ticket to some winter sun and time spent riding with the biggest names of the sport. It was perfect training and aligned serendipitously with the plan to go to Ghent. Caribbean track cycling was growing in popularity; the national velodrome in Jamaica had been built in Kingston for the 1966 Commonwealth Games. The big names in the 1970s and early 1980s were Xavier Mirander and David Weller. Mirander won silver in New Zealand in 1974, behind winner John Nicholson. Six years later, Weller won bronze in the sprint at the Moscow Olympics in 1980. He remains the only non-track and field medallist in Jamaican history. Mirander would ride at Herne Hill and Paddington from time to time and certainly crossed paths with Maurice. Of equal importance, Weller and Mirander are one of a select group of cyclists to be immortalised in song, featuring in the dancehall classic, 'Wheely Wheely', by Early B, an amazing paean to Jamaican cycling. It is a million times better than almost any other song about bicycles. It is the song sports editors should use for their montages.

David Weller, Xavier Mirander
Them ride bicycle fi we lan' Jamaica
Olympic bronze, Commonwealth silver

There were two issues with the invitation. First, Maurice needed to ensure he was fit to take part; there was no track racing in the UK over winter, only the filth and grot of cyclo-cross, which did not appeal. Second, British Cycling didn't want him to go, making clear their displeasure at the prize-giving in Blackpool in December. They weren't prepared to let him wear his Great Britain jersey or represent the country in the Caribbean, ostensibly because the invitation was 'personal' rather than via 'official selection'. Maurice is clear: 'They had no authority to tell me I couldn't wear my champions jersey.' Sour grapes and administrative intransigence became another obstacle to progress. But for Maurice, the invitation added impetus to his plan to head to Ghent and ride the track leagues. After a winter in Ghent, he would head straight to the Caribbean in February, with or without the blessing of the BCF.

Pete Verleysdonk – PV – was another one of the Australian expatriate racing community, along with Murray Hall, Danny Clark and others, all trying to break into the six-day professional scene. The Australian connection is important: they were outsiders, adrift, palpably different, they sounded different, they did things differently, and there was an easy affinity between Maurice and PV, Clark and the others. Maurice affirms this, he felt comfortable with John Nicholson – Nico – and PV, then later Gary Wiggins. Their relationship was forged through difference, through their outsider status. PV had family in Holland, with some connections in the Low Countries, and he wanted to give the sixes a shot.

I knew PV was willing to go, and I knew he didn't have anyone to go with. I got on with the Australians because they had the same mentality, they came here to win and to earn money, they needed to live, they were different from many of the UK riders who came from a background where money wasn't the important thing. But it *was* the important thing for me, and it was for Heff as well. Maybe we had to be a little bit more mercenary than the other guys, we had to make those decisions, like travelling to Ghent on Christmas Eve.

Verleysdonk stayed overnight at Maurice's home on 23 December. They packed up the bikes, wheels and kit and piled everything into Verleysdonk's red Volkswagen Variant and headed off on Christmas Eve, driving down to Dover, disembarking into grey, soupy weather at Ostend, before driving straight up to Ghent. They had barely any money and no place to stay – enough for two nights in a cheap hotel near the station – and a couple of names in a notebook, people to talk to, nothing more than that. It reminds me of Maurice's excursion to Calshot with Joe Clovis, but on a much bigger scale. 'Hi Mum, we're just going somewhere, see you in February.' They were following in the tyre treads of a long line of British cyclists who headed to the Continent full of ambition, fed up with this and that, primarily the insular nature of cycling in the UK, the dead end of time trials and endless repetition of a UK road scene that seems perpetually in crisis. Instead, they wanted the romance and privations of European bike racing. Read *In Pursuit of Stardom: Les Nomades du Vélo Anglais* by Tony Hewson, read about Brian Robinson, Tom Simpson or Allan Peiper for the Australian perspective – their narratives reflect the sense of there being something bigger and better, and a desire to be a part of it. At that time, there weren't any other routes; Athletic Club de Boulogne-Billancourt (ACBB)[2] started taking foreign riders from 1975. There was no Rayner Foundation, no UK-based Continental teams, and the anglophone cohort in the peloton was almost non-existent. Compare this to 2023, when nine UK riders lined up in the season opener, Kuurne–Brussels–Kuurne, along with ten Antipodeans and a host of other nationalities, and the contemporary global reach of the sport is clear. It is unlikely any of them opted to begin their journey into the professional ranks on Christmas Eve. If you wanted to go, you were on your own; British cycling meant very little.

We didn't know anyone, had nowhere to stay or sleep, no money. We went straight to the Christmas Day track meeting – it was a big day in Ghent. The bike shop Plum Vainqueur had a little concession at the track, and someone there pointed us to Rosa Desnerck,[3] who with her husband owned Plum. Sometimes foreigners would come over and they'd help. She either didn't have space or didn't want us in their house, especially me, maybe they didn't know who I was.

[2]Stephen Roche, Phil Anderson, Robert Millar, Paul Kimmage, Sean Yates, Allan Peiper, Seamus Elliott, Graham Jones, John Herety and Paul Sherwen all went through the ACCB.
[3]Pierre Simoens, current owner of Plum: 'They all came to Ghent. If you talk with any of the old foreign riders, and speak of Rosa Desnerck, they will say, "Ah, Madame Rosa!" Tom Simpson, Allan Peiper and Gary Wiggins – all stayed at the Desnerck house.'

We stayed in a hotel that night and shared a bed. The next day, Rosa showed us along the Sint-Kwintensberg to a butcher's shop. He didn't do meat anymore, he collected newspapers and was a Seventh-day Adventist, this man, not an average bod. But he had some rooms, so that's where we lived.

It's a post-Christmas fever dream, staying in the butcher's that isn't a butcher's, the rooms slowly filling with yesterday's newspapers, waiting to ride bike races. I have to ask again about the newspaper thing. I don't quite follow.

He collected it; if you have enough of it, it pays. He just had newspapers everywhere, he would gradually fill up this big container and then they'd take it away. I lived there. Other riders would stay there, it was a known place. A few years later, Allan Peiper[4] lived pretty much in the shop window, until his riding partner Eddy Planckaert dropped him home one day, took one look at the set-up then took him home to live with his family.[5]

Neither Maurice nor Verleysdonk spoke a word of Flemish. The first race was the Saturday after Christmas; an amateur track league sponsored by *Vooruit*, the Communist newspaper. Verleysdonk, who had turned professional, could not ride. Things started badly in the Devil; Maurice was disqualified for 'riding underneath', moving down on to the blue strip at the bottom of the track, known as the Côte d'Azur, then back up on to the track. However, he had shown enough of his talent on the track, and was spotted by Oscar Daemers, the promoter of the Ghent Six Day. Daemers, like Norman Sheil and Bill Dodds before, saw something in the young Londoner. On the circuit, the promoter is God. They organise the six, pay and pair the riders, which

---

[4]Australian professional, 'super domestique', and latterly sporting director of some of Europe's biggest professional cycling teams.
[5]Planckaert's house wasn't a palace either – there was no bathroom or running water and the two shared a bed. The butcher's must have been quite the hovel.

in turn shapes who wins and who loses. Maurice became a regular at the track throughout the season.

> I was racing every week as an amateur until February when I went to the Caribbean. My last race was the Nacht der Vedetten [Night of the Stars]. I went to see Oscar after I'd done my training that day. He said to me, 'I'm going to give you a *cadeau*.'[6] There were two races for amateurs on that day. He put all the good riders in one race and me in the other. I was nineteen years old, in the national jersey. I won the race.

Daemers had the power to lift a rider up out of the depths of the winter circuit, to ensure visibility, regular rides and income. The nature of contracts, promotions and PR meant that the fate of the rider rested in the hands of the promoter. This was true of any track; for example, Ron Webb promoted at the Skol Six, Herning and Hanover. A good showing at the Skol Six could lead to contracts in his other races. The directors held the cards, first in issuing the contracts, then in shaping the racing. For Maurice, the tacit patronage of Daemers was a way in. It offered the tantalising prospect of riding in the November amateur six, the next rung on the ladder. While not certain, Daemers indicated that a ride in November was very much a possibility. Maurice headed back to London, strengthened, in form and ready for Trinidad.

At the end of February he flew from Heathrow to Trinidad and Barbados. Ted Gray, the Welsh track coach for the Jamaican team, made sure he had everything he needed. The group of riders included Olympic gold medallists, riders of the calibre of Niels Fredborg and World Champion sprinter Daniel Morelon. For Maurice, still just nineteen years old, it was an intense experience:

> You have to remember that before I went my experience of international racing was quite limited. I'd been to Munich for the

---

[6] The power of the promoter includes the capacity to choose the line-up, thus favouring one rider with a gift, or '*cadeau*'.

Junior European Championship, but that didn't end so well. In '74 I'd been to New Zealand for the Commonwealth Games. I was finding my feet in and among riders like Fredborg, Nicholson and Morelon. A couple of years before, I'd been at school.

The riders were amateurs; the clear distinction between the professional and amateur scene was enforced by Olympic regulations at the time. An Olympic medal was a means in itself, but also seen in part as a ticket to the professional scene. Fredborg and Nicholson turned professional not long after their trip to the Caribbean; Nicholson signed with Jolly Ceramica, home to Giro and Vuelta winner Giovanni Battaglin, going on to win the professional World Sprint Championship. Much of the racing seen in public, on television during the Olympics, was amateur and the riders attracted recognition in the eyes of the public; certainly in terms of cycling.

Trinidad, 1975. Maurice front right, next to John Nicholson,
then Xavier Mirander. Directly behind Mirander is Ted Gray.
David Weller back row, fifth from right

Maurice raced at Arima and San Fernando in Trinidad, then Waterford in Barbados. The outdoor tracks were huge, with shallow banking and long straights. Arima was a 'proper track, cement, with seams', both were much closer in look and feel to Herne Hill and Paddington than the indoor tracks at Antwerp or Ghent. While he was away, the BCF registered their disapproval by sending someone round to Maurice's house. The official encountered a nonplussed Rennal at the door. It served to emphasise the contrast between the shoestring operation and cold diffidence from the BCF, based at Park Crescent, with the warmth and generosity of the welcome from Ted Gray in Trinidad:

The BCF only had about two or three people working at Park Crescent: Len Unwin, Brian Wotton and maybe one other. It was Brian Wotton who was instructed to visit the house. Dad said he was very upset because I'd gone. Brian wasn't one of those who were against me, it was just the way the rules were laid out, and he'd been instructed to come and visit. I definitely got the feeling there were people who were saying, 'Let's get rid of this guy,' but to be fair, it was never Brian Wotton. The Federation were upset that I had gone to Trinidad, without going via them, in that official capacity if you like. They struggled because it was a personal invitation from the federation of Trinidad and Barbados, to ask for *me*, Maurice Burton. The thing is, if the invite had gone to the BCF then they would have put forward Ian Hallam, Mick Bennett, any of those guys, anyone but me. That was how it was, certainly how it felt back then. Every time they could have endorsed me, they didn't, why would this be any different? Ted Gray came to me because they knew they wanted me.

I was only a young fellow; I didn't really get the politics of the whole thing. All I know is that my dad said the guy came to the house and he was upset that I'd gone over there and I didn't have a manager with me or anything like that. They'd made it clear at the outset with the comments about the jersey that they didn't want me to go. It was too late anyway: I was already there.

Everything was paid for – flights, accommodation, the lot. The riders stayed in a holiday camp, more Butlins than Sandals, if the pictures are anything to go by, but the shimmering heat and timetable of races made it an idyllic week away. He won 'more than a couple of races', in fact, he beat both Fredborg and Morelon at Waterford and received his prize from Louis – known as Toto - Gérardin, the pre-eminent French national cycling coach and Edith Piaf's lover.[7] Maurice wore his national title jersey on the podium. No one booed. He returned to the UK in March.

I never went back to work. In 1974, I was an apprentice electrician. In 1975, I was a full-time cyclist. I never even told them I wasn't going back to work. I just never went back.

[7]Apocryphal Gérardin quote: 'Forty eight hours with Piaf are more tiring than a lap in the Tour de France'.

7

Kazemattenstraat

In the mid-1970s, the Good Friday Meeting was the definitive early-season indicator of form and fitness. The event is still held yearly, having moved to the shiny new Olympic velodrome. It has gained reliable weather – it doesn't rain indoors – but lost something intangible along the way: a sense of London cycling culture, of clubs, heritage and memory, stories shared in excited tones while standing looking over the hoardings as the race unfolds. New myths will be written, I'm sure, but it has yet to reach the 'I remember when Wiggins won the points race' level of cultural memory, and it doesn't have the stayers' event, a primeval death-race, where riders hold on at 50mph behind huge Thunderbird motorbikes with pilots standing upright.

Maurice got off the plane full of confidence and form after Ghent and the Caribbean. Having won the White Hope Sprint the year before, he was keen to move up a rung by targeting the Golden Wheel, a prestigious points race, followed by the scratch race later that day. The points race features a sprint every lap; it unfolds with a constant burst of speed and then a lull, then a roar – a brutal pattern of unrelenting effort and concentration. 'It was hard. I was riding for Archer Cutty Sark. There was me, Heffernan and Gary Wiggins. I remember the team manager at the time asked them to help me out a bit but it never felt like I got any help anyway. The long and short of it is I won the Golden Wheel, and then I won the scratch, which was easier in comparison.'

Maurice knew at this point that Ghent in November was a certainty. It became a case of riding to win, and riding to live, scraping a living through primes and prizes, doing just enough to keep everything in balance. The idea of turning professional was on hold until after the Montreal Summer Olympics in 1976. Riding as an amateur wasn't without financial reward, paradoxically, but it wasn't paid employment – it hinged on prize money, not contracts. Everything was about value, building for the future, aiming for the national title, another win, and the big one – an Olympic medal. Any kind of medal delivered cachet, your name higher up, bigger on the poster, a better contract, or more contracts across the Continent. After Good Friday, Maurice headed back to Northern Europe at the behest of John Nicholson to race at a series of track Grand Prix meetings in Paris, Berlin and Hanover. These were squeezed in just prior to the National Championships in Leicester at the end of July. Again, the excursion was separate from the Federation, 'who couldn't organise stuff like that'. Nicholson arranged the accommodation in Aarhus at university halls, and he negotiated the contracts for the races for the riders, including Dave Le Grys, Gary Wiggins and Paul Medhurst. Burton rode under the Jamaican flag. Being outside of the Federation had its advantages: 'The difference was at Berlin I got 500 deutschmarks whereas the British guys got 200.' Medhurst travelled and stayed in a camper van with his wife Linda and baby son Darryn as he tried to make a go of it. After winning one of the races, Nicholson brought the flowers back for the van, 'to make it smell better'.

The series included a four-hour Madison in Odense on the outdoor track. Maurice was down to ride with Wiggins, who was delayed whilst travelling on the train and missed the start. 'I had to do the first twenty minutes on my own. Gary got there, went straight on to the track and into the race, and we came second behind Gert Frank. The total distance was 218km.' It was the first time Maurice had ridden with, rather than against, Gary Wiggins, who would become a key part of the narrative in Ghent, along with Medhurst.

Even Wiggins found the Madison a stretch, using what sounds like an Australian slang phrase, 'a la nasty' in an interview. I assume he means it was a no-holds-barred, Antipodean grunge fest. The key imperative was money, earning enough to get by, to pay the rent, often a couple months in advance if a big prime came in.

By mid-July, the riders had returned to the UK and they came together at Leicester for the Nationals. Memories of the crowd response a year ago seemed to hold in the air, a miasma of latent hatred and otherness. This year, Maurice had three targets: the 20km scratch, 80km Madison and the Team Pursuit. Things immediately went awry in the scratch.

In the final, Heffernan boxed me in. He said that he wasn't working with anyone, I mean, that's what he told me beforehand, but he was holding me in, and I had to get out, so I pushed him out of the way. It was late and I was trying to get round. I might have just about made it but down the home straight this guy came up alongside, his pedal went in my wheel and that was the end of it. Hallam won the race. I wouldn't be surprised if there weren't some arrangements between riders, but then that's fairly typical, and that wasn't what upset me, it was what happened next.

I was disqualified from the race because they said I pulled Heffernan off his bike. The truth is I didn't pull him off his bike. Regardless of that, I crashed and I didn't even finish the bloody race. Why would you disqualify someone who didn't even finish the race because they crashed out in the first place? What is the point of doing that?

I can't get my head round why you would want to disqualify someone. Put it this way, if I'd have won that race, because of that situation with Heff, then they would have disqualified me, to some degree that makes sense, from their point of view. Fair enough, well actually not fair enough, but still, that's bike racing. But I didn't even finish the race, I crashed, so where does the disqualification come into it? I'll tell you why they did it. I was already down on the floor so they decided to put the boot right into me. And you know what? It worked because I never went back to ride another National Championship. It's hard to escape the way these things are, given everything else.

Being booed on the podium, the result coarsened in the press, trying to prevent him riding in the Caribbean – these were just some of the many incidents that undermined his efforts to succeed as a cyclist. Undaunted, Maurice picked himself up off the floor and went again, this time in the Madison with Heffernan. Maurice had the legs to take it to the others, in this case Mick Bennett and Ian Hallam, but Heffernan struggled. It was 80km with a sprint every so often. The key to success would be to take a lap, get ahead of the other riders, then hold it there for the win.

> Whenever I took a sprint, we won it, whenever Heff took the sprint, we lost. I was trying to take a damn lap on those guys because I was on form, and I think if he let me take all the damn sprints, I would have beat them, but in the end we came second.

That's the truism of the Madison: both riders need to be on form. He added the silver to his championship title from the year before, and lined up in the team pursuit with Heffernan, Robin Croker and Alaric Gayfer. They rode brilliantly, won the title and broke the British record in the process, giving Maurice his third national jersey. He is generous in his praise for Heffernan in particular: 'Heff was some rider, and it's a pity he never made it on the Continent.' There is an affinity; both struggled, to a degree, neither fitted in. For Maurice, the disqualification was another blow to his confidence. The prospect of equality was receding further on the ebb tide of petty officialdom and prejudice.

> I came away from the championships with a gold in the team pursuit, making it my third British championship after the junior sprint and the 20km scratch, and I had a silver in the Madison. It's quite a good return, looking back. After the disqualification,

though, that was it, I never went back to a National Championship again. I try to be optimistic, most of the time, the glass is half full you know, but sometimes it gets you down, just the way things seem to be going, especially when it's one setback after another like that. I never understood the disqualification, I was nineteen years old at the time. I just felt that this whole thing wasn't going anywhere, and I guess that made me even more determined to go elsewhere.

I ask a friend about the race. He is a high-up commissaire in British Cycling. Would they disqualify someone from a race if they did something maybe a bit dodgy but crashed out anyway? Say there was some back and forth but it had no bearing on the race, and the rider crashed out, would they then go through the disqualification process? His response: 'Probably not. It would very much depend on what the incident was. Did it affect the safety of other riders for example? Most likely as a commissaire I would make sure they understood the implications of any argy-bargy in a race situation. Also depends on if it's a youth, junior or novice rider who I might want to encourage to keep racing or an experienced rider with a "history" of being a troublemaker.'

I get a second opinion from a track official; he cannot think of any equivalent incident. He cannot understand why a rider who has crashed would be disqualified for a racing incident. Both officials find it hard to think of any precedent.

The team pursuit at Leicester was Maurice's last race in the UK. He worked at the Skol Six at Wembley at the end of September for Keith Robbins, a larger-than-life figure in British racing circles. Keith knew everyone, he was involved in almost every aspect of bike racing. Maurice's partner in the team pursuit, Alaric Gayfer, was also working, Alaric's father was the editor of *Cycling Weekly* at the time. Maurice helped with the signs, setting things out, moving stuff around, any aspects to do with the running of the event. The Skol Six was one of several races to feature a temporary track dropped into a multi-purpose venue. Temporary tracks look very cool from underneath, a carpenter's dream of criss-crossed beams and parallel pine, a matchstick model. However, these venues are different, compromises are made; like Antwerp, where the track was built on top of an ice rink. The wooden boards for the Skol Six had a coping section and hoardings almost encroaching on the lower seats, with netting to prevent 'mishaps'. For the drop-in tracks, the line of sight is different, the seating shallower. The track is a squeeze, the best they can do, and they lack the singular identity of Ghent, which is a velodrome first and foremost. Without permanence, the event lacks wider community engagement, the sense of a constant cultural space in the centre of the city, radiating cycling. In Ghent, cycling is prioritised, physically, architecturally, spatially. London was always subject to the vagaries of fashion, money and finding a willing promoter – it required a huge amount of work and the finances were precarious.

Working at Wembley for the Skol Six provided a close-up of the intensity of the six-day circuit. While Maurice was racing and training full-time, he was reliant on prize money and primes, but these tailed off towards the end of the season. Helping at the six covered his costs to go to Belgium and to buy a car, putting his 'driving lessons' with John Nicholson to good use. Maurice somehow managed to part-exchange a bike for a VW Variant with one of the other people working at the event.

I bought this car on the Friday of the Skol Six, took Joe Clovis with me. I hit a little wall, put a small dent in it straight away. The next day, Sunday, I drove up the Edgware Road and picked up Gary Wiggins, who was staying with Bradley's mum, Linda, in Dibden House, where Bradley grew up. I then drove the car up to Wolverhampton, where we rode a race at the Aldersley track. I'm fairly sure Gary was planning on coming over to Belgium at that point, but something happened, he broke his shoulder or something and couldn't come. The next weekend, I loaded up the car with the bike, wheels and everything and drove across to Belgium.

He went straight back to the butcher's shop, home of Jan 'de Papers' and host to a revolving cast of itinerant non-Belgian cyclists, all looking for a bed and board and the opportunity to break into the professional circus. This time it was the Americans staying in the front of the shop; Roger Young and a few others were bedding down among the newsprint. There was no room at the inn, so a week or so at Madame Bernon's in Wondelgem ensued, before sorting out a place back at the butcher's. The history of cycling in Ghent is told through names like Madame Bernon, or Staf Boone, or Albert Beurick at Café Den Engel. Their support was essential for those new to the city, especially anglophone riders. Most cyclists from Australia, New Zealand or the UK passed through one or more of the digs at least once. Madam Bernon's was popular with Antipodeans starting out on the Continental scene, from the mid-1970s onwards. In 1975, Staf Boone had a corner shop on Bijlokevest, not far from the Citadel Park. He still brings riders over, some forty years later, through Kingsnorth International Wheelers, a hybrid Anglo-Belgian club that acts as a launchpad for aspiring neo-pros. Boone has a reputation for honest feedback in the wake of kermesse (circuit race) victories or losses, like 'sell your bike'. Most share the same view of Boone, including Maurice: 'He was quite a character, still is.' Boone would ride the derny for Maurice, taking time out from his big farm, where he had 'pigeons the size of chickens – they were huge.'

Steve Heffernan was also in Ghent, but not at the butcher's. The key attraction was the prospect of a ride at the amateur six, followed by the prospect of turning professional and earning contracts for the winter. Heffernan was paired with Paul Medhurst and they were funded by the BCF, unlike Maurice, who had the money from the Skol Six, a £70 VW Variant he had swapped for a bike, and a bed in a butcher's shop. The BCF would fund riders, and they still do, just not Maurice. 'The same thing happens now; when my son Germain rode the amateur six in 2015, I was looking after him and his partner Mark Stewart, and everything was paid for by British Cycling: fuel, hotel, costs, the lot.' It is progress.

Ghent in winter is cold. It feels like a peculiarly Belgian form of cold, an unrelenting wind and an unwelcoming slate-grey sky. Wind-blown sleet settles on the surface of grey, cold canals, cafe windows are constantly fogged and dripping with condensation from customers sheltering from the outdoors, the allure of a thousand different types of lambic too much to ignore on a glowering, cold evening. It is quiet at night, aside from one or two streets, the Vlasmarkt and historic centre come alive, like scenes from a Dardennes' film. The Butcher's is a short stroll from 't Kuipke, ten minutes on foot through the silent city, collar turned to the cold and damp. The heat and intensity of the velodrome is in stark contrast to the deserted streets afterwards. Things didn't start well.

I rode the first race in Ghent and I only came fifth and I thought, You know what, I'm going to have to pull my finger out here, because otherwise I'm going to run out of money. I was still an amateur, reliant on primes and prizes. If I wasn't winning anything then that was a big problem because I didn't have contracts. I sat down at the butcher's and wrote all my expenditure down and basically made a budget: rent, food, bread, cheese, everything, how much it was going to cost to live. When I worked it out, I then decided on the training programme. I had my track bike, but I also had a road bike with me, it was a fixed wheel, because in the winter it was always good to ride fixed, there is a lot less to go wrong. There's a place outside of Ghent called Zelzate, with a long road linking the two. I'd have five minutes of warm-up, then just go flat out all the way to Zelzate, about 20km. I'd do five minutes at an easy pace over the bridge then go flat out all the way back. I would wash, eat, lie down and rest, and then in the afternoon I'd go to the track and do about an hour. There were groups of riders looping around and you could just get in the line and ride. I did this solidly for two weeks. The next race I entered I won. That bought me the form I needed for the amateur six.

It's another glimpse of Maurice's determination. I see it in so many things, a quietness, a matter-of-fact way of just getting things done. Don't talk about it, just plan it out and make it happen. If it's not happening, work out why, do something about it. Get the train to Southampton. Pay your way. Go to Milan. Drive to Copenhagen. Head to Ghent on Christmas Eve. Within this, there is a sense of the transaction, that these things have a cost – and yes it can be a clumsy metaphor, everything has a price, and this is something we keep coming back to throughout our conversations, but also there is a literal price, a budget, a deal to be made. I admire the clarity of Maurice's business mind, not getting caught up in the romance of something but knowing that a deal has to be done in order to succeed. I don't think I work like that; I always look to think my way through it, then get bogged down in the endless possible outcomes, usually with me being somehow the participant in the novel of my life that will never be written. I came across a great interview with Maurice by Keith Bingham and one quote sticks out. Maurice says something like, 'Well I could be working in the cigarette factory.' The cigarette factory for Maurice was equivalent to the coal mine for Belgians. Cycling in Belgium is the national sport, and this isn't glib romanticism, it's the national sport because everyone loves it and is invested in it. It is equivalent to football, an immersive, community activity. Across the northern France and Belgian heartlands, if you weren't a cyclist then you were a farmer above or coal miner beneath the Ardennes forest; it is the Jean Stablinski[1] narrative, and it holds a lot of truth. Go and see the Ghent Six Day or Paris–Roubaix, in fact, any of the spring classics, from Kuurne onwards, and experience the way the sport reaches out from the city into the countryside, how it is a part of Belgian culture, community and life. Maurice had turned his back on the prospect of working as an electrician to join

---

[1] Stablinski worked as a miner from the age of fourteen after his father died. He later rode above the mines as a professional cyclist. He is also responsible for the most French thing I have ever come across: he won a bicycle in an accordion-playing competition.

this community. Under no circumstances was he about to return to his previous life.

> You know what, Paul, it's never left my mind: when things start to look bad, if I see I'm sliding away a bit, then all of a sudden, I know that I have to get hold of myself. I'm on this same stretch of road from Ghent to Zelzate all over again. It doesn't matter what it is, even now, I just say to myself, *Listen, you better pull your finger out boy, you got to pull yourself back on track.* Otherwise, put it like this, if I didn't get my act together and start winning races, I was looking at going back to work as an electrician in South London. The Belgians used to call riders 'ploughboys', as though they were, working the fields. In those days when I was out training, tapping along that road to Zelzate and back, I'd see people with a horse pulling the plough along. That was the alternative. We ploughed a different furrow, I guess.

Yves Lampaert, Tour de France stage winner in 2022, provides lasting, current evidence of the cultural force of Belgian cycling; his comment while holding up the fluffy lion and flowers in Copenhagen after a breath-taking win in the Tour encapsulates this context beautifully: 'I'm just a farmer's son from Belgium, eh.'

Burton became friends at the track with Alain De Roo, a Ghent local. De Roo's parents were supportive, would feed Maurice up with hot meals, delicious home cooking, and they helped out with logistics. A positive profile in the press at the time is captioned '*Verblijf*', meaning 'residence', focused on his new life in Ghent. It refers to Burton as 'the coloured Londoner'.[2] It jars that this is the defining feature. If nothing else, it highlights the casual racism of the time, the notion of 'normal' or 'White' vs 'other' or 'coloured', and contributes to a vicious cycle of racist representation, a cycle of negative semantics. The portrait is otherwise kind and supportive. The language, in

---

[2] 'Verblijf in Belgium', *Cycling Weekly*, 17 January 1976.

hindsight at least, is not. It is how things were framed, and at the time it was not questioned.

De Roo had hoped that he might pair with Burton in the amateur six, but Oscar Daemers had other ideas, putting Maurice with Hans Koot, a Dutch rider and 'a good one'. De Roo wasn't happy but settled for a ride with Burton at Antwerp instead, although in hindsight, Maurice says, 'I really shouldn't have done.' De Roo wasn't strong enough for the pairing to work. Daemers knew what he was doing, Koot and Burton led the standings from the off, despite the strength of the opposition. It included Ferdi Van Den Haute, who went on to win the points classification at the Vuelta and Ghent–Wevelgem in 1978, as well as a stage at the Tour in 1984. Also racing was Frank Hoste, who later became a multiple stage and green jersey winner at the Tour. On Saturday night, after a week's racing, Koot and Burton were two laps up. Van Den Haute and Hoste were Belgian Madison champions and needed to take three laps in a one-hour Madison in order to win the overall. It was, by most metrics, a remote possibility. You mark, or follow the riders carefully so they don't get away, maybe they'll take a lap, but not three. However, they did it.

Cabin Skol Six

The report in *Cycling Weekly* praises Burton and is sceptical of the result. Maurice was a favourite with the crowd, 'they cheered him and he gave them plenty of chances to do so'. Den Haute and Hoste are cast as pantomime villains, 'the crowd booed when they attacked when Burton fell one evening, they cheered when Burton got up'. It ends by describing Maurice as the 'moral victor' after Koot was seen 'mysteriously weakening' in the last chase, enabling other riders to gang up on the pair. Despite this, it was a spectacular result in Maurice's first six; winning the elimination race and a Madison. Crucially, it led to further invitations to ride in the amateur sixes, but also marked a move further away from the British scene. Heffernan and Medhurst came fifth, on the BCF ticket.

> Heff and Medhurst were there with the Federation, whereas I was in with the Belgians and the Dutch. I was now the outsider; I was doing my thing. I didn't really know what they were doing and it didn't matter, I was moving forwards from that point and no longer thinking about the UK, I didn't see any point. It was a tough scene, there were no wooden cabins at the side of the track for the amateurs, I didn't even have anyone looking after me, no chamois cream, nothing! I just got on the bike and rode. It was a Madison every evening, that was it, a one-hour chase every night. Paul Medhurst realised there and then that I was going places, so he got involved, whereas Heff went home. Heff could have made it over there, he was strong. I rode with Paul Medhurst at the Rotterdam three-day race, a compressed version of the six I suppose – there was derny racing, primes and all that. I felt like I was in the circus, moving to the next place, the next track meeting, or six, or whatever. No one questioned me, no one booed me, they booed Hoste and Van Den Haute! No one disqualified me for this or that.

More races at Ghent followed, a steady diet of track meetings, racing, primes, some training, then more racing at 't Kuipke, as Maurice gradually settled into the rhythm and routine of being a track cyclist.

Daemers gave a contract to the American Roger Young to ride with Maurice at the Christmas Day Madison; they were the only amateurs in a professional race. The start line was crammed with talent, and the velodrome was a sell-out. Latecomers were stuck outside, the doors were closed two hours early because of the numbers. Maurice compares Oscar Daemers to Norman Sheil. They both supported him; both saw something in him and took a chance.

> It was a great experience and it was all down to Oscar. He put me in the race, even though the pros wouldn't have liked it either, amateurs riding in their race. It was another step up, and it definitely made me realise the gap between professionals and amateurs. I got cramps as well. Roger came out in the end, he wasn't up to it, so I rode with Cluzeaud – his partner, because Alain Van Lancker had also dropped out.

Maurice was becoming a part of the cycling community within Ghent but was also detached from it. It was an informal network dedicated to allowing young men, often from really far away, to ride their bikes. Many benefited from supporters' clubs who rallied behind a particular rider, raised money through events, met in cafes to watch them race. Maurice didn't have a club, but he did have a team who helped out, providing assistance with both bike riding and the practicalities of living in Ghent, like looking for housing. It ameliorated what would have been an isolated existence for Maurice, but also Paul Medhurst, Gary Wiggins, Danny Clark and others who went to Belgium, following a dream.

For Maurice, there was a further layer of detachment: Ghent in the late 1970s was not Brixton, where the Black community, while suffering at the hands of sus laws and racial discrimination, at least had a communal strength in numbers and an emerging sense of place. In Ghent, the Black community was small, part of a very slowly changing, complex country, where identity was already fractured along linguistic and cultural lines, via Walloons and Flemings, with little space for other discussions around racial and ethnic integration.

Ghent, 1975

The next race for Maurice was the Silber Adler, a one-day meeting for amateurs in Cologne. It was a curtain-raiser for the Cologne Six-Day, which ended on 4 January, 1976. Staf Boone drove the car, taking Maurice and partner Dirk Ongenae. Although Ongenae was never a specialist track rider, he turned pro the following year, and would go on to win two stages at the Vuelta. Given Ongenae's lack of pedigree, Maurice targeted the sprints, hoping to win money and prizes.

There was nobody who could come close to me and I won *everything*. They gave me all sorts of things, appliances, bikes, you name it. Staf got the bike and sold it. I got a little something from it, but not much. I did so bloody well but still couldn't get a ride at the six, I couldn't get my head round it. Maybe I rode *too* well. Danny Clark was riding the pro six and he suggested I come back down in case someone dropped out. It seemed like a good idea at the time. I got on the train, turned up with the bike, but it was a waste of time, and I had to head back again. Roger Young was riding, but not me. I was head and shoulders above the other riders, but it

71

didn't matter because Germany was different, there was no Oscar Daemers. Oscar didn't care where you were from, he supported you, it didn't matter. For example, there was an Australian, Jack Hoban, riding in the Olympics, Oscar was coaching the Belgians. He let Hoban train with the Belgians, then Hoban went and won the race. That was Oscar.

The conversation loops back around to Oscar Daemers and the debt Maurice feels he owes. Daemers was the Belgian coach and an influential figure, involved in World Championship wins and Olympic gold medals. He lived in accommodation within the grounds of the Citadel Park, practically in the velodrome, where his role extended to almost all aspects of managing the facility. Maurice makes clear the link between Oscar Daemers and Bill Dodds:

They were similar, Bill and Oscar, what they did for me. We were talking about Bill at the Pedal Club, there is a Golden Book, signed by important people in cycling, people who have made a difference. I feel like Bill should be in that book – if you look at VC Londres, he started it, the whole set-up, and now look at it, the two Hayter brothers are in the world tour, Fred Wright, they all came from VC Londres. How many of them know about Bill Dodds?

He returned to Ghent from Cologne, before heading to Rotterdam at the end of January for the abbreviated three-day race with Roger Young and Paul Medhurst. At Rotterdam, he worked with Gust Naessens – slowly the characters from the magazine were becoming real. Naessens was a mystical soigneur on the circuit who worked closely with Merckx and Sercu. The riders stayed with the family of Juliette Seraus-Oelen; she recalls it with excitement. 'It was definitely the good old days! Mostly foreign cyclists stayed. My mother was busy day and night cooking and washing for them so they could be back on the track the next day; she did it with a lot of love for them, my dad used to do the massages for the cyclists. It was such a fun time.'

Rotterdam

The picture she sends through is glorious. Everything about it sings, yet nothing sings more loudly and beautifully than the mid-1970s' Dutch decor, the fantastic lino floor. But within it is a long table with her father at the end, immaculately dressed, with the riders, Roger Young, Maurice and Paul, Noël Dejonckheere, Stan Tourné, Michel Vaarten – all key characters in this narrative, sitting down, eating potato and steak, breaking bread. Paul takes his fill. It's pre-professional, golden amateur days, Maurice in his first full season, and it is an image rooted in community and family, and it touches my heart.

After Rotterdam, the Six Days of Antwerp was the last one of the year. Over the course of the 1975/76 winter there were sixteen sixes in total from London on 19 September to Milan on 20 February. Each professional six was preceded by an amateur race earlier. Typically, once racing finished on the Sunday, riders would pile into cars and drive to the next event for a Monday afternoon start. It's a relentless, inhuman grind; huge effort and intensity from 8 p.m. until 1 a.m. every night, six days in a row, with the riders on track for up to five hours per night. It is nothing like the weekly meetings at Paddington, or the track league at Herne Hill. It is wall-to-wall shift work, a different circadian rhythm entirely, and it is not healthy. Having done four amateur sixes in twelve weeks, with Madisons, races and training in-between, Maurice was beginning to flag.

By the time we got to Antwerp that winter with De Roo, I was feeling it, definitely. We didn't do well, and Alain De Roo's dad was poking me, you know, looking at me, as though I was fatigued. I probably shouldn't have ridden with De Roo, but also, I was a bit tired. It's one of those things Paul, you learn those lessons, you might feel you're doing someone a favour but it's not helpful. The promoter in Antwerp would have paired me with someone else, but I'd given him my word. At the end of the day it came back on me; it finished my season anyway. By that point I was thinking about turning professional, for sure, but wanted to wait until the following November at least. This was because of the Olympics. I had two things I wanted to do. I had to go back to the UK and get selected for the Olympics, then after the Games I wanted to turn professional. I could see the other riders in the sixes were doing quite a bit on the road, riding kermesses, town centre races, all of that, it gave them the stamina for the season. I knew I would have to do that sort of thing; you can't make it just by riding on the track.

Maurice came back to the UK in March 1976 to target selection, receiving an endorsement from *Cycling Weekly* in an interview later that month:

'At the age of 20 Maurice Burton seems to have everything to gain. He appeared to be one of the smoothest riders … he picked his way through the field with confidence, looking at one with his machine while others seemed to fight with their bikes. A man with fair sprinter's speed, proven stamina in bunched races on the track and now agility on the boards, Burton must have a valid claim for consideration as one of Britain's team pursuiters in Montreal, and when that's over, as a welcome member of the six-day school. He's already halfway there.'[3]

Despite this, there was a latent anxiety that as a Black rider, other forces might intervene: 'in spite of the situation that I felt I was in, I knew I had to try.'

---

[3]*Cycling Weekly*, April 1976

8

Herne Hill

Throughout our conversations we come back to the importance of belief, how self-belief is one thing, but it cannot mask entirely the need for belief from others, no matter what we tell ourselves, how confident we seem. For Maurice, that belief came from people like Oscar Daemers and Norman Sheil. On hearing these stories, listening to Maurice talk, I begin to reframe my feelings about self-belief, and the empathetic power of believing in someone – how for them, the strength in knowing that you care is empowering. Absent-mindedly, maybe when out cycling, I fall to thinking about Bill Dodds and how his intuitive kindness was utterly transformative for others. I don't think I changed, at least not consciously, but looking back at the things I was doing around the time of the interviews, I can see my practice has changed. It feels like the phrases I use in the classroom have started to shift, not that I was some kind of savage, strict teacher before, but I am aware that I'm now saying things I wouldn't have dreamt of saying a few years ago; telling an angry teenage boy that it doesn't matter what they do, what errors they might make, because of course they will make errors, it doesn't matter because nothing can undo the unshakable belief I have in them to do great things, to be a brilliant person. I don't know what's sparked this shift – maybe it's incipient old age and maturity, less of the seat-of-the-pants, hit them with dynamic lessons and they'll all be galvanised approach, more nuance, depth, more emotion; a slow nagging feeling that there is more to it, much more. Maybe it's just that I always lacked that self-belief and I regret not having it, or that I overcompensate by appearing confident. Maybe I'm just acutely aware that opportunity is everything and without action it is meaningless. Deep down, I suspect it's maybe that these conversations with Maurice, about Bill, Oscar and Norman, have made me say these things out loud.

We are at Maurice's house. The cat comes in, looks friendly, rubs his back against my legs, turns, hisses and growls, walks away. Maurice's cat does not believe in me. However, Norman Sheil and Tommy Godwin, both Olympic medallists, believed in Maurice. The same was true of Reg Harris. They proved this through action. However, Sheil and Godwin weren't in charge of the squad or involved in selection for the Montreal Summer Olympics in 1976; this fell to Tom Pinnington and Bob Bicknell. They were much more circumspect. They did not believe in Maurice. The early messages in the press were flinty: 'Maurice has never quite come to the training sessions and shown us that he is worthy of a place. If he wants to, then he can contact me and I'll invite him.'[1] I can almost hear the gritted teeth; the modality of it, the strange choice of 'quite', the demand that he must speak to them, Maurice must earn this, the notion of 'worthiness' foregrounded as an essential criteria, rather than skill, talent or pace. Riding in Belgium made it difficult to get to the training sessions, but no allowances were made. Notwithstanding the lack of an invitation, the sense that it was Maurice who must approach them, must demonstrate his worthiness, is troubling. It's also apparent that no one else was singled out in the press in this way by the Federation. The journalists at *Cycling Weekly* were supportive; writers like Keith Bingham focused on his progress. He was featured on the front and back pages of the press, double-page profiles, news reports, images. In January 1976, he appeared in a full-page image with Dave Le Grys.

---

[1] *Cycling Weekly*, 3 January 1976.

When the initial squad was announced on 7 February, 1976, Maurice wasn't in it. A terse statement followed from Bob Bicknell, the manager, shared in *Cycling Weekly*.

'The in-form Maurice Burton, currently making a name for himself on the continent, who has expressed an interest in gaining selection, will be invited along with several others to attend training sessions, but it will be at their own expense.'

Again, it's notable that only Maurice's name is mentioned, apart from the obvious corollaries in the sentence itself; 'in-form' and 'making a name for himself on the continent' are not enough to ensure selection to the initial squad. Tommy Godwin came out in favour of Maurice, stating in the press that he thought he deserved a chance. The squad announcement caused controversy and confusion. Maurice is clear about why, but also the subtext:

I wasn't even in the squad, before you talk about selection for the Olympics. It was because of Pinnington. They hadn't been inviting me to training sessions, then they said I should ask for an invite, then they said I could go but I had to pay. I don't know what they were trying to get from me, what they wanted me to show, what they thought my 'value' was. Who else had to pay their way? I had to pay to show them what I can do?

Steve Heffernan was also omitted. Heffernan was a hugely successful domestic rider, a serial winner at the Paddington track, but there is a hint of discord between the selectors, the rest of the squad and Bickerton, a lurking animosity – like Maurice, he didn't fit.

Heff got a rough deal. He was a very strong rider, he didn't quite fit in with the others, and he got treated badly. Here was a guy who won the ten-mile gold medal at the Commonwealths, but what the other guys on the team did, they wound him up, he was a bit naive. One time they told him he had to pay for his blazer, got him to hand over money – no one else did, it was free. They didn't treat him well, I haven't got a degree in psychology or anything, but they could see how strong that guy was, how individual he was, so what they did was they worked on him because he was a threat to them. Later down the line, there was someone else they did this sort of thing to, a kilo rider, he was so unbelievably strong. He had steel handlebars and from a standing start he bent the handlebar out of shape. They took the piss out of him, they were relentless. Even Bob Bicknell joined in with the riders, whereas as a coach he should have put a stop to it. You can't imagine Brailsford allowing that, intimidating a rider, they would have nipped that in the bud.

In short, these are institutionalised behaviours; difficult to challenge because of the collective buy-in. It's reminiscent of Yorkshire Cricket Club. Questionable alleged actions are dismissed as banter. Then when the shit hits the fan years later, people are appalled to find they are implicated, that the things they allegedly said or did, which seemed 'harmless' at the time, were in fact toxic, unpleasant, prejudiced. Maurice contextualised his treatment and is quick to dismiss it as a feature of the time, 'how it was back then', which it might have been.

With me they made jokes like, 'Oh when they sprayed you, you had your hands and your feet on the wall,' but that was something I was used to anyway, from ever since I was at school. I never quite fitted in with anybody, I've never tried to fit in to be honest with you. Even at school, the uniform – like I said before – when we didn't have to wear it I carried on anyway, I didn't feel the need to have to fit in. I just focused on what I had to do and got on with it.

It comes back to determination, single-mindedness, even bloody-mindedness. But surely, defining your existence by 'not having the need to fit in' is a rational response to not being allowed to fit in. It's pre-emptive, *I don't need this, I can live like this, you can exclude me and be racist, but I will carry on, on my own.* There were opportunities ahead to prove he was 'worthy of a place', starting with the Good Friday Meeting, and Maurice duly set out to prove it.

I hadn't been back that long, and I went and rode the Good Friday Meeting. I came second in the Golden Wheel to Paul Medhurst. A day or two later, I won the distance race at Leicester, beat Herman Ponsteen, who was the eventual silver medallist at the Olympics, and beat everyone else. Essentially, I was beating all their riders and it became an embarrassment to them to the extent that they let me into the squad. There was even an article in *The Times*. In today's world with social media, it would have been a much bigger thing, would have blown up. People would have rightly questioned it, their motives. In those days, you could hold the line, these things didn't get out in the open. But it got to the point where they had to bring me in.

Zerny Two-Day, 1976

The squad were expected to ride in road races. This included the Zerny Two Day, the Leyland Classic and the Lincoln Grand Prix.

> Even when I got into the squad, I still didn't feel it was going to work, but I had to follow it through. Heff and I rode the Zerny Two Day, I got a puncture on the first day, that blew my chances, but I was strong and I rode with Heff in case he needed a bike – he went on to win the first stage and the GC, beat all the squad members. It might have been the only stage race I ever rode, certainly I never did that as a pro.
>
> I followed it all the way through, I had to give it my best shot. If it didn't work, well at least I tried. It would have been worse if I hadn't at least tried, then always wondered about it. Well, I did try, and it didn't work. If Norman Sheil had stayed on, things might have been different for me. I don't say that I would have got in there, to Montreal, definitely, and I'm not disrespecting the riders that did get in. It's not whether I would have made it, it's that at one point I wasn't even in the squad and there were guys in that squad who hadn't even won a race.
>
> What I'm trying to say is that I don't think I got a fair chance with it. If I'd got a bronze at the Olympics, or even better, I could have come in as a pro on a higher level, because that's another reason why I wanted to go to the Olympics, because it was a passport to a professional career.

The final selection call was made late, on 5 June 1976. There was no place in the Olympic team for Maurice Burton. To add insult to injury, that same week Maurice won a ten-lap points race easily against all of the Olympic Senior Squad, including Ian Banbury and Ian Hallam. Accompanying the squad announcement was an interview with Bob Bicknell in *Cycling Weekly*; it makes mention of everybody who was not going except Maurice: "'You won't see me at any more training sessions,' said Maurice Burton, the rueful smile on his black face hiding a world of disappointment, 'I'm off to Belgium and as soon as I can.'"[2]

---

[2]'Staying at Home', *Cycling Weekly*, 12 June 1976, p15.

The language is unnerving; his role as the 'other' among the squad emphasised by the laziness of the printed phrase, a caricature. I doubt a similar phrase would be used for Ian Hallam. The experience proved formative for Maurice: 'I never thought it was going to work, but I saw it through. It didn't work. I never raced in a UK championship again.'

9

Zelzate

Maurice rode once more at Paddington, later that week. He cleaned up, winning the Devil, the 20km, and came second in the sprint, winning £56, or £350 in today's money. The next day he went straight back to the butcher's with Alaric Gayfer, who was also keen to try his hand as a professional in Belgium. The plan was to ride on the road for a few months, earn money from primes, then turn professional the following year. Also at the butcher's was a young rider called Mike Tanks. He is a supporting player in the story, a brief candle that flares and burns brightly, before disappearing into darkness.

I came across Mike Tanks while in the depths of research, surrounded by back issues of *Cycling Weekly*; there was a big splash on him, then seventeen years old, the text driven by the idea that he was something of a loose cannon: 'The Wild Days of Mike Tanks Are Over'[1]. He had a reputation for 'rambunctious riding', and a long charge sheet of crashes and injuries. The subtext is that for the seventeen-year-old Mike Tanks, zero fucks were given. Like Maurice, he was riding for KVC Deinze Bruggeman, a local team on the road, tackling kermesses. The kermesse is the Belgian town centre criterium, a hectic race around a tight circuit. Tanks was also hoping for assistance from a supporters' club – a uniquely Belgian proposition

---

[1] 'The Wild Days of Mike Tanks are Over', Dennis Donovan, *Cycling Weekly*, 19 February, 1977, p6.

where groups of people get together behind a rider, paying a subscription for a T-shirt or a cap, then meeting at a certain place to watch the races. It demonstrates the depths of community involvement in Belgium, the familial reach of cycling as a grass-roots, community sport. The supporters coalesce around a rider and have a designated bar where they meet. Like Maurice, and Steve Heffernan, Tanks saw himself as an outsider. He was keen to do things the Belgian way, where amateur status is a stepping stone to turning professional, not a means to an end, as it pretty much is in the UK. Arguably, those who had most to lose had the strongest desire to succeed and to cross over into the professional ranks. I mentioned him to Maurice in our first meeting, whereupon he suddenly sat up, breathed in, formless memories emerging out of the mist of the past.

'Mike Tanks! Let me tell you about Mike Tanks!' A string of stories follow, as Maurice tells me about a fast bike racer who did breathless exciting things, someone who lived life to the very fullest, and, as Maurice puts it, 'did all sorts of stuff.'

I search, tentatively, slightly wary of what I might find. I ask a few contemporaries. No one knows anything. Nothing appears. He became a footnote in the pages of the press, burning out and disappearing into myth; a novel waiting to be written, going by what Maurice says.

Maurice and Alaric Gayfer spent the summer racing on the road. The pro-am Madison on Christmas Day had given Maurice a clear sense of what being a professional entailed:

It opened my eyes, and I knew I needed a season before I was ready. It was why I wanted to try riding on the road in Belgium, because you can't make it as a pro just by riding on the track. Look at the six-day riders too, most of them did reasonably well on the road, and that gave them the stamina they needed.

Maurice came second to De Roo in his first race, the two of them getting away early. The list of kermesses is a roll call of provincial Belgian cities and towns – Mechelen, Zeveneken, Lovendegem – all featuring the same listless, flat, windswept courses in and out of the irrigated farmland, across polders with water courses at right angles, through provincial town centres crowded with people.

> I had ridden on the road earlier in 1976, when I was based in the UK, trying for selection and doing a bit with the Archer GP Race team. They were invited to ride Ghent–Ypres, an amateur classic, all paid. I went over with my bike, rode my race, but when they came back, I stayed on. The problem was earlier in the year the races weren't as close together, and you had to get the train sometimes, it was expensive and I was running out of money. I didn't have enough money to get back for the Good Friday Meeting. I rode in a race in a place called Bredene, somewhere near to the sea. It was a huge race, something like 250 riders and I came second and with the primes I was able to come back. It's surprising what you can do when you put your mind to it. It was like with the Zelzate loop – I realised I had to do something to get through, so that's what happened.
>
> I hardly ever won, but a lot of the time I came in the top ten. Typically there were twenty prizes, so there was enough money in the top ten places, and occasionally I'd take a prime during the race. This meant I was earning money, I could pay the rent, afford to live. I had to earn, whereas for riders who lived there, it was clearly different, they were at home. Alaric had a bit behind him, his dad was editor of *Cycling Weekly*, so that would have helped. For me, if I ran out of money, that was it, game over. It was hard to survive on the money I was winning, I had to make it work.

I ask him about Alaric, about a specific race at Drongen, just because I've researched it, waded back through an archive, looking for the details. Maurice looks at me, slightly bemused. 'How did you know that?' It's the detail, I guess. This is the writer's thing, find out the stuff, be prepared. I live in a state of constant anxiety, that if I don't know something then it's insulting to the person you're speaking to, turning up and not knowing a thing, asking the wrong questions. But sometimes the weight of research has the opposite effect – it unsettles people, insofar as you're asking them about a thing, or a name, that has, for one reason or another, been hidden in the recesses of memory for thirty or forty years, only to resurface with a sudden synaesthetic potency, with smells and sounds and feelings. It happened a bit when I mentioned Mike Tanks in our first meeting, and it happens again, not so much with his name, but the mention of Drongen, another shapeless, windswept Belgian town. It was a place visited briefly, for a pre-race number pin, a piss in a hedge, then a relentless kermesse. Suddenly he is remembering the break, the wind across the polder, a deal with De Roo, the conversation, Barry Hoban[2] in the bunch, coming twentieth. Memories sit there, undisturbed through time, unopened for years, until called upon.

The aim was always the track. Back at 't Kuipke, things had changed. Oscar Daemers was no longer the promoter; André D'Hont was in charge. He didn't take to foreign riders in the same way, which made things more difficult for Maurice, even though the support from Daemers wasn't always positive: 'sometimes it gets me in trouble with the Belgian riders. Some people say, whenever I go for a lap at Ghent, Mr Daemers waves the bunch to slow down.'[3] Daemers' retirement was awkward, as Maurice recalls:

He wasn't a young man. Even so, I don't think he went voluntarily, he was pushed. When they put Oscar out, I think it broke his heart to tell you the truth. He bought a house in Mariakerke and I used to go and see him from time to time. I don't think many other people saw him after he wasn't the man any more.

[2] Hoban is a pioneer of British Cycling, riding twelve Tours and winning eight stages in a successful career.
[3] 'Verblijf in Belgium', *Cycling Weekly*, 17 January 1976.

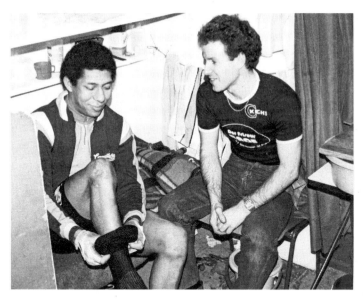

Cabin at the Skol Six with Steve Snowling

Having become immersed in the Belgian scene, Maurice found there were other offers and ways into the circuit. Informal affiliations with riders and their supporters were essential. Maurice became friends with Dirk Heirweg, whose father was a wealthy factory director. Heirweg (Senior) paid 'a fair amount of money' for Maurice to ride with Dirk at the amateur six, instead of his intended pairing with Stan Tourné. The money was enough to see him through the winter, making the decision straightforward. Tourné was paired with Noël Dejonckheere instead. There is a sense throughout this period of riders cutting their teeth at Ghent and in the kermesses, before going on to have storied careers on the road. Dejonckheere is a case in point, going on to win six stages of the Vuelta, before ending up as the directeur sportif for 7-Eleven and then Bicycle Manufacturing Company (BMC). He died in 2023.

The 1976 winter season, Maurice's last before turning professional, saw a steady adjustment to life in Flanders, with new ways of living and different cultural demands. The outright institutional hostility of the BCF was replaced by a combination of curiosity, novelty and ignorance. The UK was going through a paroxysm of prejudice, from Eric Clapton's rascist tirade onstage in Birmingham in August 1976, to the 'overzealous' policing of the Notting Hill carnival. Waves of racist moral panic churned in the tabloid press, the ripples evident in protest and counter-protest. In contrast, in Belgium immigration had been strictly controlled, with movement from Rwanda and Burundi actively discouraged. Without the same patterns of immigration – no 'Windrush' – and an active repression of the country's colonial past, the brutalities enacted by the regime of King Leopold, wider attitudes were not framed by a tentative, complex dialogue around race, but by repression, novelty and otherness. Professional footballer Paul Beloy recalled his experience growing up in Mechelen: 'People came to our garden to look at little black kids who were five or six years old. They would say, "Look, their parents are Africans and still live in trees!" We were a novelty.'[4] The same gaze applied to Maurice and the one other Black rider at the time – Paul Tachteris, a Rwandan professional.

Paul Tachteris

[4]www.newframe.com/paul-beloy-lambasts-racism-in-belgian-football/

Back in Britain, Maurice's progress was followed by a handful of journalists, including Keith Bingham, who wrote several supportive articles. Maurice was successful in the regular track meets at 't Kuipke, with a string of second places in the early season omniums, a multiple race format typically involving a devil, scratch, madison and other disciplines. Mike Tanks and Alaric Gayfer were also racing day in, day out, but it was Maurice who took the headlines back home: 'Burton Promises Much at Ghent'. Maurice took two wins in two days: a 20km Madison with Michel Vaarten, followed by a win in the Devil – one of Maurice's favoured events; the regular sprint from the back to avoid relegation seemed to suit his power and style of riding.

The sense of form and strong placings augured well for his second amateur six at the end of November, riding with Heirweg. Maurice broke the derny record for the track in one of the paced heats, riding at 37mph. However, the overall result was a step down from the previous year, coming sixth, at five laps, despite Maurice being identified as 'one of the strongest'. The professional event was won by Patrick Sercu and Eddy Merckx, who had won in Grenoble, came second at Dortmund and Munich, and went on to win Rotterdam and Antwerp. In 1976, Merckx was in the twilight of his career, but still managed to win Milan–San Remo for a seventh time. He was indisputably the biggest star of the era and is seen as the greatest cyclist of all time. For anyone starting out in the sixes, his presence was intimidating; the pairing with Sercu was dominant.

As soon as the racing finished on Sunday, Maurice headed to Zurich with Stan Tourné driving. He had been paired with Tourné, who was also starting out as an amateur. It was a curious set-up, the promoter lined up national teams, with Tourné wanting Burton to ride as a de facto Belgian. It led to the improbable sight of him wearing a Belgian national jersey. Just eight months earlier, the BCF wouldn't let him wear his Great Britain jersey. The Belgians had no such qualms. There is a curious but clear sense of pride – 'Tourné wanted to ride with *me*' – the sense of being in demand, being wanted as a bike rider, not subject to institutional exclusion. Burton and Tourné lost the chase – the rider's name for the Madison – with twenty laps remaining after a collision. Amateur riders weren't allowed to use a handsling, instead having to grab the shorts and throw. I can't see why one is deemed safer than the other. Both methods are terrifying; having someone grab your shorts at 35mph is arguably worse than a handsling. Rather than neutralise the race, as per normal, they let it run, with pressure for a 'home' victory coming from the Swiss coach, Oscar Plattner. Zurich was a fast track and Tourné and Burton broke the track record for amateurs, as Maurice explained:

> We did 52.25km in the hour. It's very wide but whereas most tracks you have the track and the transition down to the duck board, at Zurich it was really sharp, and that was what made it so fast. Vienna was the same. It felt like riding the rollers with a really high cadence, spinning the gear round.

Zurich

From Zurich, it was back to Maastricht on 17 December, with François Cathoeven. Things were relatively quiet until the Six Days of Antwerp in February 1977, where Maurice rode with Gabriel

Minibo. Primes were targeted, races won, and he made enough money to live. It reinforces the notion of the amateur in Belgium being an 'amateur professional' – a class just below the full contract, rather than the more Corinthian and rigidly enforced code in the UK. It is complicated, the conventional idea of being an amateur, yet making money. Maurice explains it in more detail, when suddenly the phone rings, interrupting our chat. Someone is asking about a Brompton. It leads to a detailed and factual breakdown of the Cycle to Work scheme costs from Maurice, with percentages, the role of the distributor and the big bike firms. The deal is weighted against the bike shop, and Maurice is open about this with the customer; he tells him the supplementary cost and reasons why, and says, 'That's how it is, sir,' when they query it. I sense the control of money, the importance of business, the way his brain works, and feel that this sharp-eyed fiscal necessity was at least partly forged in Ghent in the late 1970s.

After Antwerp, Maurice returned to the UK in early 1977 for a few months. There were no races to speak of; it was too early in the season for amateurs in Belgium, or the races were too far away. From the end of February to early May, he trained in the roads south of the capital – short, lumpy loops around Westerham, Biggin Hill – building up steadily to seven hours a day. Immediately prior to heading back to Belgium, he entered a criterium at Crystal Palace where he got away with two other riders and dropped them for the win. It was a dominating, aggressive result, a clear indication of his strength and raw pace.

He returned to Belgium in May 1977, this time staying at Albert Beurick's lodgings in Destelbergen, on the outskirts of Ghent. It was called Vel'Hotel Tom Simpson, exploiting Beurick's links to the British rider who stayed with him when starting out. Maurice was building up a support network, working with some familiar figures, enlisting new people to the cause. It's a slightly murky world full of fixers and soigneurs with magical skills and a kit bag no one is allowed to touch. Burton's group at that time included Etienne Bauwens, Raf Dierickx and others. They lived in the same suburban part of Ghent and were immersed in cycling and committed to helping cyclists succeed. They all have nicknames, enhancing their familial and mythical status. Jacky Schaubroeck, occasional soigneur and involved in the group, worked laying cobbles for the municipal council, he was known as Jack '*Cassé*', or 'Cobble'. Beurick was rotund, so he was known as 'Fat Albert'. Maurice also roped in another mystical Svengali figure, Bernard Stoops, who worked in the graveyard where he also lived – the house coming with the job. Stoops had previously helped out with waves of Australians coming over, as well as UK rider Vin Denson when he made his way into the professional peloton. The support was manifested sometimes in slightly strange ways, a soigneur's sleight of hand, support with living arrangements, mysterious hand-me-downs.

Bernard got me a pair of shorts, they were Brooklyn, with the sponsors' logo on there. I thought they were spare, turns out they were a pair of Patrick Sercu's shorts. When I broke the derny record I wore them, and in Zurich. Sercu was on the track at the time and he looked across at me and looked down at my shorts. I don't think Bernard told him who the shorts were for. He looked at me strangely and asked me where I got them.

It was a strange time; I didn't turn professional until the following year. When I stayed with Beurick I was the only rider there, it was quite an odd set-up. There was me and three random pissheads; one of them, every time he saw me, he used to look at me, he used to go, 'vrrrr, vvrrrr, bunga bunga', I'm guessing because of my colour, but either way it wasn't nice. They weren't on top of things, we had a shared toilet and they'd miss the toilet, piss all over the floor, the seat, it was really unpleasant. One night they all went off for the weekend and there was just one guy left. He knocked on my door and mumbled something, he looked a bit anxious, said he'd heard the chickens say that he was 'going to die'. I didn't understand it and didn't like it, so I just kept the door shut and didn't get involved. The next day they found him at the side of the road in the drainage ditch, head in the water. He had killed himself. That left only me and these two guys and Albert's mother who had Parkinson's. It wasn't the best set-up to tell you the truth. The one good thing was that Albert was a supporter, and we had a deal that when I raced, I'd get steak, so I would race most days. In fact, it marked the point where I started racing on the road a lot.

Maurice did more than eighty races in Belgium between May and when he turned pro in October, including kermesses and criteriums, three or four times a week. The training load was intense, not just in terms of fitness and recovery, but the heavy Belgian roads took a toll on his equipment: he broke two steel frames in six months.

One race I was in, Frank Hoste was riding. He was very strong, won the green jersey in the Tour; but he was not a pure sprinter. I was away with Frank, thinking about the win, when I heard this noise. I didn't pay too much attention to it, until he pointed out that the frame had come apart, you could see it flexing and the crack opening up. It was a damn shame because with only four of us up the road I could have won. With the amateurs, you'd have forty riders, but ten or fifteen are strong and once the break went you never saw them again. In the pros, if you get away, the team gets on the front and they pull the damn thing back. It was good for me because with there being twenty prizes you knew that you were going to be earning alright that day. That was the main concern for me, putting bread on the table.

Maurice was growing in strength, his conditioning sharp, a constant diet of speed and distance making him a formidable prospect. It became even more noticeable when he came across riders from the UK.

A couple of guys, Mick Lee, Peter Shaw, they had come over to make a go of it. Mick was staying in Holland. They thought they were going pretty well, getting some placings. They came and rode at Hansbeke, just outside of Ghent. The race went along the side of the railway line near Aalter, and there were 2km of cobbles every lap in this kermesse. With the amateurs, there was a Belgian rider, Johnny De Nul, he had a chrome bike with a single fifty-six-tooth chainring, and he'd just attack and attack, churning it, until eventually there would be nobody left. As soon as any of us saw Johnny on the start list, you'd try your hardest just to stay with him. At this kermesse we hit the cobbles after 1km, that was it; he attacked, pushing this enormous gear and I stuck with him, about the width of a Rizla paper off his back wheel, trying everything just to stay there, telling myself to hang on, head down. This carried on full gas for the 2km cobbled section, before going back on to the tarmac. I looked over my shoulder to see who was with us. It wasn't even that they were down the road a bit, or stringing out, I literally couldn't see another rider. Johnny won; I was second. Mick Lee told me about this race many years later: 'Yeah, we thought we had a chance, we saw you on the start line with Johnny then suddenly it exploded and we never saw you again. Basically we got the shit kicked out of us and went back to Holland.'

Even the edgy Mike Tanks was wary of De Nul: 'he rides a gear of 114 inches and he is pure strength'[5]. After a summer spent having his head kicked in by Johnny De Nul, Maurice was ready to turn professional.

[5] 'The Wild Days of Mike Tanks are Over', Dennis Donovan, *Cycling Weekly*, 19 February 1977, p6.

10

Bommelstraat

Eddy Merckx and Patrick Sercu were unequivocally the brightest stars in cycling, featuring on magazine covers across a continent. Merckx was even known in Britain, where cycling was a niche sport, barely scratching the back pages of the broadsheets, and only then because of sleeper agents like Graham Snowdon at the *Telegraph*. There were other galacticos from the road scene who could also be found plying their trade through winter in the sixes. Broadly speaking, there were the Belgian superstars: Freddy Maertens, Marc Demeyer, Roger De Vlaeminck and Ferdi Bracke; then there were the Germans: Albert Fritz, Günter Haritz, Udo Hempel and Dietrich Thurau; and swarming around the edges were the Antipodean expatriates: Graeme Gilmore, Don Allan and Danny Clark, all regulars on the circuit, vying to join the 'Blue Train', the rarefied group getting regular contracts across Europe. Also within and without could be found the global superstars turning out for their local race at the request of a promoter, who knew the surest way to get bums on seats; tempting out Felice Gimondi and Francesco Moser at Milan, Bernard Thévenet at Grenoble, or Gerrie Knetemann at Rotterdam and Herning. The six was pure performative theatre, a compelling series to enliven the darkest of winters, providing the opportunity for people to get up close to their heroes, see them in prolonged action over a whole week, watching every second of the race. As a spectacle, it was in stark contrast to the Tour, where watching the peloton typically involved a four-hour side-of-the-road picnic followed by a three-second blur of whirring colour. Edging into the midst of this revolving cast, standing nervously in the wings, was Maurice Burton, a boy from Catford. For Maurice, it seemed surreal to see his name on posters, to ride out and line up on the presentation lap, to look across the track at Eddy Merckx and Patrick Sercu, those two-dimensional black-and-white heroes pressed into the pages of *Cycling Weekly* magazine.

The Dierickx family helped with logistics upon Maurice's return in August 1977; he escaped from the butcher's and the slightly sinister lodgings with Albert Beurick, moving into a worker's terraced house on Bommelstraat. It was perfect for Maurice. Dierickx Senior fixed it up for him, the family mucked in, including fourteen-year-old Luc. They supported the Londoner as he prepared for a full summer on the road and a winter on the track, the standard diet for six-day professionals. Paul Medhurst had turned pro the year before: he rode the Ghent Six Day with Dirk Ongenae, they came eighth. He had been pestering Maurice to turn pro because he knew Maurice was quick and there would be more opportunities for a pairing. Medhurst also knew that with Burton there was a chance of more contracts, better placings and he was more likely to make it.

All that summer he'd been badgering me to make the move, but once you've done it there's no going back. It wasn't an easy thing, I was doing OK on the road but I wasn't head and shoulders above those guys, and even though Paul was pushing me to commit to it, it's a big step.

It's not a truism; if you turn professional and find it sucks, big time, and you get spat out of the back week after week, you can't hold your hands up and say, 'Well that didn't work out, I'd like to be an amateur again.' The process of reinstatement was arbitrary and could take years. It was all or nothing. If things went wrong, it would be back to the electrical apprenticeship or even the Molins tobacco factory, dragging a suitcase full of regret. Even so, turning pro was inevitable. Maurice did a few last criteriums as an amateur, riding with Alaric Gayfer at Zelzate in August, where he came tenth, with Alaric second. His first race as a professional was at Aalter, on 8 October. He finished twelfth, took some primes, the win going to Herman Vanspringel – a Tour green jersey winner, who came second at the Giro and third at the Vuelta. This was the big league.

Turning professional changed things, moving away from the opportunism and pursuit of the individual race, the sprint prime, to a concerted effort for contracts. It exacerbated the underlying tension between making use of his colour – as a draw, as a novelty, to get contracts – with being taken seriously – not reduced to the role of the other, to be gawped at and caricatured in an overwhelmingly White environment. In fact, there are waves of paradoxes. Maurice Burton and Paul Tachteris aside, there were no Black professional track cyclists in Belgium. The dialogue and the language in British press at the time highlights a systemic racial inequality, sometimes explicitly, at other times through using crass phrasing, framing skin colour as the defining feature: not being White. Maurice returned home briefly to see family and spoke to *Cycling Weekly* during his visit. They reported it as 'the black Londoner was home for a few days'. There is no doubt, looking back, that many at *Cycling Weekly* were big fans of Burton, that they wanted him to succeed, they saw him first and foremost as a hugely talented bike rider who struggled to overcome obstacles. And yet, those obstacles are encoded in the use of language. The response is evident in Maurice's choice of language, the way he frames his experiences; how he reframes isolation as a positive: 'I was happy on my own, I did my own thing, I took on the challenge.'

The paradox became more complicated in Belgium. He knew that he was more visible, the only Black guy in the bunch: 'I get recognised quickly when attacking, there is no hiding.' He needed the prizes, needed the top ten placings, the licence was much more expensive, overheads were higher. His road diet was kermesse after kermesse, and after turning professional, was enhanced with monuments,

Belgian classics and semi-classics – the Tour of Flanders, Het Volk, Ghent Wevelgem, Kuurne–Bruxelles–Kuurne – staples of the early season calendar.

To be honest, at the beginning I didn't take riding on the road that seriously. When I rode Het Volk, I picked up the bike the day before, then all the spokes came loose; I hadn't checked it properly. I had to do it, but I had no illusions, I wasn't thinking that I was going to be up against Maertens or De Vlaeminck in the final. It's not that I couldn't, but more that I knew it wasn't possible. I've ridden them all, I've got up there in Kuurne, twentieth or something, but to be in a team and have riders that are going to work for you? I used to do business with this guy who did Sidi Shoes in East Flanders, he said that Johan Museeuw is from West Flanders and he had riders from Antwerp in the same team, and they *wouldn't work for him*. So how is that going to work for me? How do you think I would be able to get anyone to want to work for me? A Black guy from London?

We've been talking about it for years but it's only now, fifty years later, you see Biniam Girmay[1] cross the line first with the support of his team. But back then? I don't think so somehow. The only way for me to ride in those events was because I was something of an attraction, because I was different, because I was the Black guy. The promoters liked something like that. And it was the same for the sixes, later. At the end of the day, you still have to be able to race. If they put you in the race and come in 100 laps down then that's not going to work. The thing is, I could do it, and they knew that, but it really wasn't easy to get in, not at all; being Black helped me get in, while holding me back.

[1]Eritrean Biniam Girmay became the first Black African rider to win a Grand Tour stage at the Giro D'Italia in 2022, beating Mathieu van der Poel into second place. He also won Ghent–Wevelgem.

There is a different challenge, but one also rooted in prejudice and ignorance. Strength and resilience was required to fit into an allocated, tokenistic role, from where Maurice could exploit his position to become established as a rider of physical merit, not solely predicated on colour.

The races and training were in the service of one overarching aim: getting a ride at the Ghent Six Day in November. Maurice had missed the Skol Six, having turned professional too late. He teamed up immediately with Paul Medhurst, who had moved out of the camper van and was living with his wife and baby boy at Kazemattenstraat. 'It was very basic, pretty cold, the toilet was at the end of the road, that kind of thing. With his family there it wasn't easy, there's a different pressure when it's not just you. The street was rundown, I think it was condemned. Rosa [Desnerck] owned pretty much all the properties.' It was hard for both riders. When not putting in miles on the road in the frigid Belgian winter, track training sessions were held in an unheated, dark velodrome. The hope was that it would be worth it and they would be able to make the step up. The road to the six-day circuit is littered with the abandoned bicycles of those who didn't make the grade. For some, the breakthrough took years, a stop-start process as they fought to adjust to the increased physical, mental and emotional demands of the circuit.

Medhurst and Maurice got off to a flyer in their first race in the Ghent track league. There were three teams in the opening omnium, including Gerrie Knetemann with Gerben Karstens, Rik Van Linden with Van Den Haute; Medhurst and Burton won. It had the potential to be a long, gruelling night. Burton and Medhurst won the 4km pursuit, came second in the kilo, and placed highly in the Devil to lead the standings. Their place at the top of the scoreboard unsettled the other riders, who were edgy at the prospect of two total noobs taking away the spoils. The collective response was to sit on the pair in the Madison, forcing them to chase every single attack. They lost their lead and two laps in the process to finish third overall. It was a spectacular result, both an indication of what you can do, but also perhaps an indication of what you can't do if people don't want you to do it; the nature of the six, how alliances and enmities shape the outcome, often through written and unwritten rules (and how even these sometimes get torn to shreds). One thing is clear: Maurice Burton and Paul Medhurst had done enough to gain selection for the Ghent Six Day at the end of November. Maurice also picked up a contract for Cologne, with Raaf Constant. After a summer of relentless training outdoors, then indoor laps, getting in the line, riding in a shadowy, frigid velodrome, the dream of becoming a fully-fledged six-day rider was about to come true. And not a moment too soon, as Maurice explained: 'I couldn't face another winter as a taxi driver', i.e. being paired with slower riders, providing a mentoring service through the amateur ranks, helping others get a foothold. After the omnium, Medhurst and Burton formulated a strategy for Ghent.

> We were wondering what we could do. Realistically, we knew the overall classement wasn't possible. Merckx and Sercu were riding, along with Danny Clark and Freddy Maertens. These were the fastest riders in the world, indoors, outdoors, the lot. Marc Demeyer was there, he had won Paris–Roubaix the previous year. It was crazy really. Gary Wiggins was also riding his first six, with Staf Van Roosbroeck; he finished on about sixty-three laps, he was completely out of it. We targeted the points race on the first night and then the overall points competition, aiming to wear the green jersey and win it at the end of the week. I mean, we knew it would be hard, but what we didn't know before the start was that we were riding into the middle of a grudge match between Merckx and Maertens, and then pretty much everyone else. That made it even harder than it should have been.

Any ideas that things might start steadily, building up to a crescendo, were shattered on the very first lap, due to a simmering antipathy between Merckx and Maertens that sucked in everybody else. The last time Clark, Maertens, Demeyer and the others had come up against Eddy Merckx was at the Radstadion in Munich, where Merckx had opted to go hard, early. He had warmed up on the rollers – something unheard of on the circuit – on the opening night. Riders ordinarily settle for the rolling half-hour presentation as a loosener and then ride steadily into the evening. Merckx had exploded out of the blocks, gone on the charge and immediately taken eight laps on everyone else. It was a brutal assault and it went down like a cup of cold sick. Fast forward to Ghent and Freddy Maertens wanted revenge. For the record, if you're going to pick a fight with any rider at any point in history, I'd argue that 1977-era Freddy Maertens is probably not the rider to go for. Having read his chaotic/brilliant 1993 autobiography, *Fall From Grace*,[2] I would probably avoid a fight with Freddy Maertens under any circumstances, and from any era, but the 1977 iteration of Freddy Maertens was on the hottest of very hot streaks. He won eight stages at the Tour in 1976, thirteen stages and the overall at the 1977 Vuelta (terrorising the peloton like 'a South American dictator', according to one writer) and seven stages at the 1977 Giro D'Italia. On Tuesday night at Ghent, he roared on to the track in a demonstration of force and barely controlled anger, motivated by wounded pride, with a score to settle. Maertens did sixty seconds for a flying Madison 1km time trial, a demented paired race where the tension builds lap by lap, accompanied by squawking, percussive music, until the pair hit the last three laps at full speed and one of them is catapulted into the last two laps to bring it home. It's a visceral thrill to watch; a handsling from Maertens feels like it could reach escape velocity.

Maurice remembers it vividly. He sighs, then laughs. 'Yeah, he just smashed people to pieces', he says. Keith Bingham's report for *Cycling Weekly* at the time has all the hallmarks of an embedded reporter at a war zone; the crowd were on edge, unsure of what was happening, the violent, untrammelled force of racing, the lack of a warm-up, a savage first evening of racing, no theatrics, no deals, just punches flying. It seems enhanced somehow by the journey, the adventure, the fact that it's the legendary Bingers (to me at least, and other people brought up on *Cycling Weekly*, who also place Bingham firmly in the 'legendary cycling journalists' box, along with Jock Wadley) doing the writing, having taken a thirty-six-hour coach and ferry journey, then somehow wangling a seat at a trackside cabin. He captures the raw pugilism of the opening exchanges, comparing the Six to a boxing match.

Gary Wiggins, like Maurice, was riding his first professional six. He described to Bingers what it was like to see Danny Clark move from the top of the banking, by the rail, to the black line at the

---

[2]Freddy Maertens, Manu Adriaens (transl. Steve Hawkins), *Fall From Grace* (Ronde Publications, 1993).

bottom: 'he came down so fast it looked like he was going to go through the banking and out the other side.'[3] It was a violent intro-duction to the professional ranks and caused carnage, as Maurice admits: 'I was absolutely wasted after that, there was a hell of a battle going on and we were just in the middle of this thing. Doing one minute dead for a flying Madison, hahah.' He chuckles at the memory of it, of how 'Maertens and Merckx didn't get along,' and how their latent rivalry spread outwards, dragging everyone into their grudge match, forcing them to play along, pushing the pace of the Madisons up and up. 'We did 60km in one Madison in one hour twelve minutes,' he says, simply. I work it out – it's about 54kph. For an hour. It is astonishing, frightening stuff, with Medhurst and Burton holding on for dear life. Said Bingers: 'two Britons holding their own among two kingly teams fighting over one throne.'

It was a spectacular show, featuring multiple Grand Tour stage winners engaged in staggeringly fast bike racing. Poke beneath the surface, however, even literally, in terms of the spaces beneath the velodrome, and the event suddenly seems much less glamorous. Nowadays, endurance events are managed, controlled, coped with, ameliorated, at least that's what we think, with special pillows, ice baths, enormous team buses with expensive chairs and a professional chef. It is still an unbelievable slog, of course it is, beyond the reach of mortals, but somehow it seems like the bits in between are geared precisely to rest and recovery. This does not seem to have been the case on the six-day circuit in 1977.

We would sleep at the track, in spaces or a room underneath somewhere, a dormitory basically, a windowless room with lots of camp beds. Anywhere really you could sleep, or try to. We had a wooden cabin at the track, that was standard, with our names on it, you'd rest between the races, the soigneur would

[3]"Two Kings Fighting Over the Same Throne", Keith Bingham, *Cycling Weekly*, 3 December 1977, p18.

help out. You had a bucket there to use for the toilet, to stop you having to walk out and down the ramp and across to the toilet then back again. You had a runner as well, a young lad – he would attend to things, get you what you needed, and empty the piss bucket as well. They used to call them *loopjungers*. After the racing you'd sleep at the track, maybe not so much at Ghent but certainly at the other tracks, Zurich, Cologne, anywhere you weren't at home.

I had a bit of a cough, had caught a chill, and Paul had a stomach issue. If you came down with something then you'd get more ill over the course of the week, and sometimes it would spread through the other riders. For that first one I stayed at the track. Ferdi Bracke mentioned he could hear me coughing in the night. It was such a smoky place, very different to now. You could smell the cigarettes on your clothes, the atmosphere was not good. It wasn't a coal mine, but it was ironic because the job I was offered after leaving school was at the Molins cigarette factory, so from that to this, that was the choice I made.

Ghent trackside cabin – bucket of piss bottom right

Sometimes it's hard to remember how horrible pubs were before 2007, the way smoke hung in the air in thin wispy strata, the smell that clung on to everything you wore, the stinging in the eyes, the fact that everybody smoked, that drinking a pint meant smoking at the same time. It was something that seemed so utterly normal, so entrenched and unchangeable. Then it changed overnight to be utterly abnormal; the idea that you might smoke in a restaurant, or on a plane, or upstairs on a bus, seems bizarre, a facet of a bygone era that might as well be Victorian, Dickensian even, when public health was secondary to strange notions of individual freedom. It's a step further to try and imagine this scene transplanted to a velodrome, where sixteen riders at maximum effort, reliant on huge VO_2 max, are reaching right down into the depths of their lungs while all around Belgians are smoking furiously, with sickly, murky, clouds hanging in the air, billowing, rolling down on to the track, because everybody smokes. And it is November so everyone already has flu and respiratory virus, so everyone is coughing, and everyone is still smoking, and the velodrome becomes a toxic microclimate, filled with a dense, tacky fug of 3000 phlegmy Belgians smoking and coughing.

Maurice's dad and brother Norbert had come over to watch. They drove across from London, were flagged down on the E5 on the edge of Ghent, guided across and into the city by supporters and people from Maurice's network. At the time, Norbert was awe-struck, telling Bingers excitedly, 'It's unbelievable, Maurice has so many friends. His mother couldn't be here so I've taped everything.' Somewhere, there is a Super 8 reel of Maurice Burton's first six. I task Maurice later with trying to track it down. It is archive gold, surely, if we can ever locate the reels. Rennal's attendance was a vindication of sorts, but with caveats.

He never really approved of what I was doing, back then, and throughout my riding. Even when I had the business, even with Germain, when he rode on the Olympic Development Programme, experienced success, Dad never really got it. He didn't really understand it at all, the whole thing, cycling, the track. Both Mum and Dad would come to the Skol Six, Dad used to get Wembley mixed up with Wimbledon, he'd call it Wembleydon or something. They came over to watch me race in a Christmas Day meeting one year.

It wasn't just the presence of his parents, but the revolving cast of riders and soigneurs that added to the sense that this was a significant moment for Maurice. The pictures in magazines had become real figures: Eddy Merckx, Patrick Sercu and Gust Naessens were walking around, brushing shoulders, sharing mealtimes, having conversations, making small talk. Maurice remembers, 'It all came to pass, from the pages of the magazine at Herne Hill, when I looked at it and thought, "That's where I want to be", and here I was, racing against Sercu and Merckx. And for a first six, as new professionals, we didn't do too badly.' He underplays it. They won the points competition across the week with 343 points to Maertens and Clark's 288, with Merckx and Sercu in third. On the third night, Burton won the derny event, and in the second derny race, he beat Sercu. They won the points race. It was the third night when illness kicked in, they lost laps, but stuck it out. They did more than enough to draw the attention of Ghent track manager, André D'Hont, who professed himself 'pleased'. The end result was the most important thing: Medhurst and Burton had earned contracts to ride more sixes throughout the winter. Across the week there were other moments that proved transformative.

On the first night there was an elimination race, they called it a 'Madison Devil' with a car as the prime. There were two teams left, me and Medhurst, and we were riding against Merckx and Sercu, they were coming into change and Paul took the chance, he went full gas, and then he threw me in and I went full gas and we ended up winning it by half a lap. It was unreal. We beat Eddy Merckx and Patrick Sercu, in Ghent. Later on that night there was an individual Devil, and there were two riders left in the race, me and Merckx. Eddy had ridden with us before, at the Madison champs, and he knew that we were young, keen guys. Chances are that he would win, he was Eddy Merckx! He could see we were up for it, really wanted it. He rode alongside and he said to me, 'You let me win this one?' and I looked at him and I said, 'Well, yeah, OK Eddy, no problem.' Some people don't quite get it, they think, 'Why did you do that, why did you let him win? You could have beaten him.' Well, the reason is, an hour later nobody would even remember that race, you see, but for that man, it was important to him because he had his appetite for winning. He was like nobody I had ever seen before, it didn't matter what the race, he could even be playing cards and he'd want to win, and Eddy Merckx came to me and he asked me, ME, this little boy from Catford who some years before watched him on *World of Sport* on a Saturday winning the Tour de France, in my living room, saying to my dad, 'I want to ride with that guy,' and here I was, with this same man, on the track, in a race, and he was talking to me about who was going to win the race. It was a great honour.[4]

---

[4] For the six, or any multi-day stage race, it is never about the single race, the moment in time. Some riders are in it for points, or primes, others chasing the overall classification, and others still out to please a local crowd or promoter. Tactical alliances, enmities and arrangements emerge and dissolve in a pedal stroke. To be in a position to discuss an outcome with the strongest rider in the race, literally side by side, both riders giving it everything – to be a part of the tactics of the Six-Day with the greatest rider of all time – Maurice was flattered to be asked.

11

Zurich

There was no time to recover after Ghent. After six days of worsening illness and sustained physical effort, the first time for Maurice at that scale, and for that long, it seems cruel to have to spend the afternoon and evening driving to another country to repeat the process. It's the madness of the six-day circuit: finish Sunday, get straight in the car, drive for ten hours and 1000km, another velodrome, another city. The hermetic environment of the six adds another layer of disorientation. There is no acclimatisation, just a night drive through urban sprawl, searching for the track, head in through the doors, come out again six days later, drive away. You could be anywhere, outside of time and place, only the language, beer and interlude act as an indication of wider culture and identity. Flandrian ballads and Jupiler? It must be Ghent. Oompah music and steins of Helles? We're in Munich. After Ghent came the Hallenstadion in Zurich, a very fast track. The ice rink concealed beneath the track had expected consequences.

The main issue for the riders is that it was a very cold track because of the ice rink; they kept the ice at about 4°C, just above freezing. It didn't matter how warm it got up top or how warm they tried to get it, there was a freezer sitting underneath. Then, what started as a mild flu or cold in Ghent became a full-blown illness, bronchitis ripped through everyone, we were all ill that week. The accommodation was a windowless room in the building. At the end of the night you'd lie there awake, and you'd be sweating one minute, then switch from hot to cold, shivering. I wasn't feeling the best, put it that way.

It feels like a Dickensian morality tale, riders sleeping in cells; prize fighters waiting to be called, putting on a show for the paying punters. The circus is a constant, apt metaphor for the six schedule; a literal revolving cast from town to town, the evening's entertainment replicated across the week, with tweaks, building towards the weekend and a crescendo, a matinee send-off. The riders are both the acrobats and the animals, working hard, being worked, on a treadmill, another apposite metaphor. Any romanticism around the six circuit tended to disappear quickly, replaced by a creeping fatalism, a sense that there wasn't anything else, even for some of the biggest stars, like Danny Clark, who was unequivocal at the time in his attitude towards the circuit:

> I really do hate the sixes. It's such an unhealthy way of life. You spend six months of the year indoors and if you put your nose outside for a breath of fresh air you get pneumonia. You're working thirteen to fourteen hours a day in a smoke-filled atmosphere and that worries me when I think about what it's doing to my lungs. There's also the fact that you're always with the same bunch of riders and there are lots of times when you don't get on. I have to do it because it's the only thing I know.[1]

Nigel Dean also captured the physical demands and unnatural stresses.

> You are on your knees, your head is drumming, your crotch is sore, the sweat is running down into your eyes already burning from

---

[1]'Clark: the star who hates the sixes but needs the cash', *Cycling Weekly*, 5 April 1978, p25.

the thick cigarette and cigar smoke. I rode nearly an hour's chase on the fifth night of my first six with two broken ribs and a ripped shoulder joint. In the last fifteen minutes of the Munster Six I blew completely and the track was just a blur of colour. I shredded the chamois in my shorts during a chase and took all the skin off my crotch in a matter of minutes. In the showers after the night you can see wounds in riders' crotches big enough to push two fingers into. These are the grim realities that take place behind the facade of glamour.

It is a brutal way to earn a living. Timings varied from event to event, but a split session was common. Racing took place from two until five, then from eight until the early hours of the morning. The finish was sometimes dependent on the vagaries of a city's transport system. The Skol had a harder finish at midnight, allowing people to get the last tube home, others pushed on through, in the knowledge that no one could get home after 10.30 p.m. until the trams started up again at 4.30 a.m., for instance. Rotterdam finished at 3 a.m., riders would try to sleep by 4 a.m., get up at midday for breakfast, then try to work out mealtimes and calorie intake, despite the ability to eat enough becoming a growing problem over the week, especially combined with the lack of sleep brought on by intense physical effort. It took three, maybe four winters of constant six-day racing for riders to learn to regulate their bodies and adapt to the level of intensity needed. However, this brought with it risks and long-term consequences. In short, it was spectacularly unhealthy, and long-term success too often came at a cost in terms of health and longevity.

Roman Hermann was partly established on the circuit, a couple of years further on than Maurice. He was paired with Günter Haritz, who was a regular, having won ten sixes in the past two years in partnership with René Pijnen mostly, but also Sercu, fellow German Didi Thurau or Tour winner Bernard Thévenet. There was a solidarity between Hermann and Maurice – they were both fighting to take places on the circuit that were held on to tenaciously by senior riders.

In Zurich, Maurice identified Haritz and Hermann as the pair to watch: 'We were pinning them, on the same laps, level on the standings. Whenever either of them went, I would go for it, follow them. If they tried to take a lap, I'd go straight after them; it got to the point where I just leaned in and said, "Yeah sorry to tell you Roman, but if you go, then I'm going to go with you," and just held him on the same laps.' Merckx and Sercu were in front, ahead of Udo Hempel and Ole Ritter, both household names.

Maurice, Werner Betz, Paul, Zurich

Maurice wasn't well; the respiratory virus had taken hold, weakening his lung capacity, he didn't feel good. The masseur was working with Maurice and a couple of other riders, one being a domestique on the road for Eddy Merckx. At Zurich, Sercu and Merckx were the patrons, and they were looked after by 'soigneur to the stars' Pierrot de Wit. The Sercu/Merckx pairing was formidable, as Sercu recalled: 'Eddy and I complemented each other. I was the speed, he was the strength and we were friends. That was very important. And he was always very motivated to win. Every time. As was I.'[2]

Maurice picks up the story again, with a pause, and a big intake of breath. I feel something simmering, a force of reminiscence. I've seen enough people dredge things up from the past, hidden in the silt of memory, to know when they are struggling how to tell, or even whether to tell.

One afternoon, I was in the massage room with another rider, getting a massage, waiting to go up on the track. The soigneur had this little syringe, and I said 'What's that?' and he said, 'It's vitamins.' He put it in my leg, while I was on the massage table. About two minutes after he did that I said to the other guy, 'Fucking hell man, this is not vitamins, no way.' It wasn't that I felt *something*, it was more that I didn't feel *anything*, nothing, not sick, just *nothing*. It was a hell of a shock. It was unbelievable. It was such a contrast from being sick, feeling absolutely wiped out. Suddenly it felt like I could take on the world. It was something I hadn't felt before – or since. Whatever it was I've never had that again.

We got back on the track. Once we were up riding, I got the feeling that Merckx and the others were looking at me. I felt paranoid that they were looking at me strangely, but at the same time, I didn't think it was my imagination, it was definitely different, the way they looked across. This was our second pro six, remember. The problem was that there wasn't anything I could do about it, I mean, you can't take it out, you can't quit, so I just had to make the most of it.

The others would be riding down there, on the black line and I'd be riding high up the track, overtaking, going the long way round. I've never ridden like it before or since, don't know what it was. He gave the same to other rider as well but it didn't have the same effect on them that it did on me.

[2]Graeme Fife: www.rouleur.cc/editorial/patrick-sercu-phenomenon

The thing is, you push yourself beyond your normal capacity, so when you have to ride again, the next day, you're even further down than you were before. He did what he had to do; we got through to the final day, but then the other cyclist I was with crashed and did something to his arm and we never finished the race. Even so, we were running up there, but the whole thing wasn't right, you know.

There were people out there who looked after riders, the soigneurs, it's such an important role, and everyone knew how it worked. They'd have a bag of medicine, tonics, they'd say, 'Drink this,' and they'd have taken the label off or taped it up, so you didn't know what it was you were given. You had to rely on the soigneur, that they knew what they were doing, and they made the decisions about what it was, the level of legality, I guess. Before Zurich, I knew that couldn't happen to me, and after Zurich it became even clearer. If I was going to take something – good or bad or whatever – then that had to be my decision to make, whatever it is. I didn't want to and couldn't have anyone else making that decision for me. So I had to sack him.

I never spoke much to the soigneur after that. I heard that he told Merckx, all of them, 'Oh watch out, tonight, my boys are gonna fly.' He used us as an advert to promote what he could do; if you came and worked with him this is what would happen – it came under the label of 'preparation'. At the end of the six, the manager and riders' agent Jan Dirksen came to sort out the money for the riders, to pay us and to take his 10 per cent. Jan was a professional sprint champion back in the time of Reg Harris, and he had about 250 riders on his books. He managed me, Danny Clark, everyone. He was the go-between, in the middle of the riders and the promoters. He'd be there every weekend, taking his cut. Roman Hermann calculated that over his career he rode two full winters for Jan Dirksen. Before Dirksen it was Van Buggenhout, after Dirksen it was Sercu, it was a common move for ex-pros. Jan turned to me and said, 'If you ride like this, I'll get you into every six I promote.'

As an amateur I can tell you hand on heart I never used any kind of medical substance to race. If you had to do things like that to ride with amateurs then it was a total waste of time ever thinking about or imagining you might race with professionals. We all knew the professional scene, and we all knew there were things going on, but it's different knowing it's happening, to seeing it happening and then suddenly finding you are a part of it happening. It shocked me. I was so upset about it that I came back to London for a few weeks, to the point where I reconsidered what I was doing, and why.

I'm shocked and not shocked. I am unable to comprehend the levels of fitness and stamina it took to compete. The six-day was a violent, inhuman, anachronistic construct. It placed riders under huge physical and emotional stress; no sleep, deepening exhaustion, respiratory illness, poor recovery, enormous physical exertion in the middle of it and extraordinary amounts of travelling between events. It is inevitable that a framework of support and preparation existed to help riders get through, to get to the next event, to sleep, to get up, then to sleep again. The list of infractions throughout the peloton in the 1970s is extraordinarily long, indicating institutionalised, normalised drug use. It was an integral part of a murky world where hundreds of riders were competing for just sixteen contracts, and all the earnings and recognition that came with them. It doesn't do any of us any good to judge, from the outside looking in, to stop and stare, but to view drug use within a complex framework of institutional corruption, flawed people, poor regulation, and an avaricious desire from the audience, rooted in the myths of the six-day and cycling in general to see more and more superhuman acts and physical heroism.

To go from looking in, wanting to ride the sixes, wanting to turn professional, then *within a month* reach the point where this happens, I thought, this is not for me. I came back, and it got to me what happened, I struggled with it, because everything until

114

then had been about getting to that point. But then I sat down and looked at myself and again, I thought, If I don't do this, what am I going to do? What else is there for me? What opportunities are there? The doors were closed to me, the opportunities weren't there, that's why I was in Belgium in the first place, because I wanted to be a professional cyclist and I couldn't be a professional cyclist in the UK. I had a choice, of course I had a choice, but it's not that simple, because in another way I didn't have a choice, and I had even less choice than many others! There are lots of riders like that, they turn professional, follow their dreams, then they don't like it, because it is a real challenge to everything they know or thought. That was the same for me, to be honest. After what happened in Zurich, I didn't like it, I didn't want it, but I had no choice.

Maurice went straight to Vienna for a one-day race at the Dusika Velodrome, named after Franz 'Ferry' Dusika, a famous Austrian cyclist in the 1930s. Dusika was a member of the Nazi Party and para-military group, the Sturmabteilung. He used his cycling magazine to agitate against Jews and 'Aryanised' the bicycle shop of the Jewish businessman, Adolf Blum. According to journalist Fritz Neuman: '*so war Ferry Dusika, so ist Österreich*.'[3] ('That's how Ferry Dusika was, that's how Austria *is*.')

Maurice was welcomed to the city by the back page newspaper headline, 'Will the N____ beat Sercu?'

---

[3]www.derstandard.at/story/1395363189487/so-war-ferry-dusika-so-ist-oesterreich

12

Antwerp

The soigneur in the late 1970s was counsellor, father figure, guru, Svengali, non-registered practitioner of funky medicines, horse-whisperer, and nearly always ageless and Belgian. Since then, the role has changed markedly, away from the quack medicines of yesteryear, into clinical practice and sports science. I have a friend who is a soigneur for a professional team. He is a brilliant physiotherapist, clinically trained, and works closely with riders. When not doing sports massage, he seems to spend a lot of time at the side of the road holding up musettes, bidons and ice-stockings, but the relationship remains vital: he is a listening ear, offering sympathy and support, as well as a familiar language to English-speaking riders. He is intensely loyal to his riders, as they are to him. After the madness of Zurich, Maurice Burton needed a new soigneur, someone like Bill Dodds.

I went back to Belgium, I mean, I had to, but I decided I needed to find the right person to work with. Some time back, at Rotterdam, maybe 1975, I was riding with Roger Young, and I worked with Gust Naessens. He was looking after Merckx and Sercu at the professional event at the same time. When the six finished, I checked with Gust to see how much he wanted, but he said, 'It's fine, you're only an amateur. When you turn pro you can pay me.' Gust had a way about him that was different to the others, money wasn't the key, it was a case of whether he wanted to work with you or not. I trusted Gust, so when I got back, I looked for him. I had a couple of sixes to ride, including Bremen almost straight away in early January, then Antwerp at the end of February. Gust was the one I was looking for.

The only problem was that Gust had disappeared; he'd dropped out of the cycling scene, didn't seem to be working with anyone and hadn't been spotted at any events over the winter. Rumours were circulating of a fall-out with one of the marquee names at a six; the rider had gone into Gust's bag and taken 'something' without permission. The next morning, they woke up to find a bottle of cologne and a perfectly-folded square towel, but no Gust. Eventually, Maurice tracked him down to Brussels.

He agreed to work with me at Bremen in January. Gust drove the car, picked me up on the way in Ghent and off we went. He wouldn't work with anyone else. I also recruited a mechanic, Roland, who worked with Flandria.[1] He was part of the network with Bernard Stoops. When I was an amateur, and broke both those frames, they took the kit across and put it on two new frames for me. Roland was the one who then started making my bikes, and he became my pro mechanic. Gust and Roland were watching me on the track and changing my position without me even realising it, adjusting the height here and there, then another tweak. That's the same position I ride now, I have never changed it. It was Gust who did that.

Maurice returned to the Night of Cologne, the Boxing Day curtain-raiser for the Six Days of Cologne featuring the Silber Adler, where he tested out the new partnership with Naessens. He felt Gust was worth the expense: 'his fee was a lot, but the contract was a good one. In fact, despite what some people said, contracts don't all go on paying

---

[1] All-conquering Flandrian professional road team.

for food and personnel. There was quite a bit left over, otherwise there wouldn't be any point in riding.' Alongside Naessens, Maurice had brought over Angus Fraser, introducing him to the six, where he provided massage.

In Bremen, Maurice was paired with Willy Debosscher. Every article on the Belgian rider includes the same word: 'clown'. I have yet to find a single race report that doesn't focus on some 'wacky' thing he did, the anecdotes are numerous: taking off his shoes and socks while riding, getting dressed up, taking time out to dance with the band then dragging people out of the crowd to dance with him, wearing silly hats, stopping mid-race to conduct the orchestra. Debosscher set out as an entertainer, to the extent that the role of six-day professional became his side hustle. Attitudes to Debosscher vary, from the mildly tolerant, to the tersely dismissive. The serious-minded Sercu occupies the latter camp: 'that's not entertainment. If he was such a good entertainer, he should have been at the Lido in Paris. No one came for Debosscher. He had no palmarès.'[2] Roger De Maertelaere, a Belgian cycling historian, is more forgiving: 'he entertained thousands with his jokes and pranks. During the Devil, where his speed came into its own, he performed jokes that made the audience roar with pleasure. At times, his humour was a bit greasy – Debosscher entertained the crowd whether they liked it or not –but he could perform. After Debosscher, the era of the six-day clown was over.'[3] Maurice didn't mind the antics, as long as when the race was on he did his bit. However, there is a suggestion of tension from Debosscher towards Burton that belied his 'greasy' outlook.

Debosscher didn't want to ride with me. There's a lot there. I don't know if it's that he saw me as a threat because I was Black, or because I was the new fast rider, or something else. Generally, established

[2]https://www.rouleur.cc/blogs/the-rouleur-journal/patrick-sercu-the-phenomenon
[3]Roger De Maertelaere, *De Mannen van de Nacht* [*The Men of the Night*] (De Eecloonaar, Eeklo, 2000), p201.

riders were suspicious of newer riders, they are always going to be a threat, but there were definitely layers to it with him. Outside of the fact that he was a clown, he was alright as a rider but he wasn't quite at the highest level. He rode me into the ground in Bremen, until in the end I had a crash and the stem hit my undercarriage. They neutralised it and we didn't finish the race. I ended up doing three sixes with him in the years ahead, the last one was Madrid, in 1982, and he was alright with me by that point.

Debosscher, and others, were wary of anyone new, regardless of difference. One of the truisms of the Six is that the group at the top always guarded their positions intensely and were unhelpful to those riders on the way up. With Maurice, it was easier to dislike, to project, because of difference and otherness. Attitudes towards Maurice varied within the circuit. There were those like Albert Sercu – Patrick's father and a regular at the track – who 'knew what I had to do, and the things I had to go through to get there', who gave support and recognised the challenges faced by Maurice. Others were less welcoming:

> Some of the riders, at the track and when riding, they didn't ever talk to me, they never said a thing. I was excluded. Nowadays they are friends with me on Facebook, and I wonder if they think about it differently, they see it differently, the world has changed a bit, maybe they think, 'You know that guy, what he did, that was something.' Maybe they don't even recognise themselves back then, the people they were. Maybe they don't even see that they were like that.

Considering the crash, it seems odd that Burton viewed the Bremen event as a success. An early crash presents an issue for the promoter, with patched-up pairs or new teams cobbled together to ensure the racing continues. Completing the event, or getting near enough to complete, putting on a show, earning an affinity with the crowd – these are the things the promoter was looking for and that ensure further contracts to ride from the cartel of promoters. Hence Debosscher taking on the role of class clown, appealing to the audience, carving out a niche where promoters saw value over and above the event, allowing him the space to do stupid things in the Devil, or anywhere, for that matter, because it sold tickets.

Debosscher entertaining. Photo by Bill Kund

In one respect it didn't matter if a rider won or lost, the contract was a guaranteed payment, with additional primes and prizes split between the riders. Maurice earned good money, ergo Bremen was a success, to the extent that he was able to buy a new car – another variant of the VW Variant.

We were contracted in advance, and at the German sixes – Munster, Berlin, Bremen – it was 1000 deutsche marks per day. You only got paid for the days you raced; if Otto Ziegler pulled you out then that was that. It was a lot more than you could make on the road unless you were a protected rider, a star or a GC contender. The six-days were always good money, maybe apart from London, but even then, you'd still come away with £1000 for the week, but it just wasn't as much as the Continental sixes. Some of the kermesse riders who weren't track riders at all used to try and get a ride in Antwerp, they would earn more in the six than they'd take home in a month on the road.

I was riding the road at the same time, doing classics in March, stuff like Het Volk, the Tour of Flanders, but I really didn't have any illusions about making it big as a rider on the road, at least in part for those reasons I mentioned earlier, having no support. I didn't really want to ride those classics, but I had to because I was riding for Fragel-Norta, a local team, and that was a part of the process, you had to go along. It wasn't a big team, so the idea of doing well enough to earn big money on the road just wasn't there.

Things have changed significantly – or haven't changed in inflation-ary terms – and this is perhaps another reason for the steady decline in six-day racing; however, there is a baseline salary in the road teams, removing the imperative for stars to ride the track in winter. Furthermore, teams blanch at the possibility of their £1 million signing hurtling around a 154m track with all the promise of dislo-cations, collarbone fractures and season-ending smashes. There are still those who see the six as a romantic, exhilarating event, who tap into the lineation of six-day racing over time. These include Bradley Wiggins, who always felt an affinity with Ghent, the city of his birth, but also Mark Cavendish. Both are keenly aware of the significance of the past, how narrative and myth shapes and mediates our view of cycling in the present.

From Bremen, Maurice went with Paul Medhurst to Antwerp at the beginning of February to round out his first season on the profes-sional circuit. It provided the opportunity to cement the relationship with Naessens, who agreed to continue working with the pair, on and off. He became a mentor of sorts, untangling the hidden complexi-ties of the circuit. The Sportpaleis at Antwerp is another huge venue with an ice rink in the middle. It held 18,000 spectators, in compar-ison to just 3000 at Ghent. It was built in 1932 during the heyday of

European track cycling by the legendary Apostel-Mampaey family, who also built 't Kuipke in 1922. It more than fulfilled the central requirements for an indoor velodrome – the capacity to transform into a broiling nocturnal cauldron full of drunk Belgians, beer, hot dogs and Europop. The track was lost in 2013 when the Sportpaleis was refurbished. The customary slot on the calendar now echoes to the sounds of Imagine Dragons and Kendrick Lamar, the Madison squeezed out by globalised sound.

Maurice at Zurich

In 1978, Clark and Maertens continued their breathless assault on everybody else, winning the six at a canter, with double the points of their nearest rivals, Pijnen and Allan. For Medhurst and Burton, rounding out their season, eighth place at twenty-two laps was a strong showing. As he drove home to Ghent, Maurice began to plan the next season, sketching out a trajectory: ride the road throughout March and May, both the classics and kermesses, build strength and endurance in readiness for the sixes, kick things off at the Skol Six in London. With Medhurst seen as the aggressive sprinter and Burton the smooth endurance pedaller, the combination had potential for further success, but neither rider was under any illusions, with Burton saying that it would take him at least three years to get to the top. Off the track, though, there were differences. Medhurst was more outgoing, and had a tendency, according to Burton at the time, to 'get a bit worked up'. The main difference was in circumstance, with Medhurst labouring under the additional weight of family commitments, the need to ensure that wife Pam and son Darryn were comfortable, on a basic level, that they had somewhere suitable to live. Keeping everything in balance, the demands of training, the need for money, for time, was a tough challenge. His second season gave a glimpse of what could be: both Medhurst and Burton bought new cars; Maurice's parents came over for Christmas and stayed at his house in Bommelstraat. They were learning the idiosyncrasies of the circuit, the dietary habits. 'You have to learn to eat raw meat when you race in Belgium.' For Maurice, it was simpler without the attendant pressure of family; he was here to race and at twenty-three years old, the alternative was never far away.[4]

It isn't an easy job by any means, but then neither is going to work every day. When things get hard, I go back to thinking about the cigarette factory. I'm content with my first winter as a professional, everyone else seems satisfied. Naessens says I'm only 50 per cent fit so far, and do you know what, I'm half a stone lighter than I was when riding as an amateur. Riding a bike as a professional is like all other jobs: sometimes you like it, sometimes you don't. It's much worse when you're not feeling well, like Zurich, when I had a really heavy cold. This is the first year since I was fifteen that I've got something out of riding.

I fixate on the phrase 'get something out of riding'. He was twenty-two at the time, and I wonder if it's symptomatic of the struggle of the previous five years, battles with authority, the institutional and overt racism, as much as a statement about earning enough to ride and live. The ambivalence of Maurice's status in Belgium was

[4]Dennis Donovan, 'Down in the cabins someone stirred', *Cycling Weekly*, 19 February 1978, p. 12.

never far from the surface, with Danny Clark recognising bluntly that alongside his athleticism, the novelty value of colour was Maurice's defining asset: '...because of his colour, Maurice could make it. One thing they've got to learn is to stay in the chase. It's not good when the race directors have to keep telling them to get on the track.'[5] It reaffirms the circus trope – come and watch the race, this year featuring a Black man. Jan Boesman, in his book exploring cultural stereotypes in Belgian cycling, argues that frequently African riders were objectified and othered in Belgium; welcomed for their novelty value in the first instance. Referring to Paul Tachteris, Boesman writes: 'usually he escaped, led for a few laps and took a shower before the race was over. In exchange for a free cycling outfit, he advertised for small companies'. Similarly, Duncan Seko rode for RDM-Flanders in 2002. Directeur sportif Frans Assez emphasised the commercial value of the deal, 'If he wasn't black, we wouldn't have offered him a contract.'[6]

I'm also keenly aware of the pioneer status, the visibility of Maurice Burton, the sensational joy in watching a Black cyclist from London make it in the most challenging sporting context imaginable; that this is a narrative of superlative achievement, it is not defined by bigotry and prejudice. The path to Continental success was fraught with difficulty, very few made it – Brian Robinson, Vin Denson, Barry Hoban, Tom Simpson – but none of note in the six until Tony Doyle, later. Many riders set out to race, only to return home, overawed, beaten. For Maurice, there was no alternative, it had to work, hence the affinity with the Australians, Danny Clark, Gary Wiggins, those who had travelled halfway round the world and could not afford to go home if it didn't work out. They were pioneers, paving the way for the next generation, creating visible role models, allowing youngsters to aspire to be what they can see. All of which is well and good, provided that the grass-roots model allows those chances for success and builds on their experiences.

[5]Dennis Donovan, 'Down in the cabins someone stirred', *Cycling Weekly*, 19 February 1978, p. 12.
[6]https://www.nieuwsblad.be/cnt/gin38upcf

13

Melbourne

The year 1978 was important for Medhurst and Burton, with the Skol Six in September being the prime opportunity to land contracts for the year ahead, especially with the advantage that comes from being a 'home' pairing. Maurice continued to race on the road for Fragel-Norta, a company that somehow made both frozen food *and* bikes. As Maurice said at the time, 'It's only a small team and my name seems to get mentioned more frequently than the other riders. The contract gives me enough to live on and there are no equipment worries on top.'[1] He returned to the UK in April to see family and took in some races at the same time, heading back to Herne Hill for the Good Friday Meeting, with British Airways sponsoring the professional omnium, featuring domestic professionals: Ian Banbury, Ian Hallam, Robin Croker and Steve Heffernan. Maurice won the one-lap time trial from a flying start in 35.6 seconds, came second in the Devil and third overall. Russell Williams won the White Hope Sprint. Williams' success, along with Joe Clovis, provided an indication that cycling just might be becoming more diverse. Later that year, Williams won the national junior title on the road. Over time, he might have expected further success at the highest level; his palmarès, like Burton's, stood out. Interviewed by Caley Fretz in 2020,

---

[1]'Keeping Faith with the Promoters', *Cycling Weekly*, 1 April 1978, p14.

his story has strong echoes with Maurice's experiences. Both came through the ranks of VC Londres, but it's at the juncture at which the British Cycling Federation became involved that things seemed to go backwards. In a bruising testimony he made in a short documentary, Williams is unequivocal about the reasons why he was not selected.

'It was because I'm Black. It's hard to say sometimes. There's nothing else I can think of. You're doing the times, you're beating the best people, and they just keep coming back and going 'Oh, no, no, not quite.' It's sort of devastating when I say it out loud. I could never ride fast enough, or win enough, because of one thing I couldn't do anything about: the colour of my skin.'[2]

The treatment of Williams and Burton exposes fully the systemic racism at the heart of British cycling at that time, and in society as a whole. Both cyclists were ignored for selection despite doing everything they were 'expected' to do, and more. The odds were stacked against them. You don't need direct causation to know that this was the case. It's one of the central tenets of Dr Marlon Moncrieffe's exhibition and 2021 book, *Black Champions in Cycling*[3], which sets out to challenge the exclusion of Black cyclists and to reassert these narratives as important, vital, personal stories. Maurice showed there was an alternative, a way into cycling that wasn't subject to the British Cycling Federation's gatekeeping. It consisted of moving out of the system entirely, confronting novelty and otherness head on, and forcing the issue by dint of being a very quick bike racer and having unfathomable reserves of determination and resilience.

The prospect of a renewed all-British pairing at the Skol Six in 1978 caught the imagination of the press but brought additional pressure: 'Burton and Medhurst have staked everything on breaking into the

[2]cyclingtips.com/2020/02/in-allegations-of-institutional-racism-a-black-british-riders-quest-for
-change/
[3]Moncrieffe, M. L., Black Champions in Cycling (2021). *Desire Discrimination Determination*.
London: Blue Train.

big time', 'the home duo need success'. *Cycling Weekly* sponsored the pair for the event. The top Continental promoters and agents were there, circling the riders, manilla folders full of contracts, pens at the ready for signatures. For professionals, the contract is everything; not the win or the prime. The evening's races are one part of a festival of cycling, among the music, the drinking, hot dogs and strange pizza bread, sponsors' stalls, and opportunities to catch up with people from the past, those who once rode the boards but now watch and comment, sage-like. It is a part of the cultural life of winter in a European city, a way of getting through the short, dark days, into spring. The promoter holds all the cards; a floating mist of gossip and intrigue swirls in their wake as they lurk silently beneath the stands, prowling through the cabins, standing trackside. At least 250 or more riders lurk in the pool, waiting to get a ride at the track, alongside the numerous potential home pairings, the local stars. How can we have Milan without Moser? For every contract taken, five riders missed out – on a payday, on the potential to earn more contracts, on a place in the 'Blue Train', as it was known, the elite cadre. Ron Webb directed the Skol Six for twelve years, but also Herning and Hanover for a brief period; impressing in London could bring at least two more contracts. Peter Post was also a promoter, his presence at the Skol Six was enough to provoke riders into supporting the Dutch team, chasing down threats to their success, in the hope that Post might view them favourably for Rotterdam. In among the friendships, enmities, old hands vs newcomers, there were plots and subplots, endless possibilities for intrigue and chaos, brawls, hurt feelings, grudges and lingering animosity.

Medhurst and Burton were out to ride as many sixes as possible. This meant taking risks, riding hard on the drop-in track, built by Webb and also used at Herning and elsewhere. They came tenth overall, not the placing they had hoped for, but not a disgrace by any means. There were some comments on Maurice's riding style, a tendency to drift up when looking behind, acknowledged by Burton: 'we all make mistakes at first'. The editor of *Cycling Weekly* qualified it without nuance: 'Comfort yourself, Maurice; compared with some

past British riders you were a black angel!'[4] Evans was an important editor for *Cycling Weekly* and a supporter of Maurice. He wrote
a double-page interview feature as early as 1975, with some awareness of Maurice's position as an emerging role model: 'Maurice does
occupy a special position as the hero of a growing band of Black
riders at Herne Hill, most of them in the VC Londres, the school-
boy-angled club he has just left.' Ken Evans and *Cycling Weekly* were
a part of that society, as were professional teams and the British
Cycling Federation. The sustained failure to reward riders like Russell
Williams, Joe Clovis and Maurice Burton is one and a piece with glib
phrases like 'the coloured Londoner' or 'black angel'.

The opening meeting of the Ghent winter track league in 1978
featured many familiar names: Dietrich Thurau, Patrick Sercu,
Willy Debosscher, Ferdi Van Den Haute, Roman Hermann, Walter
Godefroot (reigning Tour of Flanders champion), along with Marc
Demeyer, Roger De Vlaeminck and Freddy Maertens. It was a spectacular line-up of stars. Burton and Medhurst 'beat them all'.[5] It sent a
timely message to André D'Hont that they would be a force to reckon
with at Ghent in November and a contract was forthcoming. The pair
were a year stronger and wiser, better able to cope. Without the fire-
works of the Merckx vs Maertens grudge match, the racing was more
straightforward. However, it still featured one of the strongest fields
of any of the sixes, including the world road race Champion, Gerrie
Knetemann, who was paired with Sercu. All bets were off; it became
Sercu's sixty-first win in the six-days. Medhurst and Burton finished
fifth, a fantastic result, but Gary Wiggins was still some way off the
pace. It augured well for the pair, and Medhurst was positive about
his prospects: 'I really feel I'm breaking through. Getting plenty of
rides means I've got the racing tempo in my legs, and of course this
helps my form'[6]. They had an archetypal Belgian sponsor, a small

[4]Ken Evans, 'Skol 6', *Cycling Weekly*, 25 September 1978.
[5]'Burton and friends beat Belgians', *Cycling Weekly*, 21 October 1978.
[6]Ibid.

central heating firm, and they had contracts. They rode together at Zurich a week later where they finished ninth, going on to Herning the following week – contract courtesy of Ron Webb – where they came tenth in a tight race, at nine laps. At Cologne, straddling the New Year, Burton rode with Frits Pirard, Medhurst with Stan Tourné, but it wasn't a success: 'Pirard was never going to be a rider that you were going to get a result with. As good as you can be, if you haven't got a decent partner, then it's not going to happen.' Medhurst fared slightly better.

At Antwerp, in an unusual three-rider format, they were teamed with Alex Van Linden. They came ninth, beating erstwhile scourge of the kermesses and all-round hard bastard Johnny De Nul, who thus far had failed to make the transition from amateur tyro to professional beast. Come Milan, and again Maurice wasn't paired with Medhurst; this time riding with Nazzareno Berto. It's hard to escape the sense that both riders were looking for the right combination, either together, if it got the promoter's eye, or apart. They managed to get a contract for one of the few non-European sixes, at Montreal. It was an unusual event, geographically out on a limb. It also enhances the sense of the six somehow being a thing that happens outside of space and time, with riders flying across the ocean to hang out indoors for six days before coming back again. For velodromes, read airports, no-places where beer is drunk at strange times. The Montreal six had parallels with London; both were outside of the circus, looking in. In 1978, the Montreal six was organised by Willy Debosscher and provided an opportunity for the clown prince to achieve an elusive six-day win.

Debosscher didn't bring the top riders. Martin Venix was riding with Gerben Karstens, there were a few Dutch riders there, and Gary Wiggins was riding with Avogadri. Venix was world motor-paced champion, so he thought he was going to win, which wasn't how it happened. When we got off the plane there were quite a few Italian riders there; we got in the minibus they laid on, whereas the Italians were picked up in chauffeured Pontiac

Plymouths, like something out of *The French Connection*. It soon became apparent there was a slightly different thing going on. One of the nights was for Italians only, the crowd were all Italians, the sponsors were Italian, and the Italians had a lot of influence on the outcome. Before we went, I'd heard a story – who knows if it was true. They had their riders' meeting before it started, then they all filed out. A man was standing directly outside the door, waiting, and he told them who was going to win. The riders were insistent, 'Oh, no I don't think so, so-and-so will win we expect,' right up until the point where the man opened his jacket, showed a revolver and said, 'I'm sure you understand what I'm saying here,' and they all said, 'Ah yes, we do, no problem.' That's a bit how it was there. They paid us, we did the ride. Debosscher and Algeri won that year, the next year it was Debosscher and Algeri again. Neither of them won another six, before or after. All we got to see the whole time was the inside of the velodrome, that and the minibus to and from the airport.

After a strong start, the season petered out for Maurice and Medhurst. They finished tenth and last at Groningen in the final six of the season, in April. The result is deceptive; Groningen was another outlier, like Montreal:

> It was a *chasse patate*,[7] it wasn't full speed all the bloody time. Some nights, there were twenty-five people in the audience, you just rode what someone told you to do and put the money in your pocket. And you can't compare that with the proper six-days.

Both riders turned their attention to September, hoping to go again, to bag a seat on the elusive 'Blue Train'. The tricky question was whether the partnership between Medhurst and Burton was working,

---

[7] Potato chase. One of the best phrases used in the lingua franca of cycling – a pointless race or chase.

or whether they were better off with other riders, a more freelance proposition. A ride at the Skol Six in September 1979 suggested things might fall into place. They did much better than a year previously, coming sixth, at nine laps, while in the same event Sercu broke the outright record held by Peter Post for total wins. But then nothing – no contracts, no races, not even Ghent. The only contract received was for Munster, on 19 November, which normally overlapped with Ghent. This year there was a strange swap, the Belgian riders went to Ghent, and vice versa. Burton and Medhurst won the points classification comfortably, despite a series of crashes. Maurice came off five times over the course of the week, in what seemed like an unusually crashy six for most riders. Roman Hermann nearly broke his back. 'The track was terrible,' Maurice remembers. They were racing well, pleasing the crowd and the promoter, but again it failed to translate into contracts. Medhurst was downcast, in marked contrast to his self-belief just a year before. It was picked up in the press, who sympathised; recognising that in the capricious world of six-day racing, 'talent is not enough', the article in *Cycling Weekly* is imbued with a pervasive feeling of melancholy, stating that both riders were 'depressed'.[8] Only Maurice got a ride at Herning, not even Ron Webb would provide for the pair. Medhurst held out from returning to work, but his language suggests he was at least thinking about it: 'I don't want to have to find a job, because if a contract does come up, it isn't so good to have a job. If the money runs out then I'll have to work. I get the feeling it's not what you know, but who you know.'[9]

Maurice was slightly better off; without the pressures of family he was better placed to be able to stick it out, take a contract here and there. However, it put more pressure on their partnership, particularly when it came to the demands of keeping form and fitness when

[8] 'Talent is not enough for Burton-Medhurst', *Cycling Weekly*, 8 December, 1979.
[9] Ibid.

not racing regularly. Maurice recalls the sense that things were drifting towards the end for both of them.

We went into it together, as a pair, it was a good partnership, I knew him from when we were both amateurs. It carried on until there was a point when [sigh] things just started to change. The last time we rode seriously was at the Skol Six in 1979, and we were going well there. The year before, I definitely wasn't going so well, but it was different this time. However, we didn't get any more contracts, all we had was a ride at the European Madison Championships in Copenhagen, which wasn't until early November, a good six weeks away. The question was, how do you stay in shape for a race like that without racing? There was a man from New Zealand I knew, he was called Maurice Brown. He had raced as an amateur on the road, not the track, but couldn't earn a living. Staf Boone had a derny he would use to train his riders, so I paid Maurice to pace me. I would go out and do 160km behind the derny at pace. We would go up into Holland and all around, don't forget I was on the fixed wheel at the time. I would do this regularly, just to stay in shape, doing really big distances at speed.

You used to get this sugar beet in all the fields, and one day there was a huge sugar beet which had rolled on to the road. He managed to go round it, but I didn't and hit it straight on, buckled the front wheel and I went straight over the bars. I ended up sliding along on my back along the edge of the road, and because it was so cold, I'd layered up with about five jerseys or so. You could see each layer like a cutaway drawing. By the time I'd finished sliding along there was only one layer left. The bike was unrideable so I took the derny back to Ghent, got the car, and picked him up. That sort of thing seemed pretty normal at the time, you had to ride and get the miles in; if you crashed, you crashed.

A day or two later I went to see Paul. The thing is, you might ride as a pair together, but you both have to ensure you are in condition, because it's not just about you. I know what I need to do to be in condition, and the other rider, they have to know what they have to do, that bit is nothing to do with me, it's a matter of trust. Paul had moved into a better flat than the Kazemattenstraat and he was playing cards with his wife. I had a little mark on my head from the crash; in those days we never wore a helmet, just had a woolly hat on. Paul looked at me and said something like, 'Well, if you didn't go out training it wouldn't have happened.' I think because he wasn't racing or doing much proper training at that point, he wasn't motivated.

Maurice sensed that there was an opportunity to raise their profile in the European Madison Championships. If they placed it would provide something for the commentator to shout about on the presentation laps at the six, a line on the poster. It was a potential route back into the circuit. On the way to Copenhagen, they discussed a strategy for the chase. They would attack straight from the gun, gaining a lap quickly, and take it on from there.

It happened exactly as we had discussed. Once we had the lap, we could wait for the big teams, every time one of them went we would go with them, shadow their moves. One of the teams went, I went with them, held on, then put Paul in. When he got back around, he wasn't quite on the wheel, the gap was opening, so I closed it. The next time I put him in, he came round, but they were gone, he was pretty much back in the bunch, we were both in the bunch and the plan wasn't working. The next time I put him in he didn't even stay with the bunch, he lost the lap we had gained and from that point the race was done, it was over. We came eleventh, when we could have been up there. After that, when we got back to Ghent, I rang Jan Dirksen and just had to tell him not to put me with Paul any more, I couldn't ride with him.

It feels painful, even after all this time. I reconcile the businessman Maurice with the version in front of me, a young man who had to make difficult decisions, not personal ones, in order to get through. With no ride at Ghent that year it felt like things were falling apart. Paul openly questioned whether he could keep pursuing his dream, and it felt like the beginning of the end. Maurice was reduced to doing the track league, living and riding in Ghent, hoping for another contract. He had Herning at the beginning of December 1979, Paul didn't. Again, he lined up with Debosscher. A host of riders were carrying illness from Zurich, the curse of the ice rink had struck again, this time it was bronchitis. The race was accompanied by the sound of constant coughing from the cabins. An under-par Sercu scratched early on. The first day for Debosscher and Maurice was fine, but on the second day things changed suddenly after a bizarre incident at the side of the track, culminating in 'stormy scenes and Debosscher's eventual withdrawal from the race'[10]. Debosscher was standing at the side of the track, shouting instructions, when Maurice 'rode down the banking with the intention of knocking a plastic cup out of Debosscher's hand. Instead, he accidentally caught him in the face with his elbow, much to the Belgian's annoyance.'[11] When Maurice attempted to apologise afterwards at the cabin, Debosscher kicked him. The Belgian funny man didn't find it funny; he refused to contest any of the races, just sat in the wheels and followed, leaving Maurice demoralised. The Belgian back pages ran the story the next day, criticising Debosscher, which upset him even more. Added to this were mystery headaches and a general sense of misery, prompting Ron Webb to act: 'it was mutually agreed he should come out,' remembers Maurice. Burton rode solo, but didn't place, appeasing Webb in the process: 'he did what he had to do and I was pleased.'[12] Forty years later, Maurice can't remember much about it, but he does confirm that riding with Debosscher was hard work.

Maurice was driven by a desire to succeed, but he also made sure he was frugal where possible, retaining a sense of fiscal prudence.

[10] "Debosscher Gets the Elbow", *Cycling Weekly*, 29 December 1979, p2.
[11] Ibid.
[12] Ibid.

He travelled light, often with a soigneur only, with nothing like the presidential entourage who seemed to accompany Sercu or Pijnen, the kings of the circuit.

It wasn't always simple at some of the races. I remember at Groningen, Sercu was there with Fritz, Pijnen with [Wilfried] Peffgen. They had their full entourage, the mechanics, soigneurs, the boy, the lot. All we brought with us was a boy that we used to change the wheel, no mechanic or anything. Everything else we did ourselves. There were days when there can't have been more than twenty-five people watching. A six is fantastic when it's busy, but stating the obvious, it's six days, that's a lot of cycling. Not everywhere is Ghent. The promoters on occasion might make a loss. We would be paid a little something which covered our costs, but for the bigger riders it wasn't enough to pay all the people they had taken with them. I had a feeling that sometimes something like this might happen. On occasion it took nearly a year or so to get the money, and Groningen certainly never ran again. But I had no one to pay, so it was OK. Groningen was the only one like that.

With no contracts forthcoming, it made sense to look further afield – much further. Tasmania and Australia have a tradition of track cycling in their summer, including the Tasmania Christmas Carnivals, an annual Christmas shindig with all the occult *Wicker Man* vibes of an Antipodean Highland games. It's an eclectic and scary mix of cycling, running and wood chopping action around Tasmania. A modern pentathlon for the good people of the far South. Jan Dirksen was on the lookout for a group to take down at the request of the organisers, who wanted European professionals to sprinkle some stardust on the meetings. Dirksen was limited to those not under contract at Cologne or elsewhere. He paired Noël Dejonckheere with Burton, squeezing out Medhurst. Paul felt aggrieved, but Dirksen was worried that Medhurst might not come back if he got the ticket out, thus losing a rider from his roster. It wasn't far from the truth: Medhurst was struggling to reconcile the demands of the circuit and thinking about returning to Australia with his family, but he didn't have the money at that point.

Things like the Tasmania Christmas Carnivals, i.e. things you've never heard of, usually spark a frantic Google search. I typed it into the search box on 31 December 2022, stumbling, serendipitously, straight into a live feed of an actual Tasmania Christmas Carnival, happening at that moment, on the other side of the world: the 'TasCarnival', live from Burnie. I was transfixed and lost well over an hour watching a brass band, a strange running race, followed by women and men chopping tree trunks in half with massive axes. The TasCarnival is a folk festival, one of my favourite things – a living, breathing anachronism, a thin ribbon stretching back into the past when this was entertainment and nothing else would suffice and people jousted and prizes were proffered on velvet pillows. This isn't quite what Maurice encountered on arriving, but it's close enough.

It was pretty hot out there; just imagine the change from Belgium to an Australian summer, about 30°C hotter. I won a couple of races out there. Although most of them were handicaps, they were still bloody hard bastard races, no quarter was given by the other riders. You had to attack, really go for it. We were staying in Davenport, then raced in Latrobe, Burnie and Hobart, all on big, shallow, outdoor tracks. The last race was on New Year's Day in Burnie. It was a scratch – I won the whole thing. After the races finished, I had nothing in the calendar until Antwerp in February and I didn't see much sense in heading straight back in the middle of winter. I got in touch with this guy I'd met through Verleysdonk at the Skol Six, called Eddy Ziedaitas; I remembered he had shaken my hand and said, 'Look me up,' so lo and behold, I did. He was in Melbourne. Eddy had this house with a caravan out the back so I stayed in that, it was alright. It was a strange place. His old man was a Lithuanian, he'd built up this big wall made entirely of beer bottles. Luckily, Phil Anderson[13] was around at that time, back from riding for ACCB, just before he turned pro. A bike shop owner called Dangolo lent me a road bike for the duration and we went out training in the sun every morning.

Some weeks later, a comment pops up on Facebook, someone mentioning the time Maurice was out in Australia, how they rode early doors, avoiding the heat with 5 a.m. starts, tearing each other's legs off, training rides, and then drops the comment, 'Yeah that one time he ran over a wombat, that was quite something.' I ask Maurice about it the next time we chat, straight out with it – it's not something you build up to, after all. And a wombat collision is just the content I'm looking for. 'No, I don't recall anything like that, I don't remember hitting a wombat. We did see some strange creatures dead at the side of the road though. But I think I would remember that.' I am disappointed. I wanted wombat-death.

Maurice flew back via Sydney to London, then back across to Ghent, ready for the Six Days of Antwerp, with three rider teams. Maurice paired up with Paul Medhurst, and they rode again with Alex Van Linden. They went one place better than the year before, finishing in eighth, but were off the pace. Maurice then headed straight to Milan, riding with Paolo Rosola, who was just starting out in his career. They finished last, low on points, down on laps. Maurice, along with Stan Tourné, were taxi-driving for Italians in their local six. It took place in the avant-garde Palazzo dello Sport, a serious chunk of quasi-fascist futurist architecture. At Hanover, Maurice rode with Pietro Algeri. Paul Medhurst rode his last six of the season at Montreal, with Gary Wiggins. Unable to live off of the disappearing contracts and a lack of

[13] Anderson was at the forefront of a burgeoning group of Antipodean riders: Tom Sawyer, Danny Clark, Gary Wiggins, Graeme Gilmore, Paul Medhurst and Allan Peiper were just some of his contemporaries. Anderson was arguably the brightest of them all: the first non-European to wear the yellow jersey in the Tour, where he came fifth two years running, with an extensive palmarès in prestigious races.

prize money, the dream slipped away. He reverted to his previous job as a welder in order to earn enough to move back to Australia.

> Paul had the ability but it got to the point where he didn't want to do it any more. Pam [his wife] was a really important part of it, she was the driving force. Certainly they were a partnership, at one point she went back to Australia for a break, and without her, Paul found it more difficult. It was hard with a family to feed, two young boys, trying to become a professional to earn a living riding bikes. Antwerp was pretty much the end of it for Paul. We could have won the Madison championships if he had done the training, but he'd given up on it by then. Paul got demoralised by it all – we'd be riding well but not get the breaks, whereas other riders who were not as good got in and you didn't. That's the way it is. Paul's heart wasn't in it any more. Maybe that's the difference: with me, I never give up, it just doesn't come into my vocabulary. There have been times in my life – not just on the bike – when I have really struggled, it felt like it was impossible, those were difficult times, but you keep going and, in the end, you get through. What else is there to do?

Paul Medhurst got further than most. He spent six years building towards life as a professional in the sixes, followed his dream and rode the circuit for three of those years. He won bronze at the Commonwealth Games, rode at the Olympics, won prestigious races and mixed it up on the indoor tracks with some of the best riders to have ever lived. Just when it looked like the breakthrough might happen, it slipped through his fingers. Maurice stayed on, determined to see it through.

> It was hard enough to look after yourself, let alone when you've got a child and a family, that's a different perspective. It was hard for Paul. For me, I was on my own, and I wasn't ready to stop. I've never climbed off my bike on a hill before. I just can't. I don't know, I just don't think I'd be able to live with myself. It's something in

me, I don't let go easily. I'm not talking just about riding; I won't give up on anything. Sometimes I can recognise something is not a good thing, but it doesn't come easily for me to do that, it's not easy at all. I don't know where it comes from, you're just born with it, it's a determination, whatever you're going to do you want to see it through. That's how it was for the six. It was pretty far from easy, and you knew that you could do it, but it was so hard to get in.

Medhurst, Stam, Maurice, Peffgen, Sercu,
Texas Instruments GP Copenhagen

14

Ghent

No one told me that if you want tickets to go to the Ghent Six Day you have to buy them the day after the event finishes the year *before* you actually want to go. It sells out in less time than it takes Yoeri Havik to complete a flying lap. I didn't realise, carried on in blissful ignorance, assuming that at any point, once I'd got things sorted, I could bag a ticket. I missed the one two years ago because of Covid-19, and then again in 2021 because of uncertainty, waiting for the green light on the project before I bought my ticket. I watched the live stream on my phone, saw Mark Cavendish tearing around until he broke his collarbone. Watching it on my phone is not enough. I know I have to go there, that this is where the story is written, and this is where this book ends up, in the little bowl, surrounded by animated Belgians drinking from small cups of very strong beer, but there are no tickets. Somehow, I have to find tickets, otherwise I'm going to be writing about the most amazing bike race in the world that means everything to this story and making out like I've been there when I haven't in fact been there at all. The dread hand of inauthenticity will strike me down.

I attempt to circumvent the problem by emailing the press officer at Ghent, drafting and redrafting a hopelessly long email, over-explaining my life and project, talking about Maurice, begging for a ticket, explaining my credentials, mentioning the fabled name 'Bloomsbury'. He replies almost immediately: 'Hi Paul, no worries,

I'll put your name on the press list. See you in the fall.' I breathe a sigh of relief. I shall go to the ball.

This opens up another problem. The Ghent Six Day is in November, in term time. Fortunately, I've got a brilliant boss who recognises that work and life and living are uneasy companions when it comes to schools and she allows me two days of unpaid leave. I have to resist the impulse to post relentlessly on Instagram from the start to the finish of the weekend – pictures of trains, places, people, altar paintings. I worry that my colleagues or students might read this and realise that I spent a long, grubby, exciting weekend in Belgium when I should have been teaching them; except they won't know because they have literally zero interest in my tales of niche cycling cultures and extraordinary people.

I can see why the Ghent Six is such a hit with British cycling fans: it is a glimpse of an alternative cycling universe, one rooted in place and community. There is a palpable sense that at any given time most people in the city are invested in this one thing, as opposed to the UK where everybody hates cyclists, and even cyclists hate other cyclists. Ghent is also very easy to get to: the Eurostar rushes you across northern France and into Brussels in two hours. A quick change and half an hour later, you're at St Pieters Station. It is both easier and far cheaper than getting the train from Bristol to London. I feel an ache of melancholy at the European project, at everything we have lost in our myopic transference of anxiety, the Brexit heist perpetrated by racists and xenophobes, designed to stop people from doing what Maurice did, to keep us here, and keep others out. I arrive in Ghent on a day when the cost of living crisis crunches ever harder and realise my train home on Monday from London has been cancelled because everyone is on strike in our melancholy, Brexity corner of the world. In contrast, the Belgians I meet seem impossibly friendly, but somehow exude pity, looking at me as somehow representative of a sickening nation, a part of the contemporary ideological clusterfuck that is the UK. Rather than saying, 'I'm English,' I feel like I have to preface everything: 'Sorry, I'm English.' Maybe it is all just melancholy and projection.

I head straight to 't Kuipke because somehow, I've wangled an interview with Fred Wright and Ethan Hayter, who are riding the six, and I have to catch them before it all kicks off on the Friday night. Both are bona fide professional stars. In fact, they might be the most famous cyclists I've ever met. Ethan Hayter – multiple track World Champion, Olympic silver medallist, National Champion, fourth in the Worlds – rides for INEOS. Fred Wright – National Champion – is a Grand Tour rider for Bahrain Merida. Both started out with VC Londres. It feels vaguely symmetrical, seeing VC Londres young-sters ride the six for the first time, following Maurice Burton and all the others who went before. Maurice fixes Ethan's bike and helps him out; both their pictures feature on the wall of De Ver. Fred's mum and dad are regulars at Herne Hill. They feel intense pride at Fred's progress, but also at the link to Herne Hill and to Maurice, their inspiration. The sense of community courses through, from the outdoor sessions as youngsters with VC Londres coaches, through the different layers of the sport, before landing in 't Kuipke. The sense of a lineation is quite strong – Ben Wiggins is riding in the under-23 event, son of Bradley, grandson of Gary. He is riding along the same section of straight, around the banking, in front of the same seats, just like Gary did with Maurice in 1981, taking the fight to Sercu, Tourné and Fritz, or Cavendish and Bradley Wiggins against Elia Viviani and Iljo Keisse, Wiggins finishing his career in the city where he was born. Now it's Fred and Ethan's turn, mixing it up with Iljo, with Yoeri Havik and Robbe Ghys, the current stars of the six-day scene.

When I check in at the hotel, the proprietor guesses I'm here for the six. It is a cultural highlight of the city calendar. The circus is in town: six days of bike racing, from 7 p.m. until 1 a.m. every night, with music and drinking and singing and drinking and hot dogs and more drinking. What's not to like? Everything up until the beginning of November – the track league, kermesses, everything – leads to the six. I drop my stuff, get my recorder and camera, emergency snacks, and head out. It's a short walk across the city from where I am staying. Place names chime with transcripts written at home: the Bommelstraat, Sint-Pietersplein, every street imbued with stories of the past. That's how time works, clearly, but here I'm aware of Maurice's past written in these streets, forty years ago, wheeling his bike across town, from Sint-Kwintensberg to Citadel Park and back again. It is a city teeming with cyclists, where cars wait – happily, patiently – because the primacy of the motor car has been severed, and again I feel a pang of melancholy, a lost sense of betterment, how the UK seems permanently on the wrong side of a view of what makes a liveable place, at war with anyone who thinks safety, respect and tolerance are virtues to be celebrated.

'T Kuipke sits austerely in the middle of Citadel Park. It is an unassuming, boxy 1960s building with high windows; the shape functional, a leisure centre, a secondary school, a municipal rectangle. I head to the door marked 'press' and cross my fingers, toes, everything. I'm convinced that I won't be allowed in, that the brief email will have been forgotten, my credentials revoked. I once tried to get a press pass for the Tour of Britain for a genuine assignment and had to jump through a staggering number of hoops. This seems so much more relaxed that it can't be true. The people behind the desk, a team of older gents, are friendly, welcoming, and they usher me in, present me with the Lanyard of Dreams and a glossy programme. I say I am here to meet Fred. It's all OK, they couldn't be more helpful. They won't let me go to the cabins though, and although I'm sorely disappointed, remembering how Bingers 'bagged a seat from Jacky Schaubroeck', I have to remember I'm definitely not Bingers, I'm just me, a teacher who writes books and takes wonky photos with a cheap SLR. I told Bill Kund, a professional snapper, that I had an SLR and a prime lens, no zoom. 'Well, you're just going to have to get very close, aren't you,' he said, with clarity.

It's 5 p.m. and the stadium is empty, the doors not yet open, the space echoing to the sound of things gearing up, stalls getting ready, heavy things being moved, urgent conversations, beer barrels scraping across the floor. I walk under the banked concrete seating, past the wooden hydraulic door that allows emergency access to the ambulance, or as it once did, provides the finish for Ghent–Wevelgem. It was an awkward dog leg on to the track at high speed, from outdoors to indoors in a second. It was not repeated. The velodrome is redolent of a lower-division football club, the same stark, communal functionality of space, how everything seems geared towards watching sport, but in a space devoid of the moneyed trappings of modern, globalised sport. I can imagine the equivalent tribes, the ultras, the hardcore, the amateur fans and those just visiting, all drawn by a sport wrapped around and reaching out into the community. It is the last of the real sixes, a spectacular event that speaks of heroic things, a stadium that leans over and whispers about the past, when this was the greatest show in town, in Europe, even. The Ghent Six Day is embedded in the cultural memory of the city, in Flanders, in the national psyche. I breathe deeply, inhale the smell, the colour, the sound, and I am baptised fully in the timelessness of this unique place.

I walk down some concrete steps, underneath the track and then up a sweeping ramp as it arcs into the middelplein (the area inside the track), stepping into the photos I have been poring over, a palimpsest of reality upon sepia. I have ridden indoor tracks before but I am not prepared for what 166m with 46-degree bankings looks like from underneath. It looks vertiginous, impossible, awe-inspiring, the wooden striations curving outwards to the coping then into banks of seating rippling upwards in unbroken waves. The short track, high bankings and steep tiered seating make it perfect for watching bike races. Beneath the coping, riders are warming up, the stadium empty enough to hear the conversations between pairs and the sound of the tyres pressing down on the boards.

Ethan and Fred are going to meet me in the stands. They don't say where. I am petrified. I am already utterly spun out by the fact that I'm in Ghent at all, in 't Kuipke. I run up to the most likely staircase, look around, then spot two impossibly handsome, youthful chaps in the distance, waiting, watching the warm-up. We talk and they are lovely, funny, normal people. I feel spectacularly old when juxtaposed with their shiny skin, lustrous hair, smiles, athleticism and humour. Fred Wright is utterly charming, utterly real. Ethan is more circumspect, more Ethan, but also funny and charming.

Ethan Hayter

Even at 5 p.m. it is noisy. The racing has yet to start, but the music is being cranked up, super-loud remixed cheese on full blast, with a barrage of Flemish commentary as the MC warms up his vocal chords. It's nothing compared to what happens later in the evening, on and off the track, as Fred attests:

> The crowd is so completely into it, especially the sheer amount of drunk people in the middle, that's fun. There's pressure to get the lap gain, so you measure your effort sometimes at other points, saving your legs to basically go full speed in the chase to get the lap. When that happens you can feel it with the crowd, their response, and you just go. On Thursday night there was a silly

race, everyone was swinging their jerseys round, Yoeri Havik had his jersey off, topless, swinging it around his head; there's a song on the PA which makes everyone take their shirts off and wave them around, and everyone was copying him in the crowd, and you're in the middle of it, shirts off, arms up, Yoeri topless, it's just such a bizarre thing. It is a spectacle, it is mad, and it is great to be a part of it.

It is not so much the novelty of a mid-evening race where everyone showboats a bit and channels their inner Debosscher, more a constant conversation between the crowd and the racers, exacerbated by the fact that the biggest, most deranged part of the crowd is in the middle, pressing in on the cabins, watching the riders from a metre away as they warm up, looking up at the track. It is a constant, pulsing, ebbing exchange between the two – a call and response, a crazed cultural dialogue that infects the racing in a beautiful Flemish feedback loop, getting noisier and noisier, more scratchy, sensory, an acid house techno tune from 1989, that bit when the beat DROPS and everything goes batshit crazy. This, *this* is the Ghent Six.

Fred and Ethan take turns. Sometimes they say the same thing or finish each other's sentences. They live together and race together, and it shows. Both riders are a bit fried, but slowly adjusting to the demented circadian rhythm of the six. I come to the conclusion it's much harder to discuss bike racing when the Queen song 'Bicycle Race' is playing full blast over the top. They are having the full six-day experience, one of total immersion. They have a Belgian soigneur courtesy of Fabio Van den Bossche's dad. There is more to it – Fabio's grandad is Willy De Geest, who rode with Maurice at Ghent in 1982; it's another link to the past. There is a bucket in the corner of the cabin. Ethan sees me looking and admits, "They still have the bucket in the corner. That's still very much a part of the six. Part of the charm! I thought, "Ah well, I won't be using that", but I've used it every single night. Sometimes you only have a couple of minutes between races, you have to go, but you have got your

146

cleats on, and can't or don't want to go downstairs.' Fred echoes the comment: 'Yeah, it's a case of shut the curtains, have a quick piss, then off you go. It's bizarre, with the swannies, the mechanics, the cabins, buckets, you just have to integrate yourself within this whole thing, commit to it.'

This full commitment extends to taking in the demands and vagaries of this track; even the bumps can wreak havoc with the undercarriage after a week's racing. Ethan does the maths.

To be honest, it's so much smaller, it is tiny, 166m, and that changes everything really, including the way you race. The pressure it puts on your body is a lot more, because every third lap or so you're doing another lap compared to a 250m circuit. There are that many more transitions, and because of that there are a lot more changes in speed. I tried to go a little bit bigger with my gearing the other day and it was harder. The combination of a small track and small gears works really well, fits the rhythm of the racing.

I try to work this out in my mind: 20km on a 250m circuit is eighty laps. On a 166m circuit, it is 120 laps. That's a lot more laps, a lot more corners, banking, transitions, and it's a lot steeper, heavier. As if pissing in a bucket or taking on more transitions weren't enough, the disruption to the body clock is a constant struggle, as Ethan explains:

I had the worst headache ever after the first day, I just lay in bed for a while. At the end of the night, you head back to the hotel and you're buzzing from the spectacle. There's just so much stimulus going on. For instance, having to concentrate on getting the changes in the chase, because you're doing them so much more frequently than on a bigger track. You're fully concentrating, right up until 2 a.m., and you take that energy back with you. We're getting into bed at two but can't sleep until 3, 3.30 in the morning.

I express empathy, tell them how I struggle to sleep after our evening time trial round the lake, and they look at me with such kindness, such disarming kindness, as I try to compare my utterly half-arsed efforts at slow speeds for about 22 minutes once a week, with this absurd circus. I realise my foolishness but too late, the words are out. They are kind; I am charmed.

I take several bad photos. They look radiant. I feel old. I see the picture on the camera screen, the light bouncing off my forehead, my slack skin creased like discarded fabric, and I feel even older. We watch the under-23s come up to race the first Madison of the day; it promises to be a bit spicy. They watch it, and I watch them watching it, but try not to let them see me watching them watching it, because I'm fascinated to be watching a Madison with people who are experts at a Madison. It is hectic, the proximity of the riders, the constant force of the narrative, the feeling of competition, the frenzy of the commentator. We (me and Ethan and Fred!) are all on edge because, well, it looks very crashy, very much like there is going to be a crash at any minute, to the extent that I'm almost hiding my face in my hands, which is just as well, because there is a crash. I've seen enough and I am anxious not to outstay my welcome, so I go and explore the rest of the velodrome, buy beer tokens for later, take photos of everything, get ready to watch people watching bike racing.

I give in to the primitive rotating force of the track, as it begins to pull in people and light and air from the surrounding areas, compressing it into a riotous celebration and expression of Belgian cycling. The middleplein fills up as the racing starts, a rectangular solid block of people in cycling caps surrounded by a race swirling around the walls above. Tuur Dens is on the attack, trying to take a lap on the bunch, accompanied by shouted chants from supporters, Flemish show tunes and deranged Euro-house, a commentator stoking the ferocious escalation of noise and energy. It is the syncopated heartbeat of a city in love with all of these things.

15

Wembley

Without Paul Medhurst, it wasn't so much a case of being liberated, but a case of being more available. Maurice spent the summer training hard, riding kermesses for the Belgian road team, Solahart. 'At the end of July I started riding to races and home again. Some days I covered 250km. The first race I went to in the car I came second, my best placing in a semi-classic.'

Things went from one extreme to the other; where Maurice had been struggling to get contracts to get a ride, he was suddenly in demand, doing sixteen sixes from September 1980 to March 1981, back and forth from London to Berlin, Dortmund, Frankfurt, Munich, Munster, then back to Ghent, then Zurich, Herning, Maastricht, Cologne, Rotterdam, Copenhagen, Antwerp, Milan and finally Hanover. It was a gruelling schedule, race after race, six nights of work followed by long drives to the next city. It is the height of the six-day dream, a relentless, exhausting slog across a continent, punctuated by exhausting racing, full of sound and fury. Maurice had broken into the circuit, finally becoming a part of the 'Blue Train', mixing with the very best, the marquee performers, taking primes, winning races, chasing laps, earning points and basking in the adulation of a passionate crowd.

Tourné throws Burton at the Skol Six, photo by Bill Kund

The season started with a ride at the Skol Six in early September 1980. It had been a fixture for the Continental-leaning UK cycling fan since 1967, an opportunity to see at first hand the stars of the peloton. However, the event was under threat due to the costs of the venue and the installation of a temporary track. Declining sponsorship rang the death knell: the 1980 Skol Six would be the last in London for more than thirty-five years. Photographer Bill Kund was there, finding his way into photography after a career of bike racing on the Continent and on the track, including the 1964 Tokyo Summer Olympics. His sequence of images captures something essential about the six: a strange, subterranean, nocturnal dreamscape, cabin fever, the constant blurred loop of riders on the pine track.

Photo by Bill Kund

Outside, the world carries on, people get up, go to work, go out, get drunk, go to bed. Inside, the six rolls onwards across the week, an unwinding ribbon of races. In Bill Kund's photos, boys in ring-necked Mr Men T-shirts and Halfords hats clutch programmes, seeking autographs. I wonder where they are now, if they became cyclists, rode the track, were inspired by what they saw, or were shut out by the dark years of British cycling, with no indoor track, a national federation close to bankruptcy, inept leadership – those pre-Brailsford-, INEOS- and Sky-funded years, decades away and a different universe to the world-beating medal factory we are now accustomed to. It was Kund's first big photography assignment.

I had raced with both Danny Clark and Don Allan in Holland, along with René Pijnen and Willy Debosscher. Sercu won my event at the Tokyo Games and I used to see him in the peloton in Belgium on occasion, so I was not just some stranger wandering around. Typically I would pre-focus on an area and shoot, either panning or stationary, whatever came into view. The riders that were photographed, most just appeared there largely by chance. This whole shoot was a big learning experience for me – shoot, process the film, study contact sheets and learn from my successes and mistakes. You can learn a lot in six days' worth of photography.[1]

The images capture the speed and blur of the race, riders grimacing, strung out across the track, their eyes full of concentration and stress and fatigue. It looks amazing, and incredibly hard. Tony Doyle is having a hard time. Maurice is having a hard time. Willy Debosscher might be having a hard time, but he also looks like he's having a party, because, well, because he's Willy Debosscher. The photos also capture the in-between times, the dead spaces between the racing, the communal breakfast, Danny Clark in a dressing gown, soigneurs doing soigneur things, promoters chatting conspiratorially, mechanics leaning against plywood cabins or head cocked to one side in front of a wheel truing stand, the cold expanse of an empty exhibition hall both during the day and in the oozings of the early hours when the last punters have taken the last train home. Maurice was paired with Stan Tourné, both had turned professional around the same time. They had ridden together as amateurs and their partnership was a good one. They rode well, despite Maurice struggling to urinate on the last two nights; it necessitated some 'fairly painful treatment'. I don't ask more; it is enough to imagine. The hours in the saddle and the forces from the track surface, with some notoriously bumpy, seamed or irregular planking transmitting directly up through the stiff fork crown and frame into the perineum, caused havoc with a rider's anatomy. Excruciating, gaping saddle sores were commonplace.

Despite his difficulties, Maurice and Stan Tourné were a formidable combination, winning several races across the week. Most of the press coverage went to the British domestic riders, Nigel Dean, Ian Hallam, Tony James and Tony Doyle. However, Maurice had done enough to impress race director Peter Post, who promised Maurice a ride at Rotterdam in January. Post could see Maurice had stepped up, but there were anxieties about sustaining fitness because it was three

[1]pezcyclingnews.com/pelopic/1980-london-skol-6day-photo-gallery-by-bill-kund/

months away; Maurice reassured him that he would ride behind the derny, put in the effort and be ready.

Tourné, Burton, photo by Bill Kund

A capacity crowd was accompanied on the Saturday night by the Alan Elsdon jazz band. The big Saturday night Madison was disrupted by intense rain – a leak in the roof leading to a dark stain on the straight. Mick Jagger was in the audience. Apparently the Rolling Stones loved a good six and the lithe singer is a customer of Condor Cycles in Gray's Inn Road. Berlin race director Otto Ziegler was in London, planning and mapping out his pairings for the next race. Tourné was unavailable since he needed to be at home for the birth of his child; so Ziegler paired Maurice with Roman Hermann.

When we got to Berlin, Otto Ziegler came up to me before the racing started on Tuesday and told me not to worry about the sprints and the Devil, to just ride for the classement. This was the first time this had ever happened; no promoter had ever said that to me before. Most of the time they wanted me to do the sprints, put on a show, make the Devil exciting, ride for specific races. This was different: he wanted to see us come up, to see us place.

The fact that Burton and Hermann were riding for the overall win was new, and symbolic of their progress. They finished in fifth place at three laps, having challenged both for the overall and the points competition right up to the last chase. They were popular with the crowds; their style of racing, desire to chase and to take a lap engaged a partisan crowd, but also impressed Jan Dirksen. Maurice signed a further ten contracts immediately, thus doing away with the need to train behind the derny. The power of the promoters was everything.

> What the track director wants is what's important for you; he is paying you. If he says he wants you to do this or that then you have the option to look at him and say, 'Up yours!' and do what you want, but you also know that if it doesn't work out then next year you're not going to be coming back. The six is similar to road racing, think of it like the Tour. There are lots of different classifications, the green jersey, polka dot, white for young riders, then there is the combativity prize each day for someone getting in the breakaway. People target these different things, very few go solely for the GC. For me, those first two years in Ghent, Medhurst and I rode for the points jersey, we would target the green jersey, we got flowers, we showed ourselves to the promoter and to the crowds. We were saying, 'Well you're paying me and I'm going to work, not just ride round and say thanks, but I'm going to show that we're doing something and we're worth the contract.'

The results kept coming: fifth place in Berlin, followed by fifth again in Dortmund with Horst Schütz, although it was another uneasy partnership.

> I don't think Schütz wanted to ride with me, he was Roman's partner, but he had to. People used to talk about him quite a bit, there were stories. He struggled after retiring from the six for a bit, but he got through. He came across as a little bit arrogant. I remember once we were heading over to America to ride a criterium, forty-two of us on the plane. He was talking to this girl; she didn't like it, so she got a pint of beer and poured it over his head.

The string of fifth places continued in Frankfurt, riding with Udo Hempel – 'a good guy, we're still friends now', but Munich 'wasn't a great experience'. He came thirteenth with Derek Hunt. The sequence of German sixes finished at Munster with Hans Hindelang. They came seventh. The sheer number and frequency of the sixes meant that there were careful conversations, aimed at defining the different ways of winning and ways of losing. The trite assertion from the outsider is that winning or losing comes down to a handshake, people decide beforehand who wins, and how, it is not much more than wrestling. There is some truth in this, the same with most bike racing, but it is much more nuanced. In the six, it comes down to keeping control of the format, keeping the public, promoter and racers happy, and therefore sustaining the series and making it an appealing product. The six-day was a Barthesian spectacle of signs and signifiers with codes, mythologies, goodies and baddies, clowns and ringmasters.

> You don't have a choice about who you ride with, that's down to the promoter, they make the pairings. It might be in your interest, it might not. You might be driving the taxi for a week. If there's a road rider coming in, locally, you have a job to look after them. Neither of you is going to come up in the results, but the crowd are going to see the star, say, Roche or Gimondi, but you have a contract. That's partly why it's a shame London finished in 1980 – they'd pair you with a good rider in order to ensure a home rider was up the leader board. That's not a fix, that's just the pairing, you still have to ride! In Zurich, when I was riding with Medhurst, Roman Hermann was riding with Felice Gimondi – an Italian who had won every single Grand Tour, monuments, the lot. They put Sercu with Daniel Gisiger. He wasn't a six-day rider, he was a pursuiter, but with Sercu he got a placing. In London, they put Tony Gowland with Sercu, but there is no way they would do it in Berlin. Sercu's job was to win it with Gowland, to make sure the local name tops the leader board, and he did.

Within the evening, across the week, there are discussions stemming from the desire to ensure that the racing is competitive and varied, and the crowd goes home happy.

It's not necessarily decided who wins or who is allowed to take a lap, but it might be suggested. Even so, you still have to be able to do it, you have to pedal for it. Sometimes the bunch can make life hard, they can take the lap, or make it difficult, you have to really fight for that lap. Generally, there were always discussions in the last few days, once it became clear there were two or three pairings who were strongest and were the only ones who could win it. That's when the egos came into it, someone wanted to win, but another pair might have said, 'You know what, we're winning this one.'

Sometimes it comes down to tiredness. By the time we got to Frankfurt that year most of us had done three in a row with enormous distances spent travelling, everybody was really tired. Towards the end of the Frankfurt six, one particular team decided they wanted to win. Sercu was the spokesman, the patron if you like, but he had gone home. In his absence it would have been Albert Fritz or René Pijnen calling the shots. In later years, it was Tony Doyle who was in charge.

The Frankfurt track was tight; very sharp bends had the effect of making it narrow across the centre. It was slightly longer than Ghent but the physics of the loop meant it threw the riders out of the curve and required a lot of strength and skill to race there. The riders were exhausted. Discussions happened, but no one could agree on who should win: 'it was a free for all, hahaha. We all went full gas and the people that wanted to win didn't win, put it that way.' Maurice laughs, loudly, recalling the moment of triumph vs collective will. He also says 'full gas' in a very Belgian way, 'vuull gaz'.

Milan in February was another track where things sometimes happened a bit differently. Maurice draws a distinction between the 'proper sixes' like Ghent, full gas all the time, everyone on it, and the 'less serious' ones, where there might be discussions, the suggestion of an arrangement, a potato chase. Sometimes it came down to

157

self-preservation; Munster for example, where 'the track was really dangerous, if you went full gas there wouldn't be anyone left.' At Milan, the riders turned up fully fit, against Italians who were pretty much in their off-season. Both the *tifosi* (fans) and the promoter wanted to see the Italians winning, or at least doing well, which meant managing the effort.

The day before we started, the man in charge in Milan had a rider meeting and he said, '*Piano, piano*. Take it easy, don't go crazy.' This was great news to most of us, to be honest. I had no plan to go crazy. The thing is, most of the time we would get a contract to ride for the race, and it made no difference where we came, that's what we were going to get paid. The various prizes and primes would all go into a pot and were then divided 60:40, depending on where you are in the pyramid. The top riders take 60, the others get 40.

The thing about the promoter saying '*Piano, piano*' is that certain riders would allow a smaller rider to do something. They might say, 'Look, tonight you're going to take two laps, but so-and-so, the top rider, they will take four laps during the hour-long chase. It's all a careful balance. If that lesser rider only takes one lap instead of two, everyone is OK with that, no one is going to challenge them. 'Oh them, oh, why didn't you do this or that.' However, if he was told to take it and tried to take three or four laps, sneak a few extra, that's when the problems start, and that is not going to happen.

Even though there is a little agreement, the rider still has to be able to do the laps. If you're having a difficult night on the bike, or you might have been physically unable to take the two laps, they don't slow down and let you ride away, they just wait for you to speed up, you have to be able to attack and make it stick. And don't forget, the bunch is not hanging around. At the Milan Six the amateurs were going flat out at 50km in an hour-long chase, it was quick. There were no agreements, they were racing hard, trying to get primes. Now, as professionals, on that occasion we weren't going full gas, but we were still averaging 55km in the hour. Even though we were slightly easing off, we were still a full 5km faster, and that was going *piano*! The difference in speed was huge.

The bulk of the time we were just racing, flat out. In Berlin with Roman we were out there, trying to take a lap, it wasn't an arrangement, we were racing. It took us a full ten minutes of *vuull gaz* to take that lap. The whole lot of them, Didi Thurau, Sercu, they were out there and going round really hard and, to be honest, I got the feeling they didn't want us to take it. We were out there for ages. We had to put everything into it just to get that one lap, and it was only because we had it in our legs, otherwise they would have pulled us back in, they wouldn't have sat up. If the group is going round at 50kph, then you have to be able to go at 60kph for the time it takes to get the lap, and if that's ten minutes, then that's what you have to do. When the time comes, it's your lap, you have to go out there and take it, and if you haven't got it in your legs to do it then nobody's going to help you, and if you go the other way and try to be clever, then that's another story.

Milan was like that, really, you had to play the game. One year, Herman Ponsteen was there – he won lots of medals in the pursuit. He was telling me how easy it was to beat the Italians; he was cleaning up. I turned to him and said, 'Listen Herman, you might find it easy, but if you keep beating those guys then next year you won't be beating anybody. The Italian promoter didn't bring you here to beat the Italians, they brought you here to make them look good!'

When people talk of the six, that it's fixed, they are missing the point and devaluing the race. In cycling, the arrangement is everything, whether it's asking a rider to wait for another on a mountain, an agreement on a stage win over a general classification effort, or the negotiated make-up of a breakaway group on a stage when everyone knows it's going to end that way. There are always key riders – or a patron – who agree what can and can't happen for certain races across the week. This is the unwritten lore and law of the bunch. If Sercu or Fritz or, latterly, Doyle didn't want it to happen, it didn't happen. But it was never as simple as a gift: 'fix or no fix, you needed the legs, the skill, the raw speed, and the respect of the bunch, otherwise it came to nothing.'

Interlude: where James – my agent – gets in touch to ask about the latest meeting with Maurice.

15 August

good meeting with Maurice?
absolutely brilliant, lots of content, loads of texture to add in
yeah was an insane day, left super early, like 6am.
did the interview then went for a ride.
thought it would be a quick 30 mile loop
but *no*
maurice drags my ass round a 55 mile stretch of Kent. fucking hell
he can ride a bike.
doesn't eat anything all day
then just smashes it. At 67. Once a pro always a pro. #lifelesson
then we go out for dinner so he gets the convertible bentley out
i'm living my best life
he drives super fast down the A3 and asks if i'm ok and i really am
but also trying not to shit my pants
his daughter is in the back and her hair is going crazy
the wind is ripping through
everyone looking at us in the convertible bentley and i'm loving
every second
while maurice plays smooth fm full blast and it's the george michael
freedom 90 remix and it sounds perfect
got home 2am.
my skoda superb on the M4 wasn't channelling the same vibe, ngl.

16

Ghent

After a few years of getting up to speed, struggling with the mach-
inations and the demands of the circuit, things were improving for
Maurice. Having missed the Ghent Six Day in 1979, he rode with
Gary Wiggins at Ghent in 1980. It was a welcome return and their
first pairing since they were amateurs. Wiggins could see that Maurice
was becoming an established rider. Wiggins was on the same path,
Maurice recalls:

> He had started to work things out a little bit, he was coming through
> stronger that year, definitely. With Gary, I rode to the best I could,
> he did the same, and at that point he was very good with me, it was
> in his interests and we got on. The thing was, he needed people
> around him, he didn't like to train on his own. When he came to
> England the first time, he came with Dave Sanders[1], and he would
> always have someone with him. Gary could be a good friend, but
> when he moved up you wouldn't be so interesting to him, and to a
> certain degree, that's how he was, he was ambitious. He was living
> in Ghent with Linda, Bradley was born in April of that year, 1980.
> It was due to Linda that Gary could stay there; they got married,
> otherwise he was going to be thrown out of the country. As time

---

[1]Dave Sanders went on to become a revered mentor and coach, working with Cadel Evans, Simon
Gerrans and the Orica Green Edge team.

went on, he reached a point where he was going up in the world, maybe he felt he didn't have a need for Linda any more, he kept moving on. He stayed there and they went back to Kilburn.

Maurice's partnership with Wiggins, but also with Medhurst, was one of mutual support, out of necessity. However, it is a paradox: the desire to succeed means working with others, but to further your own career and ambitions. It was true of Gary Wiggins, and of Maurice, of any rider. The circuit defined these relationships through the narrow and fickle nature of success. Partnerships were fragile, transient, bound by mutuality but riven by difference. These were amplified by Maurice's status as the outsider, both among the Walloon and Flemish riders, the majority of the peloton, but also as a Black rider in an entirely White sport. But for Maurice it comes down to one thing, regardless of the motivation.

By the end of it all, I rode more with Paul Medhurst than Gary. But the thing is, Gary was good with me, as a partner, he was straight about it, he rode hard. The same was true of Roman in Berlin, he rode strong with me the whole time, he committed, unlike some of the others where there was always a sense that something was going on, say Debosscher. I was doing well at that time, and doing well in one six-day can make a difference, it encourages the others, they'll ride with you, they accept the promoters' pairing, but there were other riders who would wonder why they should ride with someone else, and someone like me, in particular.

He mentions the clown prince, Debosscher, the way there was always an underlying ambivalence, a sense of a commitment elsewhere, a diffidence surrounding the partnership when they rode together – but this wasn't only true of Debosscher, it was a feature of the sixes. From the outset, partnerships were beset by external factors, as far back as Koot, mysteriously weakening in the last laps of the last race of the Ghent amateur six. Amid the fragility of pairings, it is evident that some riders didn't want to ride with Maurice, because it didn't suit their interests. Sometimes these interests were shaped by latent xenophobia or entitlement, a desire to be riding with anyone but Maurice Burton. When the results are coming, it becomes easier, self-interest takes over, transcends prejudice, to a degree, concealing it, but it is temporary.

Maurice rode at Zurich with Nigel Dean but they didn't finish. Maurice went down with the flu; the cold curse of Zurich struck again.

> I really wasn't feeling the best. We had a 100km handicap race, and they gave us such a good handicap, that even though I wasn't feeling that great I talked to Nigel and we thought we'd better do something to provide the promoters and the crowd with their money's worth. We made a big effort and won the handicap, it was a 100km race. I'm not sure if it was in the plan for us to win that race, but even so it was their fault, they gave us too big a handicap. We had to sprint the last lap three times because the Swiss guy was supposed to win but he couldn't get past. The soigneurs were behind me and kept saying 'Go!', so I kept going. We won and got a sash for winning that one – I don't know what happened to it.

After Zurich came Herning, again with Nigel Dean, where they came tenth in a forgettable race. Maurice headed on to Maastricht and his first pairing with Tony Doyle, who was just breaking into the circuit. Doyle was a rider of considerable potential, he became a multiple World Champion and the most successful ever British six-day rider, with twenty-three wins, nineteen of them in harness with Danny Clark. Maurice fell, they came ninth. The season rolled on and on and on, a relentless grind across a continent, featuring ninety days of bike racing and more than 10,000km of driving from September through to February. Three days after Maastricht, Maurice rode in Cologne over the New Year with Hans-Peter Jakst, coming ninth, before teaming up again with Doyle at Rotterdam and then Copenhagen. Their partnership began to improve, with a sixth and fifth place, respectively. At that point, Doyle admitted to finding the transition to the professional sixes a tough one to negotiate, as did most riders. The Skol Six that year was his first event: 'the hurly-burly of a pro six was something else … it's not only the effort, you have to stay alert. With all the other riders around you on the tight banking, you can't lose your concentration for a moment.'[2] Doyle managed nine sixes that season to Burton's sixteen. By the third one, Doyle was on the edge: 'I was just smashed, I didn't know where I was. I just hung in, got round.'[3] Maurice attests to how difficult it was for Doyle to break in, despite his clear potential and strength.

> Tony was up and coming. Riding with Tony, what I found was that it was me who had to make the move, when we were going to go for a lap, if you put Tony on the front, he would just go but the whole lot would then follow him, straight away, so it had to be me that did it. I was smart, got the gap, then if I put him in, he was strong, he was good, but I had to make the jump and open the gap before I put him in. We still speak, we are OK, me and Tony. He's a special guy. Tony got a bike for his partner's son from De Ver. When he came in, he saw a picture of me and Tourné on the wall, and then another one of me and Tony in Rotterdam, he says to me, 'Yeah that was in the early days.' What he was implying was that that was before he moved up, that's when he rode with me. When he rode in London, he couldn't hold my wheel. That's how it goes though. We all start somewhere.[4]

Copenhagen finished on 4 February. Maurice flew into Brussels early the next morning, sleep-deprived and physically exhausted. He had with him a large bottle of champagne awarded for a prime

[2]Geoffrey Nicholson, *Tony Doyle: Six-Day Rider* (Springfield Books, 1992), p. 140.
[3]Ibid.
[4]Tony Doyle died in May 2023. We spoke about it at the time, the sadness that another rider was gone, so soon after Dejonckheere. Maurice said, 'I'm devastated by the fact that he's no longer with us.'

the night before. In desperation he opened it for a glass, then proceeded to drink the bottle. It did the trick; he slept for a couple of hours, got up, went straight to Antwerp and headed out on to the track.

The Antwerp Six in 1980 occupies a strange place in Maurice's palmarès. It's his best overall placing in a six-day – he came fourth with Rik Van Linden. Strangely, only his name features in some records, including the Roger De Maertelaere Six-Day Bible, *De Mannen van de Nacht*. It feels complicated, even when he explains it to me.

It's a bit of a funny situation. I mean, Rik Van Linden, he's a friend of mine on Facebook, you know, but back then there was a different Rik Van Linden, I mean, we were all different. The year before there were three-man teams, with me, Paul and Alex Van Linden, Rik's brother. This year, it was pairs and I started with René Savary. Rik was the more accomplished rider of the brothers, he won the green jersey at the Tour ahead of Eddy Merckx, won lots of stages in the Giro and the Vuelta, he was a star, no question. In contrast, Alex got around, he was OK. Obviously, I was going pretty well that year; and I started with René, whereas Rik was with Don Allan. However, Don used to have problems with his undercarriage, and he had to pull out. This wasn't good for the promoter or the crowd, because Rik is from Antwerp and suddenly he was dropping down the classement. So the promoter, maybe Alex as well, they had a word with me, asked if I would ride with Rik. As long as they paid my soigneur and the other stuff, they would have a deal. That's the way I am, I'm a businessman, it didn't make any difference if I rode with Savary or with Van Linden. They paid Savary out, sent him home, and I carried on.

So far so good, a fast pairing, just what the crowd had come to see, the pairing holding up, top five at least, then moving into fourth place, chasing the podium in the last chase, anything was possible. Maurice put in a huge stint behind the derny, took a few laps, which counted for points as well as gaining laps. It looked promising; the race was on. Maurice was up against a strong field – Alfons De Wolf, Wilfried Peffgen, René Pijnen, World Champions, the lot.

I took a lap on the whole damned lot of 'em; I lapped them, came back up to the front and won the race, which brought us back level. It was all on the final chase. Rik was a star on the road but he wasn't a really great track rider, not quite up there with the best. If he was, we would have been on the podium. The thing is though, he didn't finish, he pulled out on the last chase. He didn't look too bad to me, I'm not sure what happened, he just pulled out. The podium was there, it was the last chase, no sign of injury, and then suddenly he said he had cramp and he pulled out. So that's why on the result, it says Maurice Burton solo – fourth. The following year I came fourth again, it was my highest placing in the sixes. I've never seen it before or since, that one man can finish on his own. I didn't ask why at the time, but I am sure they didn't think it was right to put me out at that stage, to give me nothing. They didn't feel comfortable with it. The agent was Firmen Verelst, maybe he had a hand in it, maybe he insisted I get something.

I spoke to Danny Clark about it recently; he came over to London for Tony Doyle's funeral and we caught up for the first time in a very long time. We talked about the past, our lives, it was emotional to see him. Danny felt that it might have been because Rik was from Antwerp, he wanted to be on the podium, it was all or nothing, if you like, his local crowd. Looking back, I think that makes sense. It was high stakes for Rik, he had a lot of pride, he was a bona fide star of the road, in front of his home crowd, his home city. If he wasn't on the podium he may as well be nowhere, and that might have been why he pulled out.

However, the issue wasn't Rik Van Linden, it was a wider one. Things like this would happen. Each time it might have been different, for this reason or that reason, but if you notice that year and some other years I came fifth or fourth a lot of times, and it felt like that was as far as some of them were going to let me go before they started to bring it back in.

We skirt around what he is saying for a while, in the way that we do, the depth of feeling, acknowledging and ignoring it in the same breath. I choose my words carefully. The six was a closed shop, always, riders were looking to hold their place in their group, come what may. Maurice was the outsider, visibly, culturally, allowed some latitude, but not enough to break up the hegemony. We speculate, talk around it, we're both anxious not to offend, to challenge sensibilities, to explore other reasons, empirical facts like athletic skill, but context and attitudes, marginalisation, prejudice, lie beneath. I recall a phrase borrowed from David Olusoga's brilliant book, *Black and British, a Forgotten History*[5]: the subtext is race and prejudice, Olusoga argues that these are both the features *and the* consequences of systemic racism. The six-day circuit is a part of society, the riders are within the system, the institution, their actions are informed by wider values. Maurice is more measured than me, I don't know whether it's my job to be less measured, to even comment on these things, but I sense that his reticence is a further consequence. But the truth is that every individual narrative of exclusion, where someone might or might not have been acting in something less than good faith, was part of a wider string of episodes, working cumulatively. People look back and argue about context, changing times, contextualising things within an overtly racist society. Even as I write this, I listen to cricketers at a news conference try to contextualise the use of the word p___ as a term of 'endearment' to describe a colleague 'back then', and the echoes of institutional exclusion are hard to ignore.

> That's how it was a lot of the time. With some other riders, I don't see any pictures of me and that person riding together, but there are pictures of them with *everybody* else they ever rode with, and those are the things that make me wonder about this, wonder if at that time the association made people feel uneasy, that people

[5]David Olusoga, *Black and British: A Forgotten History* (Macmillan, 2016).

didn't want that. It's just … I mean nobody ever said that to me, but it's kind of how it unfolds.

You know Paul, the questions you have at the time, the way that something just doesn't feel right, they kept coming up.

It's not about pride, or injuries, or this or that, it is about how and why things like this kept happening, and their cumulative effect. We talk about Debosscher, the difficulties with their partnership, his attitude and approach.

I think among other things, for Debosscher, and for me, there was the fact that we were both a novelty, for different reasons, and fought for our place on the circuit. Debosscher got paid to entertain, and he was good at entertaining the crowd and he carved out a space for himself, he had a novelty and people wanted him to ride. He saw me coming along and he felt threatened by me, because the problem is in the six-days, it's not like you have 200 riders in a race: some tracks in the six could only take twenty-four riders, and fourteen of those might be the nucleus who earn their money. For Debosscher, entertaining and not winning, he had his space in that group. But if someone like Debosscher saw a younger person, maybe who could be a bit cheaper, filling that role, then suddenly he's in and you're out. That's the crucial thing with riders when they see the new faces coming in, they are not welcoming, everyone is watching their backs, watching their space on the train.

To some extent this is the cut-throat world of the six, the competition for contracts. It's predicated on any means or way of excluding someone else, in order to secure your place. I'd love to think that there was solidarity between riders, but it is palpably not a setting that encourages solidarity. There are some surprising similarities between Debosscher and Maurice. Both had to rely on exploiting their novelty to get a foot in the door, with one primary difference: Maurice was both hindered and helped by his colour. He had none of the innate advantages of the other riders in the peloton. Nelson Vails, winner of the silver medal in the 1984 Summer Olympics and one of the few other Black riders from the era, summarised the difference: 'When you get perceived as White, you have an advantage over someone who's not.'[6]

It's hard to clearly articulate the abstract swirl of racism, without preaching, or patronising, or leaving it open to speculation; the system enshrines values and attitudes, and individuals conform or react against it. Riders making life difficult for Maurice were acting within a discriminatory framework and culture; they were a part of it. However, some of the manifestations of prejudice were overt and shocking, and there is no space for negotiation, or whataboutery, or evasion, or for me to frame this narrative. It's not mine to frame. I ask outright, across the table, sitting in his garden in Croydon: what was it like, what did it feel like?

Some riders would play tricks on me, undermine me, they used to do things like tightening my bottom bracket so that it was that much harder to pedal. They used to call me racist names, typical stuff of the time. Albert Fritz, one day he said they were going to call me 'Bimbo', which I really didn't like. But at the end of the day, if you like it or not, the more you let them see that you don't like it, that it gets to you, the more they push it harder. So sometimes you just have to live with it, it's not something I found pleasant, it used to get used in the press, this nickname, and I didn't like it. Bimbo – what does it mean? I don't really know what it means, I just didn't like it the way it was used. There's a word here, like a woman, that was the same thing over there, but it wasn't a nice term, it definitely wasn't a friendly thing.

[6]https://andscape.com//features/ahead-of-tour-de-france-black-cyclists-remain-rare-in-the-sport/

Neither was it a temporary thing, shared by the riders. It lingers now. A cursory Google throws it up on a Flemish/Dutch cycling results website:

Tot 1981 Jamaïcaanse nationaliteit, daarna Brit. Burton was vooral actief op de piste en in het Belgisch kermiskoerscircuit – bijnaam 'Bimbo'.

(Until 1981, Jamaican nationality, then British. Burton was primarily active on the track and in the Belgian criterium circuit. His nickname was 'Bimbo'.)[7]

It wasn't just Fritz. Rumours spread among the riders about the background of some of the others on the circuit: so-and-so's dad was in the Hitler Youth, such-and-such used to listen to Hitler's speeches to get him pumped up and ready to race. I guess rumours are one thing, hearing a rider listening to Adolf Hitler's hate speech at full volume is unmistakable, it's not the swirl of hearsay. At the time it was seen as an idiosyncrasy, albeit one associated with a political movement that forty years ago deemed Black people an 'inferior race' under supplementary Nuremberg laws.

A silence drifts across the hard paving of Maurice's suburban garden. The morning sun angles down and starts to shimmer, the concrete slabs acquire a chalky brilliance and we both wear sunglasses. Maurice has been wearing sunglasses all morning, to be fair. I had to root around and find my slightly scuffed pair. His glasses are very sporty. It's half past ten and a seething Sunday is sweltering into being, another in a run of stupidly hot days. We will ride in this heat later today. Maurice shifts in his seat but he stays in the glare of the sun – he loves it. I remain under the shade of the patio umbrella. The sounds of a Croydon morning are being committed to the tape: children bursting into the garden of next door but one, Mum shouting at them to be quiet, a parakeet, more parakeets, shouting and

---

[7] www.dewielersite.net/db2/wielersite/coureurfiche.php?coureurid=2838

screeching in a way that never becomes familiar to my parochial naturalist brain. Among the suburban noise and heat of Maurice's garden, I wonder about Fritz, about that word 'bimbo', the onomatopoeic stress and unease.

The next day, when home in Bristol, it is this word and Maurice's reaction to it that resurfaces. The conversation has a miasmic haze, it sits uneasily with me, the word, 'bimbo'. I can't shake it; I think there must be more to it; contextually, it just *feels* racist, innately, maybe the sound of the word, the echoes of other lazy cultural stereotypes and insults, of *sambo*, of grotesque caricatures, of the Asterix books I grew up reading, loving, laughing at, glossing over the depictions of Black people as fat and stupid, accepting them, laughing at them, not questioning those representations because I was seven years old and because no one else questioned rampant colonial racism, arrogance and othering; Conradian natives, or shadows in the jungle. I check with Jon Hughes, professor of German and things like that at Royal Holloway University of London because I feel like he will know, definitively.

9 October

Hi Jon, can I ask a question about a German word?

Fire away Paul!

Just going through transcripts with Maurice and he mentions a German cyclist, Albert Fritz, who used to call him 'bimbo'. Maurice didn't like it but there's nothing in the transcript when I listen back that suggests he thought it was racist. But I feel like it is. Other riders picked up on it and it got into the press a few times as a nickname. It looks pretty dodgy on Google, but I thought i'd check with you because you would know?

In my view there is no question that a German using this word, a few decades back, would have meant is as a racial epithet. It's akin to something like 'sambo', in English, or other dated, racist terms. The Duden, the authoritative source on German language, confirms this - it defines it as a strongly discriminatory term of abuse for a person with darker skin colour'.

Duden.de
Duden / Bimbo/ Rechtschreibung, Bedeutung, Definition, Herkunft

I should add that the English sexist term 'bimbo' is unrelated, although this sense seems to have crept into German recently. But years ago it was a racist term, without doubt. Maurice was quite right in disliking it, even if he didn't know the term.

I try to anticipate the counter-argument, where people reject in day-long hearings, years later, that they ever said anything, or if they did, it wasn't racist and it was typical of what non-racist people said in different times. I think of my experiences teaching in London in a hyper-diverse school, with a brilliant head of department. I was driven by a youthful idealism and passion to change young lives. I made cringing, horrible, lazy comments, and I regret them intensely. I was not racist, but at twenty-two years old, I was crass, clumsy, arrogant. I was utterly unaware of my privilege, no matter how much I foregrounded the whole 'my dad's an electrician and my mum has a stall in the market' schtick. I grew up in Barnstaple. My main concerns in North Devon were an undue number of hippies, extreme boredom and a lack of public transport. I was never stopped by the police as a teenager because of the colour of my skin. I have never been followed around a shop.

I was never called bimbo. I didn't have to work twice as hard to get what other people had.

A couple of weeks later Jon Hughes messages me again. He has been reading about the experiences of the mixed-raced kids born in Germany to American GI fathers after the Second World War, and he stumbles across the word again. It emerges on the page to describe the discrimination and racism they received. It sits squarely within the frame of Fritz's life, born in 1947. I wonder who the good guys were within this setting, and ask Maurice.

> I wouldn't say 'good,' that wasn't really how it was. But certainly, I don't think that Sercu would fall into that category, of that type of thing, the bullying that went on. Sercu's father, Albert, he knew what I had to do, what I had to go through to get there.
>
> I wouldn't say they were my friends as such, because actually you didn't have a lot of friends on the six-day. There would be Pijnen, he didn't see me as a threat, he was up there, winning, but Fritz, he obviously had this thing, it was different, he saw me as a Black guy first and foremost whereas from the likes of Sercu, or Clark, or Pijnen, they saw you as another human being, a bike rider, not just a Black man.
>
> I don't know if I ever had friends, the best out of them all would be Roman Hermann. If ever I had to have one of them for a neighbour it would be him. As it turns out, he actually is my neighbour, he has a house just down the road from me in Lanzarote.

He laughs, again. It's clear he has a lot of time for Roman Hermann, and also that after the race things are different, motivation shifts, the heat of competition dissipates and reminiscence reshapes and reframes the past for everyone. But the past doesn't change, it is the present that changes, and thus we are forced to revisit our past, our historic tweets, our assumptions, our prejudices, our actions, and to own them now.

Gracie, Maurice's daughter, has come out to the garden. Both Gracie and Maurice's wife, Mia do a lovely job of making me feel welcome, despite the fact I've interrupted their Sunday, dragged Maurice out of bed with punctilious exactitude, and made everyone feel a tiny bit awkward in their Sunday house clothes. It's a timely pause, we make small talk, I had bought everyone some biscuits. Mia says, 'Mr Burton will eat those if we leave them unattended.' I am unsure about this, I have yet to see him eat anything. They disappear back into the cool of the house, leaving Maurice and me – and the cat, who is pretending to like me – with our conversation, disentangling the past and the present.

From Antwerp, Maurice finished the season with back-to-back sixes. He came eleventh in Milan, with Venix, then ninth at Hanover with Betz. The racing wasn't entirely done – he came fourth in the European Madison track championships, just missing out on a medal, then broke into the top thirty at Kuurne–Bruxelles–Kuurne, an early-season Belgian hardman's classic. As the winter sixes lurched into the road season for the following year, things were looking good.

17

Annerley

The morning is submerged by the afternoon and we take a break. Again, Maurice hasn't eaten. He has more herbal tea. His diet is intense. As far as I can tell, it consists of a tub of yoghurt for breakfast and a can of Coke for lunch. He seems to take it all entirely in his stride. I am ready for this, this time, I have prepared sandwiches and they are in my bag, secretly.

We are going for a bike ride. I have been training, desperate not to make a fool of myself, to get dropped, to crash the bunch. I have put a new chain on, I have even cleaned my bike. I am wearing my De Ver jersey, it says that I went to the Lanzarote training camp, even though I didn't. Maurice gave it to me last time we met and it instantly became my favourite new jersey. I wear it on club rides and hope desperately that someone will ask me about it, where I got it from, so I can say with pride, 'What, this old thing? Maurice Burton gave it to me.'

First, I have to drive Maurice to the shop, which is where he keeps his bike, obviously, because if you had a bike shop you wouldn't do what I do and keep a bike in every room of the house. My car is a mess. The footwell is disgusting. It is because I have children. We throw food at them in the back and they eat messily and the car is full of crumbs and the torn shiny plastic ears of sweet wrappers. I am embarrassed. Maurice doesn't seem to notice. I also drive my car really badly because I feel nervous because Maurice Burton is in my car.

I haven't been out to the back of the shop; it is a labyrinth. A small tunnel and low roof leads to an extensive courtyard, there are bikes and parts of bikes everywhere. The cottage is just about recognisable as a living space, it is a cottage of sorts, it has a kitchen, stairs, bathroom. Every exposed bit of flat surface is covered in stock. More bikes, more bike parts. I get changed in a narrow alley between two stacked cardboard bike boxes and I eat my sandwich, furtively, because I cannot risk the bonk, under any circumstances. I squeeze into my jersey, hold my tummy in, and I am ready. I have even shaved my legs; actually, I still shave my legs all the time. I do one or two races early each season just so I can justify shaving my legs, regarding myself as a 'racing cyclist', otherwise I'm just another hairy nobody on the bun run, and my misguided forty-six-year old pride won't let me do that.

We head south on the London Road to meet with Junior, one of Maurice's regular riding partners. I have seen the route on his Strava profile, a straightforward loop around Biggin Hill and back, 30 miles or so. I am confident. Junior lives two minutes down the road, he is not quite ready. We wait in the sunshine, and it is hot. Five minutes pass and he emerges from the house, ready to go. We are all in De Ver jerseys, we are a group, we have an identity. I am the outsider because I am not a regular in the De Ver, and because, for the first time in my life, I am riding with more than one Black person. This says a lot about cycling. There are more people called David in Bristol South Cycling Club than there are Black people. I love my club, the way it is ineffably Bristolian, a part of the cultural heritage of the city, and I will talk about it until people glaze over, moving through stories about South Bristol and the Wills tobacco factory and Bristol industry, aircraft and cars, how cycling emerged from these places, and how it is woven into the social fabric of the city. But, for all our talk of visibility, of inclusivity, we are failing to make cycling a visible activity for people of colour in Bristol, a city with a dynamic multicultural community and an important part of the Caribbean diaspora in the UK. I don't know what to do about it, how much energy I have to change this. I went out on the club run last week and it was all White men, mostly within a narrow age bracket, and I felt embarrassed.

Right now, I am riding with Junior and Maurice under a sky-blue sky. I am aware that this jaunt is going to be a part of the book, that this is about context, background, texture, but equally I am having a blissful time, riding my bike in the sunshine, heading into the Kent countryside with Maurice Burton; it's a thrilling, dreamy experience. I write these books because I love cycling, the lore and lives of the protagonists, and here I am participating in their lives. I am on Maurice's wheel; his compact pedalling style and aggressive riding position speak of years spent riding a bike for a living. He is fast, ridiculously so, every slight incline is treated with disdain, but also seized as an opportunity, a chance to mix things up a bit, to see if I can keep up. I realise quite quickly that what I don't miss about living in London as a cyclist is the ride out of the city, the car-clogged roads, the anger.

Once we get through the city suburbs, beyond Croydon and Addiscombe, towards Shirley, things lighten up, colours shift, sunlight drifts in soft golden threads through the canopy of London plane trees, as they give way to deciduous woodland and narrow lanes. As soon as we turn on to the first proper wooded lane, we stop. Apparently, this is where Maurice stops every single time, on every ride, to take a piss. Junior reckons he cannot remember a ride during which this ceremony has not been observed. Truly, this is a blessed gateway and a hallowed strip of degraded tarmac. Whether the tarmac was degraded before Maurice made his citations, I know not, but I do know we are creatures of routine, cyclists, and we like to piss in the same place.

We are chatting, laughing, but no quarter is being given, it's a funny mix. Maurice really digs in on the shorter, sharper climbs, it is hurting me. It is hurting Junior, too. He goes straight out the back, says he'll see us up there, at the top, at this point, or over there. Junior calls Maurice 'the captain', the phrase spoken with reverence. I drift back and we talk about cycling, about the book, about the captain, the role he plays in the cycling community, and it is clear that Junior loves and reveres him, that riding with Maurice, being a part of his life and the wider De Ver community, brings him joy.

By the time we get to 25 miles, I realise we are not doing 30 miles. We are going further, possibly quite a lot further. The lanes have a ghostly quality. As a cyclist in London, I would loop out this way from Café de Paris on a Saturday morning, riding with the Dulwich Paragon in the days before the Paragon had eleventy billion members, pre-bike boom. I half-recognise turns, descents, strange public houses, a section of main road, the name of a suburban business, or a village. We loop out past Biggin Hill, a two-seater Spitfire taxis past, the guttural, stammering rhythm of the engine is unmistakable. We see the gate guardians, a Hurricane and a Spitfire, outside St George's Chapel, remnants from the days when Biggin Hill was at the centre of the Battle of Britain. It's a whistle-stop tour of Kentish history: we go past Downe House, Victorian architecture pickled in aspic, Darwin still working in the study, completing *On the Origin of Species*. It feels bucolic. We stop at Knockholt village green. Maurice eats a Mars bar and drinks a can of Coke. It is a diet I can endorse. I also feel like it might be a prelude for a bit of a tear-up. I base this suspicion on a lifetime of riding with monstrously fast people; the way out is ridden at pace, but is typically a chatty affair, but at some point on the way back someone starts to turn the screw. I have a feeling that this may happen today.

Junior and the Captain

We ride away and there is a quickening. Sure enough, the tear-up is coming. We go for launch on the way out of the splendidly named Pratt's Bottom. Junior shifts uneasily, he can sense what is about to happen. He says he'll see me up the top somewhere. Maurice starts to pedal, turns the screw, the road lifts up and keeps going, Maurice keeps on pedalling, digs in. I have to stamp on the pedals, get out of the saddle, and it's really hard work. I think about dropping back several times, but decide to try and duke it out, to hold on, wait for the storm to break and hopefully gather my breath. He absolutely has the edge on me, and I'm clinging on, trying not to slip back. In the end I slip back a tiny bit, just hold the gap, a bike wheel or so, my lungs starting to prickle, breathing accelerating, heart rate pushing up, close to max. I don't really know what is going on, apart from the obvious: I'm being taught a lesson by Maurice Burton on a tough climb and it's not going well, but somehow, I hold on and we regroup at the top. I made it. Maurice looks across and smiles. I didn't get dropped, I did alright. I bask in the warmth of affirmation. Junior arrives and says, 'That's the easy bit done.' It's really hot, 30°C and climbing. It feels hotter. We go again, and it's even harder and I realise the fundamental difference between someone who was once a professional cyclist and someone who has never remotely been anywhere near being a professional cyclist. These are Maurice's lanes. He has been riding this strip of road for over fifty years. Out and back, through and off. This is where he rode to Bill Dodd's house in the summer months, getting out of the city, working out what he wanted to do and the riding he needed to do to get there. We have another ten minutes of purgatory and suffering, until we crest the top of the rise. The high-rise serrations of the city punctuate the horizon.

We hurtle back, reeling in a fellow cyclist, they stay for a bit, then drop out the back. I wonder if they know who Maurice is. I assume everyone does. I saw him once when riding out through Annerley with my friend Nick; he was coming the other way, leading a line of yellow, the De Ver colours and logo clearly visible, a paceline of ten or more. We nodded, said, 'Look, it must be Maurice Burton!' as we went the other way, emboldened by our chance encounter with cycling royalty. Like most encounters with the past, I laugh at the thought of me, twenty years ago, writing things that no one would ever read, an endless list of spiked articles, unaware that one day I would be writing *this* story.

It is fast on the way back to London; mostly downhill on rapid tarmac. Maurice and Junior dig in, pushing the pace, and I sit on the wheel as the city encroaches on the countryside, at first slowly, then abruptly, back through Addington and Croydon. Suddenly, Maurice has an idea: 'Shall we go and see Eddie?' he asks Junior. 'Absolutely,' says Junior, and we're off on a short detour. Eddie Hughes is one of Maurice's long-standing friends, a member of the De Ver, a keen cyclist. I don't know what I was expecting, but it wasn't being served biscuits and the best ice-cold water with sliced lemon in the garden of Professor Edward Hughes, fellow of the British Academy and expert on all things to do with Proust and Camus. I don't know why I didn't expect it; professors of French in the UK have a reputation of being avid cyclists, and cycling is the second language and cultural touchstone for most French people – and Francophiles like Eddie. He is lovely. We exchange addresses and a week later I send him a copy of one of my very niche books about an unknown cyclist and he sends me a copy of one of his very well-regarded books about Albert Camus. We are in Eddie's garden because these are people whom Maurice knows and cares about, and these are the people who know and care about Maurice, intensely – people who are a part of the community of cyclists in South London, who have been helped and supported through Maurice's work at De Ver, and are aware of his stories, the past, the challenges, everything that he had to do in order to pursue his dream.

I feel acutely aware again of a responsibility to write the story in the right way. There is a wave of intense pressure, one of those moments when I feel I can't do this, I can't do this justice, I can't navigate through the complexities, capture the joy, the simplicity of cycling and community, but also the unique nature of Maurice's experiences as a Black man in an overwhelmingly White sport, and do it with integrity and diligence. But I am going to try, because otherwise I don't know what else I am going to write about. I am aware that I am sharing my interpretation of Maurice's experiences in cycling, with his blessing, that he believes I am the person to write this book with him, to give credence to his experiences and to challenge the paradigm of Whiteness, the lens through which cycling is viewed.

We head back to the shop, say goodbye to Junior, a cheery, joyful wave, and it's time for a quick shower in the cottage and then on to the last bit of the day: Maurice Burton is going to take me – *me* – for a drive through the city in the spangly blue convertible car of dreams. I wait while he uploads his ride; he shows me the stats. Maurice has hundreds of followers on Strava, including me. He follows one person: Danny Clark. I admire this. Maurice shows me his VO_2 max and fitness age according to the Garmin: he is twenty years old.

18

Cologne

After his best season at the age of twenty-five, Maurice had cause for optimism. 1981 held the promise of a further breakthrough, podium finishes, not just individual race wins, but the prospect of an overall six-day win. The absence of the Skol Six left a gap in the calendar, but also was a disadvantage for British riders; it was as close to a guaranteed ride as you could get. The action shifted later, with Berlin now the opening race of the season on 8 October, followed by Dortmund and Munster. Things started to go awry in Berlin, where Maurice was paired with Tony Doyle. Maurice's relationship with his soigneur was strained. While Maurice was struggling with his health throughout the meeting, Fraser was complaining that the floor was too cold for his feet. Their working relationship ended not long after.

I was struggling in Berlin. I had stomach issues and constipation. I had to pull out of the six with Doyle, then I didn't ride at Dortmund either. I had contracts for both but didn't fulfil them. That alone, pulling out, whatever the reason might be, if you do that, then it doesn't put you in a good light with the promoter, they might think, do we want this guy back again? Is he reliable? That's the trouble, when it goes wrong, it's hard to come back. Sercu said I should have had a different soigneur, that they would have got me through that, but it didn't happen.

Doyle came and spoke to me and we rode in Munich. He knew and he respected me, as did Sercu. The thing is, you've only got to have a few things go against you, even when you're doing your job well. If something doesn't go right in the six then they've got so many riders they can use. As soon as you're out, you're in trouble. All the riders, if they see someone new, they are thinking, if one comes in, then someone goes out, and that's why Debosscher didn't like me, because he knew there might not be room for both of us. It was cut-throat. I had to have a mechanic sleep with the bike because people had tampered with it before. In Munster, one of the mechanics for a different pair undid the lock ring on the bottom bracket on my bike and tightened the crank right up. They knew it, and they watched me. They asked me how my legs were. That's what they used to do without me even knowing, and there were clearly other things that happened.

Eventually, Maurice started his season 'proper' at Munich with Doyle, but unsurprisingly, the form wasn't there. Compounding the lack of peak physical fitness were other challenges, away from the track, both linked to cycling and not linked: issues with relationships, choices, life in general. 'That's the thing, it's never just the physical riding, there were other things going on that were upsetting to me and made it difficult on and off the track, when you are young these things can affect you.'

It's the first glimpse I have of things not being straightforward for Maurice, a situation where his default answer of 'pull your finger out, ride up and down the link road really fast' didn't provide the answer. I can sense something underneath it all. I don't know what it is, I feel like he has hinted at it before, in silences, in half-started sentences, sudden silent moments of reflection among the bravado and the sense of adventure, of control; a suggestion that around the edges, something is fraying; he refers to some time spent in Scotland 'when I couldn't race'. There is ambiguity, a tense, sharp fragility undermining years of sustained resilience.

There are a lot of things that happened to me at that time, and as a result the racing wasn't quite the same any more, but it's not necessarily that, it's not an excuse, it's just that there are things outside that can have an effect on you, especially relationships, and as a young man they can be particularly hard, especially if you're in a country where you haven't got anyone around you when it does go wrong. Sometimes, I felt alone, Paul, you know, as though I had no one.

I had a girlfriend, you see, and my relationship wasn't easy at that point, and I was on my own in another country ... um ... it can be ... it can worry you, to the point that you can't sleep properly at night. You see sometimes, in the six-days, Paul, people talk about riders taking substances to ride faster or whatever, but more than anything else what you need is to slow down, to sleep, *not* to speed up. You might finish with the big chase at 1 a.m., after you'd done all of that you'd have to lie there trying to sleep with all these wheels going round, literally, in your head, and all the other stuff creeping in, and sometimes the soigneur would give you something to sleep, because you *have* to sleep. Otherwise the next day things are worse than they were before.

Looking back, when I used to go in and prepare myself on the road, I struggled to get enough sleep. I would be fighting to get the fitness to ride in the six-days. I used to train to get to the level needed, building up the strength and the stamina to keep going, as well as the speed. Five or six weeks before I would start riding to races, kermesses on the road, say from here to Antwerp, ride there, ride the race, ride back, 250km a day, do that for five or six days in a row, every day, just get up, ride, then do the race, sitting there in the 52:16, pedalling, pedalling, pedalling, just *vuull gaz*, sitting there, then ride home, then try and sleep, then get up and try to do it the next day and the next day, and at the end of every day I'd go home and try to sleep, and I couldn't. On occasion I would take something to sleep.

I think back again to the refrain Maurice has used before, and he will use again: 'At what price?' The perception is that things were good.

And they were – the pre-eminent British six-day rider on the back of his best season, earning a lot of money. But nothing is ever secure, the six is capricious, it tests each rider's ability to cope with an extreme – or dangerous – workload; to race, to sleep, to get up and do it again and again. With Maurice, the effort involved, aligned with the stress of a difficult season and things happening off the track, was enough to disrupt his circadian rhythm. It's a nocturnal event – that's just one of the insane realities of the six – it asks people to do excessive, mind-bending physical activity between the hours of 8 p.m. and 4 a.m., the world's most horrific night shift. Ethan Hayter and Fred Wright both spoke of staring at the walls in the early hours, 'You're fully concentrating, right up until 2 a.m., and you take that energy back with you.' They were doing one six, then resting for the off-season. For Maurice, the sixes never stopped, they were just interrupted by twelve hours of travel.

Ghent would finish on Sunday at about six or seven in the evening. We'd get in the car, drive to Zurich to start the next afternoon. The soigneur would drive, so sometimes I'd take something to try and sleep through the night, sat in the passenger seat as he drove across Europe. Then you would be racing that evening at 7 p.m. in a new six-day with a fresh batch of riders, locals with something to prove. Then you'd ride Berlin, Dortmund, Frankfurt with one day in between, you'd have a night off, then the next night would start. I did three in a row like that.

For me, it was about the effort, the scale of the exercise, that was always what kept me awake, along with nerves. I would be tense in the days leading up to a six where I wanted to do well. I raced on my nerves, which meant I was in a heightened state at the end, and at night.

I can't say anything about any other rider because I don't know their point of view. The thing is with sleeping tablets, with any of this, Paul, is people don't understand it. I don't know if *you* understand it. There were guys taking things sometimes, they were no angels. When I became a pro, some riders would say what they were using: tablets, maybe an amphetamine. But for riders who might sometimes take amphetamine, they would then have to take something to sleep as well. Sometimes you might sense that a rider was using something strong every night during a six, but by the end of the week they would be completely wasted.

We talk about others, we mention names, some in the public eye, others not. We talk about Erik De Vlaeminck, cyclo-cross genius with an accompanying set of myths, some awe-inspiring: 'his handlebars cracked in two. Yet he still won the race, steering with just his right hand, waving the shattered half above his head with his left';[1] some terrifying: 'Belgian cycling authorities were allegedly so alarmed by his lifestyle, they only granted him a racing licence one day at a time.'[2] He went to prison in 1974 for falsifying medical prescriptions and fleeing the scene of an accident.[3] Maurice summarises it: 'They used to let him out to go and ride the worlds. That is a different thing altogether.' Around the edges, some riders were taking things, some to get by, some to sleep, most just to cope. It wasn't systematic, industrial doping, it was occasional amphetamine usage, it was unscientific and dangerous. As late as 1995, Frank Vandenbroucke used 'the sleeping pill Stilnocht to get some shuteye, amphetamine for the get up and go for the races.'[4]

> It's like everything. Someone might have a glass of wine, sometimes two, but rarely the whole bottle. Drink a whole bottle of Jack Daniels a day and see what happens. There's a line – some people didn't have that. They might even find the right formula for a while, but it didn't work forever. There were some guys who might be taking things on the odd occasion, they were no angels, but there were others who couldn't get up without putting something

---

[1] www.brusselstimes.com/323385/monarchs-of-the-mud
[2] Ibid.
[3] Ibid.
[4] Andy McGrath, *God is Dead* (Bantam Press, 2022), p. 83.

in. Most of the guys who were like that, they're not here anymore. *They're not here.* You just have to look at the demands of the six. It's inhuman.

The raw inhumanity of the six-day circus became a perfect storm of stress and noise when aligned with Maurice's sense of isolation in Belgium and his faltering relationship. Contracts were disappearing and form was slipping away. It started to bleed out on to the track, affecting his riding and races in an entropic spiral. A sense of pressure weighs heavily; it's never there when things are good, they feel effortless, everything is dealt with, success happens. But now, suddenly, it was there, an increase in pressure, a descent into darkness, drowning under the weight of the water. In one of the few contracts he got that year, Maurice was down to ride at Ghent with Gary Wiggins. They won the first night and were leading the event, but the second night saw Maurice crash out, dislocating his shoulder.

Even now, sometimes if there's something on my mind, I lie awake in the dark. The difference is I don't take anything to sleep nowadays. I remember in the run-up to London, especially the closer it came, the more on edge and wound up I would get. I wouldn't be so good with people around me any more, that was when I would sometimes take things to help me sleep. Maybe my reflexes weren't as sharp as they could have been because of it, and that could be why things happened at Ghent, when I crashed and dislocated my collarbone. Maybe if I was a bit sharper, I wouldn't have touched that wheel, come down. Van Den Haute pulled his pedal out, the bike went out and I touched a wheel, and there it is. Gary went on and they paired him up with Don Allan.

It was the first time Wiggins had ridden with one of the regular hardmen of the circuit; Allan was a regular partner for Danny Clark. As an Antipodean, Wiggins was in. He knew that the chance to ride with either Clark or Allan was a ticket to success, to wins, and to more contracts. It seems a turning point, of sorts: one partner drops away, the other seizes the opportunity. A touch of wheels exposes the brutal, capricious nature of the six.

> If your performance goes down in any way or form then they get somebody else to take your place, it's as simple as that. Don't forget, our agent – everyone's agent – Jan Dirksen had 250 riders on the books, so it wasn't personal, they'd just get someone else instead. It is there all the time, there is a worry about it, your performance, but sometimes things just don't go your way, and at that time it felt like it was one thing after another.

The race continues without you. Maurice made it back for Maastricht the following month, from 16 to 21 December, with Gary Wiggins. They came fifth. It was a strong result given the circumstances. He rode the Christmas Day Oscar Daemers GP at 't Kuipke, coming second, then headed to Zurich for a Boxing Day meeting, winning the 100km Madison, again with Wiggins. Over Christmas, Maurice did race after race, heading to Cologne on 29 December with René Kos, where they came tenth. Maurice finished the season at Antwerp in February, coming fourth with Willy De Geest. In total, Maurice rode only four sixes that season, compared to sixteen the year before.

> It wasn't that it was all awful, or that my performance had gone, but it wasn't quite the same as it was before. It was combined with the difficulties in my home life, and that made it hard. I'm not trying to make excuses. I was on my own, my girlfriend was Belgian, we weren't living together, but it was serious. She lived at home with her parents, but she found it stressful when we were apart, and especially when I was riding at the track. I'd go to a six and when I came back, I'd find she hadn't been eating, because she was anxious and worrying about what I was doing, and who I had been with. People would bring stories to her, that I'd done this or that, been with this woman. As a young man, all of these things can affect you, Paul. When you see it as an older, more mature person, you

might be able to handle yourself a bit better in these circumstances, but at the time it was hard.

Our conversations are illuminated by Maurice's constant desire to make things happen, to do the things that change the future, not to give up, to be active and not passive, but also a refusal to accept such things as excuses. It is a key component of his success, and it is forged in a crucible of discrimination, but later, when listening back to our conversation and transcribing, I want to offer some kind of support, to say, *You know what Maurice, that sounds really hard, on lots of levels and it's OK to say, well, those things affected me and I'm OK with that, and that wasn't my fault and that's not an excuse, it's a reason.* But for Maurice the sense is that these things happen and we still have to do stuff and therefore these *are* excuses, everything else is details, the individual should do something about it. This is what burns so strongly in Maurice Burton, and he foregrounds it at every chance. *We are what we are, there is a price, life is what you make it, I told myself to sort it out, I did this…* But I'm struck that any challenges, any obstacles, are amplified on almost every level. He was an outsider in a country, a British guy in Belgium – where British cyclists try and make it and 9 times out of 10 don't make it and come home again and never race again – but also a man of colour in a country where it held a novelty value and a fascination. Maurice was a visible representation of what was repressed: Belgium's simmering colonial past and racial identity.

I spoke some Flemish by then. I could converse with people, but I was always the outsider. I tried not to let it get me down, I wouldn't let that happen, and at the same time of course I knew things weren't going as well as they should be. But I wasn't in a position where I wanted to just throw it all in, either. I wanted to make it work. I was aware that people come and go with the six-day. If I look back, there were others at the time, like Michel Vaarten, he was with Albert Fritz, they either won Antwerp or were second, and a year or so later you didn't see him riding any races, he disappeared, but then later he came back to the circuit and he was successful. There were other riders who were in and out, some were there all the time, but many disappeared and they came back. That seemed like it could happen to me, drop away a bit, then come back.

It is rational and he was barely twenty-five years old. But the immediate challenges – sustaining a healthy relationship, competing at the highest level, keeping healthy, sleeping well – were extreme and exacting a heavy price. We're descending into the abyss of a conversation about sleeping and waking, stress, pressure, and things being out of control. It is difficult.

The thing is, you just *have* to sleep. I remember I moved into this other flat and there were these people living upstairs, and the bloody radio would go off and they'd go to work and they'd leave the radio on, and one day I knocked on the door, I couldn't sleep because of the noise, and I broke the door down and the radio was on and I pulled the flippin' thing out of the wall. It was on, it was keeping me awake. I got into a bit of trouble for that. Things like that, a radio next door, they can upset your whole balance.

It's the kind of thing that when you're older you are able to put it out of your mind. But when you're young, trying to make it, it's stressful. I don't know if you do become a better person as a result of it, but you become stronger, or harder, I guess. You carry it with you. You realise how quickly you can go up and how quickly you can go back down as well.

We pause amid the intense memories and regret, about how things worked out, how they didn't work out, and I'm finding it hard to disentangle the cycling bits from the personal relationships, the sense of where and how things happened. But there's something else, it's not some weird, writerly intuition that I have, because I don't have that. There is just *something else*. There is a pause filled with all the heft of an unopened sentence.

'Yeeesss ... Paul. Yes.'

The accompanying sigh carries with it all of the repressed memories from the intervening years.

I am not uncomfortable, but I am aware that I've done that thing interviewers do: I've dredged up memories and it's been great, they have come alive and cyclists are flying around our heads, a colourful orrery of time, people and places. In among the constellations there is something else and I don't know what it is or where it has come from. Through the dust I can see the outline of something and it looks like it holds other stories.

Paul: 'Do you want to take a break?'

Maurice: 'No it's not that. There's another part about that thing you know. About this, all of this. You haven't said anything and I don't know whether you know about this or not.'

Paul: 'Well I don't know about it then. I don't know what I don't know, otherwise I would tell you.'

Maurice: 'You sure?'

Paul: 'Yeah, I'm sure.'

Maurice: 'But I don't think we want to put it in the book.'

19

Scotland

Of course I think we should put it into the book.

When someone says they don't want to put it into the book, the phrase tells me this is a truth, this is an event that shapes and scars, and these are the events I'm interested in. I don't want to upset anyone and I know that Maurice and I will have to revisit this conversation, there is more talking to do. I try to inspire confidence, to peek through the thin net curtain of time and memory, but equally, I think Maurice wants to talk about this, because otherwise he wouldn't have mentioned this thing he is not sure he knows if I know about.

But right now he is balancing what he knows I know with what he thinks I know. Maurice knows I do lots of research, right from the first meeting, when I began plucking names out of the air, names that had been filed away for forty years, stories about people nobody talks about any more, their mark on time not much more than a footnote in a yellowing race report from 1975, emerging suddenly in a splash of colour, defined edges, a living, breathing vignette. I'm flattered and pleased that Maurice thinks I do research. He tells me again, 'The fact is, you look very closely into this, Paul...'

I always think I haven't done enough research; this is my starting point. I can't come here and turn up not knowing stuff, not asking the right questions. Maurice will think I'm not serious or that I don't care, at best that I don't do my job properly, and I'll miss the important stuff. Even when you do know stuff you still miss the obvious questions and have to make decisions about going back over things, trying to get shape and detail, trying to get the narrative right, because this is a book about Maurice, but it's also a product of the industry and the lovely people who bought it have an idea of what they think should be in this book they haven't yet read. Writing the story of someone else's life is hard. You are trying to capture their life in the way they want to see it, but also in the way that you see it, and in the way that you think others will want to see it. There is no simple way of balancing these imperatives, apart from being honest.

Maurice leans back, looks up at the edge of the patio parasol, the sun noticeably lower in the now pallid blue London sky.

I think I have missed something. I'm not sure how. I spent weeks literally knee-deep in archive material. I turned every single page of every single weekly edition of a cycling magazine, from the years 1972 to 1985, that's 660,000 pages. I glossed some, where it appeared nothing happened. I glossed over 1981 when there were long absences from the narrative. I don't know what it is I missed because Maurice is being elliptical.

Maurice: '... But at the same time you don't know about this thing. You haven't mentioned anything about this situation. And I don't know if you haven't mentioned it because you don't want to say it to me, or you just don't know about it.'

Paul: 'I suspect it's me not coming across it, why don't we talk about it now? I mean, if you're nervous about what goes in or what doesn't go in, what I do is I go away and I write, go through the transcripts, everything we've talked about. I have forty pages of transcripts, and in brackets some of it already says, 'Don't include' or 'Think about how to frame', because of a reservation, and I highlight that to myself, the need to be careful with it. And you get to read it all, agree or disagree, highlight the things I've got wrong, challenge it.'

Maurice: 'Well, if you don't know then not many other people will know.'

And he's right, if I don't know, then people won't know, those reading this book, coming to this story for the first time, they won't know anything other than what I tell them. It's not on the internet. And I know it is up to Maurice if he wants to talk about this thing or not, but I know that there is only one book here, no one else is going to write the story of this life. This is the one people are going to read, to reflect on, to make sense of, to be inspired and challenged by. This isn't a draft account to be improved on, or amended, it's the definitive telling.

> Paul: 'You know, Maurice, and I know you know, that the truth is everything, that this is an honest story, a narrative of a life lived, and people will want to read it because it tells them something about their lives, it tells them something about cycling, and it tells them what it means when things go well but also what it means when things go badly, and what it is like to live the life you chose, to cope with things that happen to you, as a result of the decisions you make. They will read it and they will draw strength from that, from all of it.'
>
> Maurice: 'Well, Paul, when it comes to it, maybe. The thing is, a lot of cyclists write books, but there's only a very few riders who have ever mentioned anything about substances … you see … and um… The reason why they haven't mentioned substances is because people know that they've had some issues with that, it's a big topic for them, it's public. What I'm saying to you, is we haven't gone down that route and talked about drugs, or anything like that.'

And he is right, we haven't talked about drugs, with the exception of a neatly walled-off section, or comments about Pervitin,[1] things administered. We talked briefly about it last time.

> Maurice: '… I haven't knowingly used that stuff, but equally, I'm not going to tell you that I was an angel.'

---

[1]Pervitin was a methamphetamine used extensively by German soldiers and pilots in the second world war. Usage in sport became widespread throughout the 1960s and 1970s

I don't think he was an angel, and I can't quite see how riding the six-day circuit in the late 1970s, at a time of significant amphetamine use in the professional peloton, both road and track, is compatible with any rider being angelic. If our conversations affirm anything, it is that the unique demands of the six-day placed extreme pressures on riders' mental and physical well-being, simply by asking people to ride for that long, in that way. Equally, I know I am not an angel, and no one I know is an angel, or can ever be angelic, because we are all deeply flawed creatures.

> Maurice: 'Yeah but you see, there are these things in people's books and people say, "Oh, he's only where he was, he got there because of this or that, the things he took, the way he prepared," which isn't the case. *You see?*'

I see he is nervous. The confidence, the laughter, it has ebbed away. This amounts to a confession, of sorts, but also a fear, a sense of anxiety about what this means, how it plays, outside of a conversation between me and him, in his South London garden on a beautiful sunny day.

> Maurice: 'It's difficult. In the world we're in, people have opinions about this, the way cycling has gone since the 1990s. People ask you if you ever took anything, as though you might be some sort of criminal if you ever did, and anyone who didn't is therefore the perfect professional. It's not how it is.'

It's a binary position – the opprobrium of the Lance years, the fall-out, the reckoning, the soul searching, an entire generation undermined by industrialised usage of EPO (erythropoietin), seven years of asterisks in the biggest race on the planet. I read Daniel Friebe's book on Jan Ullrich, a key protagonist at the heart of the EPO years. It is full of interviews with Lance Armstrong, and maybe, just maybe, the book is a turning point in our attitudes, not in the way that it seeks to absolve but in the way that it *doesn't*, in how it seeks to recognise that these are people, they were young men, late teens, early twenties, caught up in a world that was broken, and yes they made catastrophic decisions, and yes, one or two didn't make those choices and they suffered hugely, but ultimately everyone suffered and everybody lost, and in the wake of it everybody carries on living and everybody dies. And it is this that Maurice is referring to, the frame within which all discussions about drug use in cycling are seen, the accompanying curator's notes beneath the portraits of riders from the era.

> Maurice: 'The public, they see it in a certain way, that is how these things are viewed. As a result, a lot of people don't mention this side of things because of that perception. And I think probably, it's for the best that way, you know, to keep that out of it, but there was ... er ... there was an incident, something happened, a stupid thing, after a kermesse on the road at Mechelen in July 1981. At the time, a lot of the riders had positive drug tests after races. I had a positive test for Stimul and was suspended for a while. It had a bad effect on me, I really struggled, deeply.'

I realise now why he was getting away from it all in Scotland in August and September 1981. He breathes in, deeply, waits, thinks, breathes in again, shifts in his seat.

> Maurice: 'I don't think it was anything too bad, you know, at the time, and maybe even now, but it is something that happened to me, and it came to light. The thing is, other people, other riders at the time, it wouldn't have bothered them at all, others who used it regularly, or had used it in the past. But to me, Paul, it bothered me a lot, it made me feel pretty bad. It was around the time when things were really difficult and it didn't help. Things weren't the same for me at that point, I was finding it hard.
>
> I don't think I want to put this in the book. I feel ashamed, Paul. You know ... you see ... I don't know how you see me, by that?'

Maurice says, 'you see' as a filler, sometimes with a 'hmm', a short 'hum', a way of checking on affirmation. I think he is asking me what

I think about it, how I feel, my opinion, he is asking me to respond, and this feels strange, because it feels like my opinion *of Maurice* on this carries weight. We are both carefully measuring our words, each syllable. It's not a free-flowing conversation, but it has warmth, empathy and openness. I pause, say each word carefully, I don't want to be misconstrued, everything is full of modality – could, maybe, should, might have...

> Paul: 'I feel that ... there is no shame at all attached to any of this; I think I understand that you did something that goes deeply against your principles, your values, but when I look at it ... I don't see anything that is worthy of shame... I think it's very easy from the outside to look in and say, glibly, from our living rooms, "Oh these people did this and that's wrong," but we weren't there.'

I try to think of something analogous. I know I've done things that make me shudder, normal things, in my twenties, drunken impulsive behaviour, things you shouldn't do, things that I am happy people don't know about, things that keep me awake at night sometimes, but in the harsh light of the morning, are just normal things, errors of judgement, a part of living. When people do know about them, they think nothing of it, it is human frailty. We carry these things, they shape us, and are probably the most important thing about us. Would I change the foolish mistakes I made that directly or indirectly led to me being attacked with a knife at 1.15 a.m. on 15 January 1995 and subsequently changed the direction of my life completely? No, I wouldn't. But this wasn't enough to stop me repressing it for twenty-five years, carrying it inside of me like a burning coal inside my rib cage.

I am aware that Maurice hasn't talked about this in years. I doubt he has told anyone about it, even the people whom he tells everything to, maybe they don't know. But just like the drawer full of unopened bills, it becomes nightmarish, growing in size in the dark, out of all proportion, until the size and scale of something in your head far outweighs the reality of whatever it was. It is a lump of burning coal, it is too hot to touch.

Maurice: 'You didn't know about it did you? At the time it was carried in the press. People knew, but it's gone, and it's probably best to let it go. Nobody really knew or cared about it in the UK, it might have been in *Cycling*, but people in Belgium knew. Maybe it's best to leave it, Paul. I don't think people would understand, and I don't want people to think I'm using it to justify what happened to me, mentally, at that point in time.

And with all of that, this thing that happened – whether I bring it into it or not – it all had an effect on me. It was nothing in one sense, it happened all the time in cycling, it was a simple little thing, and I don't think you even felt that different after taking Stimul, in my case I don't even recall it doing anything, as such. But all the same, it was something that happened.

All of that, all of these things – and I don't even want to bring the suspension into it – it all had an effect on me.'

There is such a weight with this. I can feel it so heavily on Maurice's shoulders, and it's not about the suspension, although clearly that is laden with regret, it's something else. Maurice is someone who is so guarded about the version of themself that they put across, that even to acknowledge that something hurt, that it was hard, seems to be doubly intense. I am now the one measuring my words really carefully, I hear it back on the tape, a stilted pause mid-sentence, mid-phrase each word seems to sit awkwardly, takes time to find, like old letter sets, wooden blocks, pushed clumsily on to paper, badly kerned. I can see my spoken words in the air in front of me, a sensory mess with all the fluency of a glued newsprint ransom collage.

Maurice: '... and I don't think that it's something that we ... er... there will be people who look at it and see me in a bad light because of it, so I feel like I'd rather just...'

Paul: 'OK, I agree, I respect that, and I'm not going to go against it, but do you think that anyone at that time was riding clean in that way? In any way at all? I mean, given everything we've talked about and what's in the public eye?'

Maurice: 'I don't know, Paul, but that's neither here nor there.'

Paul: 'But it is both here and there. And I think it is here, not there, because it's about the culture at the time, not you, it was the endemic riding culture at the time, and you were a part of it. There's a massive difference between, say, the usage of basically amphetamine, pot Belge [a mixture of drugs illegally used by cyclists], in the 1960s through to the 1980s, compared to what came later: industrialised, scientific blood doping. It's night and day.'

Maurice: 'Yeah, there is a difference but there isn't a difference, it's only that... It's just something that I guess I'm ashamed of. I mean if you didn't know about it, and you're a man who looks into things very finely, if you didn't find it, then I think it's best I'd just keep that out, Paul. I'd rather keep that out. Because I didn't know if you knew or not. To tell you the truth, I wondered if you knew whether you would have done this book in the first place. It's something I'm ashamed of, to this day, I guess.

I'm stunned by the last bit. That somehow if I knew about this, I wouldn't have done the book. It's so far from the truth, or my truth. This is a counselling session now, it's about the advice people tell you to give yourself, about the secrets we carry with us, the anxieties and fears we all have, the bad things we have done, the way we treated people who care about us, the horror and the feeling in the pit of the stomach about these things, and the recognition that we can't change them, we can only continue processing, forever.

Of course I would have done the book. I would have wanted to do the book even more, because what I am interested in is people, in their entirety, not the varnished narrative that we construct, but the raw truth that makes people who they are, not who we think they should be. And my heroes are flawed, sometimes deeply, but they are heroic figures, they do incredible things, feats of mental fortitude, and they make me want to live my life better, to be better, and to cope with things better. Maurice makes me want to do better.

Paul: 'Well, of course I would have.'
Maurice: 'But you might have seen me in a different light...'
Paul: 'Let's flip this around. There isn't a single person who isn't ashamed of something in their past.'
Maurice: 'I know but I don't look at other people, I'm only looking at myself. At the end of the day, it had a big effect, a bigger effect than it might have had on other people maybe, and it wasn't that alone but it was a contributing factor to what happened to me with regard to that point in my cycling career. I left Belgium. I didn't know what I was going to do. I went up to Scotland for a bit, and got far away from it all, to think, to get some space.'

There is an overwhelming sense of self-criticism, a harsh, unforgiving self-perception. I can't escape the sense that it is linked to his outsider status, of having to fight 'twice as hard for half as much', the unseen, pressing anxiety of being within and without, of being othered, constantly, and trying, constantly, to challenge prejudice and preconception. It adds up to a feeling of vulnerability, of fragility, stemming from the precariousness of his position, of having to be better than the next person. The six is hard, exhausting and lonely enough without this context.

Maurice: 'People might have thought things about me before, I don't know, but at that point I guess it was me thinking these things, in my mind, worrying how people saw me, and it had an effect on me, Paul, and that shows in my results. It was combined with the struggles with my girlfriend in Belgium, all these things came along at that point, then the crash at Ghent, the dislocation. When things are going well, it's like in the bike trade, you know, you get up, it's good, like now things are just going along, but we have had situations when things weren't going well at all. A few years ago we had to defer our wages, things were tight, and it was really hard to keep it all going.'

He's right about the bike trade going well. Every time I look on Facebook at the De Ver page, another smiling customer is wheeling a Giant or Colnago out the door, with Maurice in the background, his presence, his blessing.

> Maurice: 'Well you don't even see all of 'em Paul. I don't put them up, take the pictures, Mia gets me to do that, that's not even half of what we sell! But then sometimes things go out of sync, and it can lead to something else, and then suddenly things aren't going as well as they should. And that was a point in my life when things weren't going as they should. I can see myself through this, because of these previous experiences I have this inner strength. I didn't let it go.'

When talking, and even more so later, when listening back to the transcript, I am struck by the oscillation between confidence and fragility. There is strength and resilience, but it veers between public confidence and private anxiety, of regret and shame. I can't imagine Maurice sees himself as vulnerable, and maybe that's not the right word, because I doubt if anyone who has ever raced against him, or done business with him, or written a book about him would find any evidence of fragility, but there is a repressed sense of vulnerability about his place in the world, his legacy, the past and present. These are the emotional scars of a lifetime spent trying to make things happen, to overcome obstacles, to cope with knockbacks, to be better than everyone else.

The day is drawing on and we need to go for dinner. I am hungry. It has been exhausting, emotional, heartfelt. I feel privileged, I don't feel like I'm writing a book, but talking about things that matter with someone who matters. In fact, I am living my best life because I am doing things that I care about, with someone I care about. Maurice leans in, his eyes ablaze with light, with excitement, maybe even with relief, a lightness.

> Maurice: 'There are two Frank Sinatra songs: "My Way" is my signature tune, the other one, "That's Life", there's a part in it, he says how every time he falls down he picks himself up, and that's exactly it, you get up, dust yourself off, and you just get back in the race.

I turned it around, and here we are, and that's it, Paul, that's it.'

20

Ghent

It is Saturday night, 7 p.m., and I'm in Belgium. I see my new best friends, Fred and Ethan, on the presentation lap. I am sure they see me, leaning over the coping, taking terrible pictures from too far away with my prime lens, Bill Kund's voice in my head. Fred waves at me, I'm sure of it. He just happens to be waving at everyone else at the same time. Ethan is maybe a bit too cool to wave at me, Mr Try-Hard, the old guy with sallow, saggy skin, waving like a lunatic. Ethan and Fred are riding for Callant Financieel Advies, which confirms my theory that Flemish is English with a very heavy Dutch accent, a theory hypothesised on the train this morning with the sign 'Welkom in deze train'. I note that every great pairing is sponsored by a Belgian hardware shop or the lottery, nothing in between.

The presentation lap takes the place of a warm-up and is a jazzy bit of spectacle. The pairs circle in a string, side by side, the commentator rolling a lot of Rs as he talks about their successes, hyping them for the crowd, while the music thuds underneath. As he reels through each rider's list of victories, there is a growing crescendo, followed by noise and Euro-house music as they wave to the crowd, no hands, and everyone cheers. The loudest cheers are for Iljo Keisse, the thirty-nine-year old patron, winner of twenty-eight sixes. He is riding his last event before retirement in front of his home crowd. Everyone knows Iljo, or knows Iljo's dad, who runs Café de Karper, a bike length from the velodrome, and everyone has come to say goodbye to this adored Gentenaar. The refrain is a long '*eeeeeel*' followed by a drop for the '*loooo*', repeated, a chime that reverberates around the seating, into the centre and back.

Almost anyone in the crowd could be a famous Belgian cyclist from days of yore. As if to prove a point, Ferdi Van Den Haute strolls past, taking his seat. Roger De Vlaeminck saunters into the press area and waves. He looks immaculate in a dark blue suit. Stan Tourné and Eddy Merckx were here on Tuesday, along with Bradley Wiggins. Some are saluted by the commentator or take on ceremonial duties, others blend into the crowd, take a seat, watch the race they once won, breathe deeply in the glorious confluence of their past with the present before them. Most of them rode against or with Maurice. 'T Kuipke is unchanged, the same fried abattoir smell of hot dogs and burgers, the same beers, merchandise and Belgians, the same beautiful cross-section of Ghent metropolitan culture. Everyone wears a cap, or a cycling jersey, or both. I make do with the 'Flandriens' cap I got from a concession stall; it is an organisation that supports all aspects of Flanders, it helps me blend into the morass of Gentenaars. It's Friday night and the people of Ghent have come out in their finest cycling caps and jerseys to get absolutely smashed on very strong Flandrian beer.

The lights fizz amid a dense, rolling cacophony of sound, propelling the riders around the track. It is a roiling soup of Euro-house, cheers, exhalation and shouted conversation. Spotlights track the lone escapee, the hare and the hounds. The light and dark polarises much more these days, no lingering clouds of cigarette smoke to blur and ameliorate the house lights, but it is also easier on the lungs, riders inhale the beery fog of people. The middleplein is full and yet somehow getting even busier as a race whirls around above, the flickering zoetrope of a Madison, the first big chase of the evening. A Madison makes no sense on the telly; you are reliant entirely on the commentator telling you where everyone is. In the flesh, the pattern is evident. It is a constant fluid motion, two pacelines, one rider in, one out. This Madison is *vuull gaz*, we are told this by the rolling R commentator, many, many times, particularly as Lindsay De Vylder and Robbe Ghys try to take a lap. They ride to the edge of collapse, arms wrestling with the bike and the camber, for about ten minutes solid, trying to first get ahead, then to catch up, to make the junction. They dangle in no man's land, but then the tempo shifts and the crowd sense they are going to do it and the roar escalates with each metre stolen, until they re-join, finally, and it feels like the Madison is the highest point of expression in the medium of track cycling, and Ghent is the canvas. I am breathless at the constant sinuous flicker of movement.

I wander around with my camera and lanyard, enabling me to be wherever I want, except the cabins. I sit in the front row. I go up to the top of the banking, look down and marvel at the steepness. I stand next to the dernies and legendary pilot Peter Bauerlein. The music shifts and changes, one minute a blazing, hi-trance version of a Fleetwood Mac song, then a gunshot heralds a shift into the most Belgian song I have ever heard. The dernies are out and the stuttering splutter of their engines increases in frequency as the race unfolds. Iljo Keisse is making a charge up the field and the crowd are in raptures, shouting 'EEEEElio' over and over. At 166m, the shortness of the track distils and compresses the race. You have to choose whether to follow the movement around and around or watch one half and the big screen. I choose both. The derny and riders create a

sound of their own. Ethan Hayter is in the race, holding off the challenge, but I know Iljo must win, and he does win, because it is his last
ever six-day. The race finishes to a crack of a gunshot and the DJ plays
more oompah Belgian drinking songs and everybody drinks.

Tuur Dens' dad

An interval appears at 10.40 p.m. and some English people complain
that the club singer is not Gary Hagger. Instead, we have Jettie
Pallettie and she is amazing. She is dressed like a majorette and she
is singing her hit songs from the Flemish Ultratop 50, 'Pinten &
Patatten' followed by 'Dubbeldik Feest in de Tent'. The songs are fast
and slow at the same time, and right now it is the highest point of
Flandrian culture and everyone is singing along.

I stop trying not to drink, stop trying to watch the cyclists in some
vaguely journalistic way, stop trying to rationalise and explain, and
instead begin to lose myself in the madness of the middelplein and
start taking photos of the mad things that are happening instead.
And there is an incredible amount of mad things happening instead.
Somewhere, there is bike racing, starting up again for the final three-
hour shift, but it has moved to the periphery of my vision, to be
replaced by a crowd from Brixton Cycles wearing Fred Wright masks,

including Fred Wright's dad. Fred Wright's mum also wears a Fred Wright mask so I can take a picture and we watch as Fred wins the scratch race and we go crazy.

The evening moves at a different pace and it is way past my bedtime. I walk through the crowd with my lanyard and camera and people don't ask, they *demand* to have their photo taken. Then a song is played and every single Belgian man takes their shirt off and waves it around their head and the whole place wobbles and beer is thrown. But something else even more deranged and athletic is about to start: the beer cup tower jumping competition. A gap opens and a drunk Belgian runs and vaults a 5ft tower of stacked plastic cups. For a moment, the real race is secondary to this event. I take photos and nearly get crushed. Someone stops me and insists I drink a cup of beer in one. It is a small glass of Primus so I oblige, without much effort. It's hot and sweaty and the drink is not unwelcome.

I can no longer work out where reality begins and ends: the Tuur Dens fan club is in full force, every single one in a blue Tuur Dens casquette, including Tuur Dens' dad. The members of the Eric Schoefs fan club have matching baseball caps. I take a photo of them and later realise one of them is Eric Schoefs. At some point I start drinking a beer called Super 8 Flandrien because the logo looks pretty. This is a mistake. It is a very strong beer.

Eric Schoefs fan club with Eric Schoefs

Someone steals my hat. They don't steal it per se, they just insist I give it to them, repeatedly, through glazed eyes, in limited English – 'give. me. the. hat. please.' – until I give them the hat because they are really drunk and big. I am sad, because I liked the hat. They give me a crappy sponsors' hat from a road building firm. I amble around, increasingly drunk, and an English fan tells me they like my hat and it's their friend's birthday, so I say fuck it and give them the hat, and now I have no hat. I meet friends from London. Christine wants a new Tuur Dens hat, this year's special blue one.

She has last year's white one. Isaac wants a Primus Haacht, as do I. We all want Gary Hagger.

I wake up the next morning with a camera full of pictures of drunk Belgians and a hangover for the ages.

21

Luna Park

The sense of something ending begins to seep into our conversations like ink in water, delicate fractals of blue tainting the clear liquid of the past. The last time we met, Maurice took everyone out for dinner in his blue Bentley convertible. I lived my very best life and my seven-year-old son's best life – he is obsessed with cars and he wants to know every single detail of the car and the drive, make, model, sound. When I get back, the first thing he will ask me is about the car, and he lives in hope that one day Maurice might take him for a drive in the blue convertible of his dreams.

We drove south on the A3 into the twilight, daughter Gracie in the back with her partner, the wind around us, exposed to the elements. We ate pizza and ice cream and talked about everything and nothing, our jobs, happiness and school. We marvelled at Gracie's postgraduate study into the aerated bone structure of birds. We drove back into the ceaseless turmoil of the darkening city, beneath the stars peeping through the incipient London haze, the ambient sound of traffic accompanying our thoughts about the future, for the shop, for Gracie, Maurice and for me. Gentle conversations closed the curtain on a day full of intense reminiscence.

After the sleepless horror show of the 1981/82 season, featuring dislocations, a suspension and fine, compounded by the terrors of taking things to try to sleep and a spiralling relationship vortex, 1982/83 offered the possibility of a new start. However, Maurice was falling away from the 'Blue Train', down the order, back into the ranks of those looking for a contract, trying to get back on board. He had two contracts, starting with Madrid on 16 November, paired again with Debosscher. The Madrid Six was an outlier, made up of Spanish riders who were paired with bona fide stars of the circuit. Danny Clark rode with Faustino Rupérez, winner of the Vuelta in 1980. Gert Frank piloted the almost entirely unheralded Avelino Perea to the win. The racing was close, Burton and Debosscher came sixth at only two laps.

Maurice with Jop Kristens at Ghent

From Madrid, Maurice went straight back to Ghent, hoping to do better than the previous year, i.e. not dislocate a shoulder. He was paired with Jop Kristens. The line-up was familiar: Allan and Clark, Sercu and De Vlaeminck, René Pijnen, Dirk Heirweg, Ferdi Van Den Haute, Rik Van Linden. Maurice came seventh at fourteen laps. It was a decent result, with Wiggins–Heirweg back in ninth, but it proved a false dawn, no contracts ensued. I look at the blank space in my research sheets. There is nothing, not a single six from 28 November 1982 until Ghent the following year. I ask him about the gap, the challenges this presented.

> Things weren't going as they should, Paul. It was one of those times in my life where I look back and see it differently. There are certain things I might have done a bit differently, taken a slightly different path, or worked with different people. I began to think about coming back to the UK to live or race, it was possible, and it was on my mind for a few reasons. First, I knew that outside of cycling there wasn't any other job I could do in Belgium. What other job was I going to be doing, apart from driving a taxi or some flippin' thing like that? At least, not a job of any significance. I couldn't see anybody employing me in Belgium. To have a business in Belgium at that time you had to have a degree in book-keeping, so how was I going to get a degree? I haven't even got a degree now! I have a book-keeper who has a degree and he does all that for me! I knew that once I was finished with cycling, I wasn't going to be able to make a living in Belgium, not on the level that I would have wanted to, that was never a possibility. The reality was that I lived there because I wanted to be a bike rider and to be a bike rider I needed to be in Belgium. Without the contracts I began to think about what else there was, that's unavoidable really.

It is clear that when the bike racing began to dry up, the results and races slipping away, it exposed a void. Belgium was a black-and-white photograph from the pages of *Cycling Weekly* in 1972, a romantic and pragmatic location, the only place to be to ride and race. As long as these things were in balance, life was good. Without the bike racing there was very little else. Despite the challenges, Maurice wasn't done yet. An opportunity emerged in August 1983 in the UK. Promoter Allan Rushton had put together a new calendar of city centre criteriums, sponsored by Kellogg's. These were a new thing for cycling in the UK, televised bike racing on tight criterium circuits, starting in Bristol on 1 August, then Glasgow, Nottingham and Manchester in rapid succession, ending in Birmingham. The line-ups were impressive; punchy domestic professionals like Steve Joughin, Sid Barras and Dudley Hayton lined up against the smooth and sinister Continental-based professionals, Phil Thomas, Phil Anderson, Francesco Moser, Allan Peiper. It also presented an opportunity for Maurice. His road riding in Belgium had been for a series of smaller teams, sponsored by local firms: Campitello, Xaveer Coffee, Tiga Sport, Solahart Hecka – builders, wholesalers, blue collar companies looking for visibility at kermesses and in the occasional semi-classic. However, none of the UK teams – Moducel, Percy Bilton/Condor or Ever Ready – were interested in signing him.

In 1983, I was looking to ride these events and did want a contract, but nobody from the UK ever came to me and offered me the chance to be in a team. I didn't go to Raleigh or anyone like that and ask. Tony Doyle rode for a British team but did the six-days in winter and that worked for him, it was viable. He did a lot on the road in the winter, because he had the chance and the team, they supported him. I had these teams in Belgium but they never paid me a lot, my main source of income was the six-days; riding on the road for me was just to keep in some sort of shape.

Even the good kermesse riders didn't earn much. They had a team, targeted the races, but then they had to go and sell soap door to door for the sponsor to make up their contract. That wasn't for me, that sort of thing. There never was big money to be earned riding on the road. As I mentioned before, from my situation, even if I had the ability, I couldn't see how all these riders in a road team would back me as the leader; not only was I not Belgian, or not from Ghent, or whatever, but a Black guy as well. The six suited me, you could be an individual, you could race on your terms. In the end I wanted to ride these Kellogg's races so I came to a little arrangement with Roberts, they gave me a bike and they gave me some kit and I thought, well I'll publicise your bike on the TV. I did a little deal with them.

In effect, Maurice had gone full circle; he was back riding a Roberts, back in the UK, trying to make it stick. The more things change, the more they stay the same. He had spent six years as a professional, racing against the very best in Europe, and yet no one was prepared to offer him a contract. He made it to the start line on his own terms. There is quite a bit of footage from the various races; it features tight and scary circuits, Sean Kelly looking feisty, Sid Barras like he's spent the winter lifting heavy machinery on the hills above Sheffield. Far right is Maurice Burton, almost invisible on the front line, ignored by a very youthful Steve Rider. There was no recognition of Britain's first Black cycling champion.

> Alan Rushton was the promoter and a lot of the British riders were getting paid pretty well. He paid me £250 per race. I did Bristol, where I followed Francesco Moser's wheel and put in an effort here and there. After the race I said to Alan, 'I didn't win, but I did something,' and I looked at Alan and knew he was satisfied, he paid me and I did a job. I didn't ask for a fortune, he was happy and we shook hands. I rode under the Jamaican flag, it was Alan's idea, he did it for publicity. That used to happen sometimes and it didn't worry me. In a sense, that was what it was about, having an identity. It's the same as the track when you look at it. I did what I used to do in Ghent, put on a show to the promoter and the crowd, I was saying, 'Well you're paying me and I'm going to work, not just ride round and say thanks, but to show that we're doing something.' That's how it was with Alan Rushton.

After the races, Maurice returned to Belgium, but knew it wasn't going to be easy to break back into the sixes. He needed other ways to make a living as a bike rider, disciplines, ways to raise his profile and spring back into the sixes. He managed to get a ride at Ghent from 22 November, with Rudy Dhaenens, his first six since April in Madrid, but without consistency of training and racing it was a struggle. A familiar face from the past again exerted a malign influence on the outcome:

> Your body is like a watch. The timing, everything has to be right otherwise you don't do well, mentally and physically it slips away,

and the promoter sees it in you. At Ghent, we were going for the win in the chase one evening, looking to make up places and take laps. At the crucial moment, Albert Fritz came between us on the change and we crashed; he crashed as well, but he knew exactly what he was doing. He could see we were going to win that bloody race, so he came in to stop it. Sercu had put me with this young guy, a good rider, went on to become World Champion, but Fritz came and screwed the thing up because he could see I still had it there, I might come back. He came and said sorry afterwards, but bollocks, he wasn't sorry, he was an experienced rider, he knew exactly what he did.

Fritz came second with Thurau, behind Pijnen and De Wilde, with Maurice and Dhaenens in seventh. It was Maurice's last ride at Ghent.

Races were few and far between, and off the track things weren't much better. It's another hard conversation to have, we talk about the gaps, revisiting a time when things weren't good, when life seemed to be full of setbacks, it leads to silences as we sit in the afternoon heat of the garden. I sense once more memories being dredged from the abyss of time, neither of us clear just what might be coming up to the surface. Planes descend heavily in lines through the Croydon afternoon, each one laden with hundreds of people, with their memories, lives and narratives, while Maurice's story plays out on to the tape recorder. Sounds float across the back gardens on layers of hazy London heat, over breezeblock divisions and wobbly fences. Without contracts, Maurice returned to the UK and trained at home. There was the possibility of a ride in the Buenos Aires Six in April 1984.

I hadn't given up on riding. Things were difficult with my relationship, and it was made worse because I was in the UK. We were talking on the phone. One day I tried to ring and her mother said to me that they'd heard something about me, and I couldn't speak to her. We had these rings, it was quite serious, like we were engaged, and suddenly I couldn't speak to her. I didn't know what was going on, or why. In the end I went over there. She was living in Sint-Niklaas, between Ghent and Antwerp. When I got there, the place was empty. After I'd been cut out, her father had died from a brain haemorrhage, and the mother was in hospital having had a stroke. She was living with family and friends. I went to see her, just to speak to her, to find out what was happening, but they called the police and I had to leave. I never got to find out what happened, or why. I had no choice. And I'll be honest with you, all of this can really mess you up, and it did.

It sounds and feels very difficult; a career on the slide, an uncertain home life and a brutal relationship break-up. Within this seething cauldron, one element offered hope. Maurice phrases it in classic Maurice terms, veering from a stark recognition of how hard life can be, straight into the aphorism, the mantra: 'It wasn't a good time for me, one way or another, but you have to see yourself through these things. The prospect of a motor-paced race was what I had.'

For Maurice, as well as having to 'see yourself through', the next opportunity took the form of niche cycle racing. The motor-paced race is *very* niche. It's also spectacular, and extremely popular in Germany. The easiest way to describe it is to take a derny bike, square and cube it, until you're left with an enormous 750cc Triumph Tiger. The bicycle used behind the big motos is called a 'stayer', with a small front wheel and reversed fork designed to bring the rider closer into the slipstream. It is a noisy, exhilarating, terrifying race, best suited to the outdoor tracks where pairs can reach speeds of 72–80kph average with bursts of 97kph or more.

Joop Zijlaard was one of the derny pacers. He came to me because he knew I was pretty strong behind the dernies and he felt I had the ability behind the big motors, even though I hadn't done it before. There were some on the circuit who came from the stayers. Joop thought I could get a ride at the World Championships; the problem was you had to ride with a pacer from your country. Even if we had a pacer in the UK, it wouldn't have mattered because the Dutch and the Germans controlled the whole thing. However, if your country didn't have any tradition of motor-pacing, then you could use Bruno Walrave, a respected pacer. Danny Clark rode behind Walrave later when he became professional World Champion. Zijlaard knew that if I rode for Jamaica, then he could pace me at the Worlds. We had plans that I would stay with him and train in Holland, prep behind the motors on the track and the derny on the road. We both felt that I could get a medal on a stayer, and even without winning, it could bring me back into the sixes. It was like 1976 all over again, chasing the Olympics, it was a way forward. It wasn't straightforward but there was hope.

The derny pacers are well-liked and the crowd love the discipline. They also recognise the skill involved when eight pairs of riders are hurtling around the track at speed; the risk is amplified, and for the moto-paced stayers, it is increased again. The Buenos Aires Six-Day on 16 April, 1984 was Maurice's first since November and became a part of the plan. 'I felt like I had gone through some experiences and I wasn't ready to give up, I was ready to try and come back in, starting at Luna Park.'

Somewhere, there is footage of the Buenos Aires race on the internet. I'm not sure how I found it, one late evening disappearing into a whirlpool of research. It was a tight, temporary track with nasty transitions. Maurice watches the footage with detachment, looks away, then says calmly, 'It wasn't an accident, you know.' In other articles I have read, he has mentioned that something untoward happened. No one else seemed to be involved on the track, it wasn't sharp elbows, or Fritz, or any of those things.

It's complicated. I can kind of remember, it just happened, the tyre blew out and I went down. I was pretty groggy. Sometime before we went there someone told me what would happen to one of the riders at Luna Park, in detail, how they would have a tyre blow-out, a crash. Afterwards, I realised that the rider they were talking about was me, it is exactly what happened. It was sabotage, they cut the tyres with a razor blade. You might think I'm mad, Paul, but how I broke my leg, the accident, the lot, it was exactly as they said.

There are many layers of complexity. I know that the six was at the same time both lawless and intensely regimented; that competition for places was fierce. I know that there were deep-rooted animosities, that incredibly dodgy stuff happened, and that sabotage took place. Within this framework the prospect of someone returning to take a place that you had thought might be your own might be enough to spark an action, a reckless act. Within the frame of amphetamine use and sleep deprivation, morality can become a fluid concept.

If the cause was complex, the outcome was simple: he had a broken thigh bone. Femoral fractures require huge force, typically a car crash or gunshot. Track racing is dangerous, a horrid fracture is never far away. At the World Cup in 2011, Azizulhasni Awang ended up with a 20cm length of pine from the track speared *through* his leg from front to back. Maurice spent nearly a month in a hospital in Buenos Aires, staring at the ceiling, thinking about cycling and, at twenty-eight years old, what might happen next. The only rider to visit him was Roman Hermann. It seemed inevitable that something would have to change.

With a broken thigh you know it's going to be really difficult to get the same strength back, and to be honest I don't even have the same power now, forty years later. I broke the other one in 2009. After that, it took me four or five years to get it to bend. The thigh bone is not a standard break. I made up my mind in hospital that that was it, I just felt that there were too many things happening, I just thought about all of it, that it was time to change direction. That was partly coming out of it alive, and in hindsight it was a good thing.

I had to go back to Belgium initially, but then I came back to live in the UK with my parents, and I recovered slowly. I'd just been fighting all this time, to move on up, to race. That was the hope I had in my mind for the future, I knew I could do it, but suddenly that hope was gone and the will had gone. Up until that point I had always been very clear about where I was going, even the years just before when things were tough, I still knew what I wanted. And you have to remember that I never wanted anything else, from an early age. Even before I had ever raced a bicycle, I knew that I wanted to be a professional cyclist. But when you take that away and stop, for the first time ever, it's hard. Suddenly I didn't know what I wanted to do any more. I felt lost.

22

Lisson Grove

14 January 1986

When Maurice returned to the UK in late 1984, everything had changed, and yet some things were the same. He returned to his parents, no closer to employment than when he was as an apprentice electrician at St Thomas in 1974. His transferable skill: riding bikes at high speed for six days in a row. He had earned and saved enough money to live for a while, but that didn't help in terms of direction. For the first time since he was fourteen years old, Maurice Burton didn't know what to do. The abrupt nature of his retirement was exacerbated by the feeling that there were better days to come, that there was a plan. In defining himself as someone who always had the capacity to make things work, to stick it out whatever happened, having to stop – suddenly – was difficult.

I wonder about fulfilment; the sense that things were unfinished, mainly because at times Maurice talks down his record in the six-day. Where others won a six – even Debosscher – Maurice never made it to the top step of the podium. He measures himself against others, more prolific winners. It doesn't matter so much to Maurice that the number of six-day participants to have never won a race far exceeds the coterie who have, or that he won numerous races, or that he was National Champion, three times. It doesn't seem to matter that he rode fifty-six six-day races, countless kermesses, classics and semi-classics, that he made a name for himself in one of the toughest forms of cycling there is, or that he achieved this despite racial prejudice. These achievements cannot be measured in terms of numbers of overall wins. There is a sense that, at twenty-eight years old, he had the potential to achieve more.

There were riders like René Pijnen, or Danny Clark, who won races when they were younger, but some of the biggest names in the history of the six, like Stan Tourné or Roman Hermann, didn't start winning regularly until they were older. When I went to Argentina, I felt like I was starting to get my act together a little bit, because if you look at the results of the riders in my age group, Roman won eleven six-days or so, but at that point when I stopped, neither Roman nor Tourné had won any.

But there is a reason why I wanted to do what I did, and it wasn't just about winning. Yes, for most it is about the glory, holding my hands up over the line, saying, 'Look at me', but that wasn't what it was about for me. I always felt that for me it was about getting into the position I am in now, to be well-off, to be comfortable, to do the things I want to do in my life. I can't buy a jet, but if I want to take you out for a meal, I can do it. I wanted to be in a position where I was financially secure, and that's why I wanted to be a professional rider. It was a way of getting a substantial income, that was the driving force behind it. So when you say about fulfilment... Yes, there is a sense of a lack of fulfilment, but I also look at things in other ways, Paul. I see everything in life as being in balance. I've said it before, I believe that everything we do comes at a price.

There is a cost to you coming here today, to do this book with me. You haven't stayed with your family or children on a Sunday. And yes, it's your work, or a part of your work, and alright it's half-term, but it's a day that you would have spent with your family and instead you are sat here with me. It might be balanced, you might have thought it through, maybe you haven't, but that is how it is. I work hard in my business, I love my business, but I still have to find time most days to go out on the bike. You have your family, your other things, all to consider. In this trade, I see people online, they have twelve shops, but they don't make the money I make with one shop. What's the point of that? What are you doing it for? For financial reasons? Or so you can say, 'Look at me, look at all my shops?' There it is. We've all got an ego, but for some people it takes over.

I recognise the price in things, the cost. I've paid that price, and Maurice is aware of this. He has done *his* research. He points at me, he says, 'You know this! Do you see where I'm coming from? You've been through this before! You were a head teacher, then you stepped back from it because it wasn't worth the cost!' It triggers me, to be honest, I got the calculation wrong. Everything became unbalanced in my life very quickly, the load shifted, like containers falling off a boat in the ocean, everything rolling and wallowing in heavy seas. I was going to lose everything, my wife was going to leave me, I was an angry asshole all the time. It was stressful beyond belief, and in the end, one day, I just didn't go to work. I sat on a log in an ornamental park, drank my coffee, then went home, it was done. I don't regret it, it was a bloody hard choice – not that I even had a choice, to be honest, but I don't regret it. And afterwards, I felt like I had thrown everything away, and for what? No money, no time, no career, just a big mess. Ultimately, it came to make sense, but for a long while things were unbalanced. I paid a price, the people I love paid a price.

Back then, I'm not sure some of us were aware of the price we were paying. Some of the riders I rode with, they're not alive any more, and those that are, they're not necessarily in the best of health, and to a certain degree, you have to ask, is that the price they paid for what they did? Riders I know have suffered, struggled with illness, died young.

It's not surprising that sustained involvement in the six can have long-term impact on health, on life expectancy. The irony is that it is exactly like 'working in that cigarette factory', after all. Long, brutal winter seasons in smoky indoor environments at maximum effort, constant respiratory illness, the use of medication to sleep, the widespread use of amphetamines simply to cope with the physical challenge. Research indicates that prolonged use of amphetamines such as Benzedrine, Pervitin or Dexedrine can lead to an increased risk of long-term serious illness.

I was talking to another rider recently about a soigneur we knew on the circuit, back in the day. He said to me, 'Yes, he's doing well, it's his birthday. All his riders are dead though.' The thing is, I didn't work with that soigneur, but others did, for years and years, and it didn't end well. I remember working with one soigneur for a week or so, I couldn't tell what I was getting from him, so I asked. He gave me these brown pills, said they were Royal Jelly, I found out they were testosterone. That's typical of the thing. And this is the key thing, at the age of twenty-eight, looking back, I could have carried on for another eight or ten years as a six-day rider, in that environment. But if I had continued, would I have the health and the condition I have now? Would I be alive? I'm not sure, so it is for the better. Things could have been better but you pay for everything one way or another – you know this, Paul – you've moved back up in your life, you get paid more, but you have to give more, they don't realise, they think oh that's nice, but they don't give it to you for nothing, they want their pound of flesh, it's always been that way.

Looking at it another way, I don't regret that I pulled out at that point. Don't forget, in 1984 we were coming into the era of blood doping, and then EPO, all this stuff, who knows what would have happened to me? I told you already I'm not an angel, who knows if I would have delved into that? I don't know, it depends, maybe not, but all the same, the fact is I wasn't there so I didn't have to make that choice, and if I had carried on, I don't think I would have the health I have now. You can have these things, you can win these races, but at what price? I try to ride most days, otherwise I get palpitations, arrhythmia, my heart is used to that and if I stop then it's not good, but it's typical in people who have exercised over many years, and you manage it. I have no major illness. I have a hemifacial spasm, where a blood vessel touches the facial nerve. They can operate, but it's risky, or you can use Botox, which I'm not keen on. I sometimes wonder if it's the effect of the centrifugal force, from hitting those bends like that, time after time. I live with it. I'm physically good, I did 115 miles in Lanzarote, still do big days on the bike, whereas a lot of the guys, they're not physically good at all.

He is right. From 1984 onwards, cycling changed irrevocably, making Maurice's retirement, enforced or otherwise, timely. The sport was falling into an era of catastrophic, industrialised, scientific doping. The intermittent use of pot Belge and amphetamines seems quaint in contrast. The EPO era destroyed the peloton, cost lives, fragmented the sport. Getting out in 1984 was probably the best thing that could have happened. Aside from these implications, it's hard to avoid seeing Maurice's view on bike racing, the pragmatism of it all, as a fairly unromantic view – *I rode bikes to make money* – but it is pragmatism that saves lives, not an absolute view of success and failure, the pursuit of winning at all costs. It is a pursuit *with* costs, of knowing what the cost is. It's the side of Maurice that prefigures meetings, the public face, a way of dealing with people, being utterly clear, whether negotiating to arrange this book, how it is written, by whom, the contract, or the up-front costs on a Cycle to Work scheme purchase of a Brompton with a customer over the phone. It is pure clarity, and a strength. But it belies the fact that underneath this there clearly is a romantic side, and it is utterly invested in the joy of riding bikes, and that Maurice Burton finds a solace and comfort in time spent in the saddle.

Maurice Burton
3 July 2022 · 🌐   •••

Read about a ride in the Cyclist Magazine in the Snowdonia National Park, downloaded the ride onto my Garmin, left the shop Tuesday night arrived there 1am. Set off Wednesday morning 9.30am got lost on the route a couple of times, Finally got back to the van 8 hours later. Got in the van drove back to London, got back 1am Thursday morning. Great adventure. Sometimes I just need to be on my own. My thoughts that day was with my mum who passed away 21 years ago on the 27th June.

He rides every day from the shop, out into Kent, or when in Lanzarote, builds up to the training camp with long days looping around the island. He has been riding since he was fourteen years old, and on his return to London in 1984, he was never going to stop riding. It was the other elements of life that caused anxiety.

At that time, I lived life without constraints. I still used to ride. Apart from injuries, I've always ridden the bike. I came back here, Paul, I stayed with my parents. Living at home with your parents at twenty-eight years old, knowing how my father was – and to be honest, right up until he died, he didn't really see the sense in riding a bike – it was hard for me to live there. I didn't know what I was going to do, where I was going to go, and it wasn't easy. For two years I didn't really do much at all. I had amassed an amount of money, but it's very easy when you're not doing anything, and you're a young man, for that money to go, and it went.

He had to find an alternative to living at home; it was causing too much friction. Maurice cites a Jamaican proverb and laughs: 'Two bulls can't rule in one pen, it wasn't going to work.' He moved out into a rented flat and carried on spending. Without cycling as a force for confidence, a prop for his self-esteem, and living a single life, his confidence ebbed and flowed. Cycling injuries had taken their toll – he broke his nose in 1972 and began to notice more and more the misshapen bridge.

I didn't like my appearance, and I thought, I'm going to get something done about it. I went and had some surgery done to take away the bulge, for my confidence. I wasn't a married man at that point. I wasn't working and was running low on savings. I needed a loan of about three grand to cover the cost. I used to go and see Peter Verleysdonk who ran De Ver Cycles; I'd known him since he came across to Belgium with me back when it all started. In order to get the loan I told them I was working at De Ver, even though I wasn't. One afternoon, I went in to see him, we were chatting about cycling, stuff like that, and the phone rang. He picked it up, looked across at me a bit funny, handed me the phone and said, 'It's for you.' They were ringing up the shop to check I worked there, right at the very moment I came in. I got the loan, but of course, I didn't have the capacity to pay it back. In order to answer that question I thought, Well, why don't I work as a bike courier? And that's what I did.

23

De Ver Cycles

The mythology of the cycle courier is an integral part of London bike culture. In the pre-digital age, the cycle courier was a mythological, anarchic symbol of metropolitan life. Traffic was a clotted mess. If you wanted something moved, you called a courier firm. In the age of rapacious 1980s property capitalism and media expansion there was a lot of stuff to move: contracts, litigation documents, film reels, photos – the importance of the package in the last days of the analogue age. The internet did for the artefact, now the courier is a zero-hours serf on an e-bike delivering food at all hours from dark kitchens on an estate in Bermondsey. It is no longer a romanticised occupation; the role written into life by Emily Chappell and Jon Day in beautiful narratives[1] of life and movement is already anachronistic, their lyrical accounts of a city in flux, informed by physical and textual rhythm as they rolled through the paper pages of the *A–Z*, are a footnote in cycling culture. For Chappell, and for Maurice Burton, it was demanding, physical, grubby work, in all weathers, but for the right people (i.e. ex-professional bike riders) it could be lucrative. Maurice Burton responded to Norman Tebbit's crass call to arms: he got on his bike and looked for work. From the Vanguard HQ in Bendall Mews he rode out across the city, carrying solicitors' papers, swatches of fabric, gifts, images, scripts, foodstuff, flowers, anything

---

[1] *What Goes Around*, by Emily Chappell, and *Cyclegeography*, by Jon Day are two beautiful, essential books about being a cycle courier in London.

THE MAURICE BURTON WAY

and everything. The controller squawked out jobs to the flock of couriers, dipping in and out, a murmuration crossing the sprawling, grid-locked city, moving from one drop to another.

> I started out using my road bike from Belgium, it was branded as a Globetrotter, it was my training bike from Ghent. A lot of the other guys working there would turn up at ten or eleven o'clock and it was all a bit of a game, but I was there at 7.30 in the morning and I was on it. When it came to the early-morning jobs, they knew they could rely on me so I got the work, I didn't care what the weather was. I was doing about £250–300 a week back then, so within about eighteen months I was able to amass myself a fair amount of money. I paid off the loan first and then accumulated some savings. It was good money if you did the work.

Cycling photographer Phil O'Connor was also a courier at the time, supplementing his income while starting out. He had last seen Maurice at Ghent in 1981, arm in a sling, when suddenly he spotted him across the lanes of traffic at Hyde Park Corner and grabbed a photo. Maurice is on his track bike, a winter fixed wheel, the mudguards bodged on, he has a dynamo lamp and a luggage rack clipped on to the back. He is wearing his Campitello shorts with a blue sponsored professional team jersey, from his last contract. He has his head down, focused, as though the race never finished, but here he is on a delivery, musette high up on his back. Surely Maurice Burton was the fastest courier ever. It feels like cheating, a little bit.

> In those days, there weren't that many fax machines doing copy and scan, so there were a lot of jobs. For some jobs, you'd do West to West 1, no distance at all, and we would get £2.50 a job. I'd walk from one side of the road to the other with a piece of paper, hand it over, and that would be another £2.50. It was all day, every day, all week. It added up quickly.

Maurice worked for eighteen months. Throughout that time Pete Verleysdonk was pushing at him to get involved in De Ver Cycles;

he wanted to sell the business and wanted Maurice to buy it. It wasn't an easy business to go into, the mid-1980s were a low point for bike shops in terms of sales, but Verleysdonk gave the impression that there were rewards to be had.

> PV didn't seem to do too badly. He had bought a house and he was driving around in a Rolls-Royce. He'd been through one divorce, was on the way to another one, and the tax man seemed to be constantly involved. I think Pete had had enough and wanted out of the place altogether. For some reason he wanted to sell it to me, to the extent that he kept dropping the price, it went down and down until in the end I just took it on, the whole damn lot. I started running the shop in July 1987.

He started out mostly selling second-hand bikes, working extremely long hours. It was a struggle to keep the business afloat and he didn't draw a salary in the early years. As a Black business owner in a White industry he came up against indifference at best, outright hostility at worst. He recalls being patronised and excluded.

> When I first came here and I had this shop, some of the people in the road never used to talk to me. But little by little, they've seen me stay here and they've opened up, at first just a bit, a nod, but over the years more, they talk to me now, they can see me, I'm here, I've been here for thirty-five years. It's a begrudging respect. We got this camper van and sometimes Mia and I go off for the weekend. We went somewhere near Bournemouth a few weeks ago, and I went to a big Sainsbury's in Christchurch, and I went in, and you know what, I was the only Black person in the whole place. It's obvious there aren't any Black people in that area. The people that live there, what experience do they have of Black people? They only know what they have seen or what they have heard or read, so they don't really know. They only really know this or that. But if you go there and you show them, become visible, they might change, away from being suspicious, or not liking people like us,

because we are different, or because they have never seen Black people in their everyday life.

A lot of Black people, and businesses, when you look around, and see the businesses that most people have, it's either barber's or food shops, they don't venture out into other things, they follow the examples of others. When I was younger and thought about being a fireman, Dad advised me against going into the fire service, he said, 'That's not for us.' And it seems to apply to so many other things. There are no Black people doing it, so it's not a thing for Black people. And here I am, saying, you know what, it *is* a thing for Black people.

Which is one of the reasons why Maurice Burton is a pioneer, has been a pioneer at every stage of his career, from those initial forays on to the track at Herne Hill, to the six-days in Belgium, redefining people's limiting prejudices. But it must be exhausting. The wider cultural landscape changes, over time, geologically, but sometimes punctuated by sudden seismic shifts, race riots, Black Lives Matter. Things lurch forwards rapidly and new fault lines emerge. Within this, people carry on, doing jobs, living their lives. For Maurice, taking on De Ver wasn't just a person taking on a bike shop, but by default became an act of challenging representation and attitudes.

By the early 1990s, the shop was doing well. Maurice's private life was less secure. He was in a relationship, in the process of buying a house. Two days before completion, she changed her mind. Maurice went ahead with the purchase, buying the house we are sitting in now. In the aftermath of two complex, uneasy relationships he struggled, at thirty-five years old, questioning everything that had happened.

I'd been through some tough experiences, but just got on with things. I used to go to Tesco's with my ex, and there was a Jamaican security guard, we used to chat. He told me how his wife was from the Philippines, how they met via an agency. And you know, I liked the idea of all that, it sounded interesting to me, I thought I might give it a go. I wrote some letters, got some replies, continued like that, then concentrated on one, and that was Mia.

It seems somehow appropriate that Maurice Burton would focus on process, on the arrangement, the most practical way of making something happen, even if it turned out to be far from practical in reality.

In early 1992, I went out to the Philippines to meet Mia. I came back in March, and by the end of the month we were married. We had been writing a long time, but I'd only known her in person for two months. That was when the struggle began, because it was really difficult to get her to the UK and to get a visa. I couldn't get her here, so we went to Belgium instead and she stayed in an apartment owned by a friend of mine in Ostend. I'd gone over with my dad, seen the place, and made the arrangements, I then went back out to the Philippines, went straight to the Belgian embassy. As an EU citizen they were happy to give her a Belgian visa, so we got on the plane the next day, flew to Amsterdam, then Brussels. I used some of my contacts from back in the day until the place in Ostend was ready, in December 1993.

For about eight months, I would visit her at the weekend. I would leave the shop on a Saturday evening at around 6.30 p.m., drive to Dover in the van. I had a car parked in Calais, so I could get on as a foot passenger, drive the car to Ostend, then arrive about 1 a.m. That would give us the whole of Sunday together, then I'd come back early on Monday morning to open the shop at 10 a.m. By that point we were expecting our first child – Germain – so I had to work out how to get her over here.

Determination, pragmatism and a desire to make things work, along with having the energy to see it through, seem to be definitive Burton traits. After trying to go through the right channels, and drawing a blank, Maurice enlisted the services of a lawyer, Larry Grant. He tells me Larry was quite a famous lawyer at the time. I check back later, and yes, Larry Grant was quite a famous lawyer at the time. This is classic Maurice; understatement, casual reference, only to find the person being spoken about isn't just a name, but a cultural heavyweight. Larry Grant was involved in the campaign for justice for Blair Peach, defended the spy Michael Bettaney and wrote the leading textbook on immigration law and practice – a text still used in court. He was a good choice, sorted out the paperwork, the plan, and Mia settled in Croydon. With Mia's involvement, the shop went from strength to strength, their partnership strong and supportive, as she became involved in managing, promoting and supporting the business. By the mid-1990s, Maurice and Mia had bought the rest of the properties surrounding the shop, including the cottage at the back and the flats upstairs. It was a significant capital investment, securing the future for the shop and using the rental income in the same way his dad had started out many years before.

The ebb and flow of the bike trade presents challenges, however. Global brands don't tend to adjust their business model for the independent trader on the Streatham High Road.

I've had times when it's not been easy, Paul. At one point I used to do a lot on the internet, it was worth it at the time, but they changed the method of payment and it didn't work with our stock control, so I got away from that side of things. The internet broadened our reach, which was good. I knew it was going to transform everything, and I needed to do it on my terms. On the internet, you have to use your brain, do a deal, otherwise why would someone in Bristol buy a bike from me? I'd give them a deal if I was selling online, but then it shifted; one of the big US brands closed the account – it didn't matter that I was selling 900 of their bikes a year, they chose a different way of doing things, so I moved to a different brand, but that brand said, 'You can't sell bikes in boxes any more, they have got to be fully built,' and that wouldn't work for me. We had to adapt and change all the time and it was hard. By 2015, things weren't looking good. I remember sitting staring at the computer on a Monday night, with my head in my hands, wondering what the hell was going to happen.

The next morning, a phone call from Nick Gritton, ex-bike racer and head of sales at Madison, threw De Ver a lifeline. They were rolling out a new 'partner store' concept where Madison held the stock and it was ordered from them as soon as a customer put in their order. It was a significant turning point.

It took me all of thirty seconds to sign up. I went down to his house at Tunbridge Wells with Mia, we talked it through and had dinner that evening, a couple of bottles of wine, ended up leaving at around 2 a.m. It changed everything. After that, I invested £36,000 in a new e-commerce system, tills, website, the lot. Mia didn't think it was a good idea at the time, it was a lot of money, but if we hadn't, I don't think we would be here now.

233

Which brings us up to 2019 and the first time we met, in a pub on Streatham High Road. We were still in a cagey post-lockdown unease, masked or not masked, jabbed or not jabbed. It was my first visit to the capital since the world changed. The pandemic led to huge demand across all areas of cycling retail and most bike shops were stuck for things, supply chains had melted away and there simply wasn't enough stock. For Maurice, the timing couldn't have been better.

> I had done some deals with a big bike company just before the pandemic, the shop was full to the brim, I had bikes everywhere. Typically, I'd do the deal in August but I had to sell the bikes by June. I have to pay by the middle of June on the dot, for all of the bikes. That's a risk, but when the pandemic came no one had any bikes, anywhere, except me. My shop was absolutely full of bikes. Not only did I sell them but I had to grab every other damn thing I could lay my hands on as well. Over the two years of the pandemic, the phone never stopped ringing, I would sell ten bikes in a morning, across all price ranges. They were going out the door quicker than I could put them through the till.

The parallels with the six-day, moving to Belgium on Christmas Day, are clear; it's about being prepared to take a risk in order to succeed, and putting in the work to get there.

> When I was a young man, I came into the sport and reached a certain level, and now in this business I'm on a certain level, because I've been there before, riding a bike is a business, there's things I know now. You have to always look ahead, what's the next idea, the next thing.

It is striking how every working element of Maurice Burton's life has involved cycling. There is nothing else, riding for money, riding for pleasure, it is all-encompassing. He still rides every day, and he still crashes, sometimes in the most terrifying way imaginable. In 2008 he was riding in Lanzarote.

I was riding with another guy, he was on the inside, on a straight road, not a bend. A car missed him by a matter of centimetres, but it didn't miss me; he came up and drove straight into my back wheel. There was nothing I could have done. The only reason I'm alive is because I didn't see it, I didn't have time to tense up. It threw me 2m up in the air, I came down and my head went through the windscreen, smashed it and I ended up on the floor. The other guy was a doctor, which was lucky. He thought I was dead, I didn't move for fifteen minutes, then I came round. They airlifted me to Gran Canaria. I had a small amount of internal bleeding, but my spine was a mess, I lost a vertebrae. It was close; at one point they were thinking about fusing my spine but I just said, let's see what happens. I had to wear a corset for six months. I couldn't sit up for three weeks; I got people to help, they held the laptop up in front of me so I could carry on running the business. I did recover, but for a long time afterwards whenever I looked up my back, my neck, the whole thing just hurt. It takes so much time, it's better now, but I still get some pain when I look up.

I remember when I got back on the bike, I was on the rollers, it was the day Nicole Cooke won the Olympic gold medal. I then went on and rode the Étape the next year, on Ventoux, came thirty-eighth in my category. I was pleased with that. When I got back, I was riding again, but then slipped on diesel, broke my other leg, and that set me back. I have a pin in both legs now. The strength is not the same, but I don't give up. It was a bout of accidents, I'd recover, almost, then something else would happen. I was on a Brompton, it was a sixtieth birthday present, riding with Mia up near High Barnet and a car came through a gap turning right, knocked me off. I broke my collar bone – which is crazy, in all the years I was racing I never broke it. They had to jack the car up to get the bike out. I had an operation in July, then was back out riding by September, when another car hit me from behind, it destroyed a Colnago C60. I think the insurers were a bit shocked by the price. I just about managed the training camp with the slower group that year. Since then, I've been OK. Things happen, I get up, I get on with it, that's how it is for me. There's always something to learn, and looking back, even the bad things become good. It's almost a spiritual thing; not necessarily religious, just that there is something bigger than ourselves, and that these things happen for a reason, even if they seem random. The people ringing about the loan while I was in the shop, the Madison partnership, all of those things. There was even one occasion when the banks were squeezing us, it was tight, they wanted £800 that day, we had to pay it. It was me and Mia in the shop. About midday, a chap comes in, he says, 'I want to buy a bike'. I said, 'How much do you want to spend?' He said, "£800". I showed him the bike, he paid cash, Mia took it to the bank. A card payment wouldn't have done it. Everything about these things gives me confidence, things become good.

Riding the Étape or the Marmotte have become latter day touchstones; a chance to ride against others, to rekindle the fire of competition across alpine passes. It is a different experience to the road racing he did in his youth, far away from the flat polders of Flanders and the inside of a velodrome. In 2012 he rode through Bourg on to the last stretch, the punishing eleven-mile climb of Alpe d'Huez. His son, Robert, was waiting at the foot of the climb, arm outstretched with a bottle, before pacing Maurice up the twenty-one hairpin bends. It was a tender moment for Maurice, riding with his son to the top of the most famous climb in Tour history.

For his sixtieth birthday, he decided to cycle to Seville with Dexter. He chose Seville because it's as close as you can get to Lanzarote on the mainland, the nearest airport. They gave themselves a week to get through France and a week to get through Spain, with two key dates en route – a night at Steve Heffernan's house near Bordeaux and a visit to Pamplona to see Dexter's daughter play in a professional basketball match. They were escorted to Newhaven by other De Ver riders, then got the ferry across to Dieppe. It was always going to be tight but became very tight when they realised their route planner, Charlie, had missed a page from the map in the run-in to Bordeaux. It looked like a 230km stage was needed.

> I said to Dexter, 'You take a rest day, get in the car.' It was one of those days where I had to pull my finger out. It ended up being 212 miles, I did it in eleven hours, 20mph average. By the time I got to Heff's, it was getting dark, they had to use the headlamps on the car to guide me in. I got off the bike, looked at Heff, and said, 'Let's have a glass of wine.' I wasn't even tired. That's the thing, with me after five hours or so, that's when it kicks in, that's when I get going. We were up until 3 a.m., talking about everything, I was buzzing. The next day we got up, did another 60 miles. It was a day I'll never forget, after everything, the injuries, now I was coming up to sixty and could still ride like that.

Over time, Maurice has gradually become immersed in the cycling hierarchy in London, the network of ex-professionals, of captains of industry, club men and women, including two of the quirkier bastions of the sport: the Pedal Club and the Pickwick Bicycle Club. Both operated until very recently as an old boy's club, no women allowed. The Pedal Club allowed full women membership in 2021. The Pickwick has not changed, but then again, it hasn't changed since 1870; members acquire a nom de plume, trumpets announce arrivals, boaters and blazers are in evidence.

> I'm a member of both clubs, and that shows that things are changing. I think the Pickwick was interesting, because some years before, I did this Ride London thing, half of it with my daughter on a tandem. There were a lot of riders in the Pickwick that came from the Willesden Cycling Club, and I saw this man, he had a

Willesden jersey so I asked him if he was in the Pickwick. He just looked at me and said, 'No.' He was an older guy, so I carried on talking a little bit about the Pickwick, and this man looked at me, and he said, 'You'll *never* be in the Pickwick.' I went to put my hand on his shoulder, and said, 'Well, they already asked me', and this man said, 'DON'T TOUCH ME.' I looked at him and I laughed at him, because it was hard to feel, in this day and age, regardless of age, that these sorts of people are still around. The truth is, I am in the Pickwick, and the disapproval tends to come from people saying, 'Why would you want to be in the Pickwick?' rather than the other way round. When they announced me as a member, the crowd cheered, and it was louder than for anybody else, but not every single person at that dinner wanted to see me there. Not everyone can like you, not everyone does like you.

A veneer of dislike, a set of excuses, hides the extent of hatred and prejudice. Personally, I'm of the camp that the Pickwick needs to welcome women into the line-up, because we're not actually living in a Charles Dickens novel, despite the Pickwick's deliberate anachronism. I see the list of members and there are people I like immensely, people who are forwards-thinking, are not sexist, whose opinions I value, people who I have written about, shared committee time with (in some cases, hours and hours of committee time that I can't have back) and yet the Pickwick is not for me, because it is not for everyone. However, I recognise that the establishment, and membership of the establishment, is an important validation, and being asked to join a closed club can be an empowering act. It is always much easier to say no when you have never been asked. I used to be like that with the *Daily Mail*, oh I'll never ever do anything with those scurrilous racists and harbingers of hate, right up until my agent told me they might be interested in serialising some stuff I wrote. Cue lengthy hand-wringing, middle-class cognitive dissonance: 'Oh but if people read my stuff in that paper, they might just change this element of how they think and blah blah blah.' And no, it didn't happen, and the truth is when I see people picking up the *Mail* in the supermarket,

I know any serialisation of any stuff I wrote will have no material difference on the lives these people lead. Maybe this book will have that crossover impact. We live in hope. I will wait for the call.

I wonder about the gentle paradox of joining a club like the Pickwick, one full of elderly White men, so rigidly patriarchal that it's treated with disdain by many others, including Chris Boardman, who tweeted, 'women are still banned; [it's] not a tradition that needs perpetuating'.

Where I ride my bike now, around West Wickham, Biggin Hill, twenty years ago there were no black people around that area. But now you see them. Somebody had to move there, to be the first. Things change slowly, maybe that's the same with the Pickwick. I've taken people along, David Clarke, Charlie Allen. When I go to the Pickwick there are people there I have been seeing for twenty, thirty years. These are people in the industry and the sport that I have grown up with. We catch up, talk, make deals. This is what matters to me. Whether it's this or that is less important.

Cycling is a White male industry, yes, but generally, it's OK. Some of my experiences haven't been OK. I recall being at the big industry show in Birmingham, wanting to place an order for a lot of bikes, well into double figures, and the woman refused to accept that I was genuine, that I had the shop or the cash to do this. And that's because I was a man of colour. She didn't look beyond that or think that I could be a successful businessman. But on the whole, the thing about business is it's about money. The main thing they want to know is that you can buy stock and pay for it, that's the only thing, it's not racial. The issues you do get are personal, the big American brands, the rep will come into the store, and say to me, 'Well we don't want you having this brand next to our brand,' and they start telling me what goes on in my store, that doesn't work too well with me. I love the industry, the people who I know, often I knew them from the sport. We've been to Colnago in Italy a few times and met with Ernesto. I see people regularly, the community is very much a part of my life, it's good.

The notion of a wider community is integral. Bike shops, and the almost anachronistic model of the local bike shop, are at the centre of a community network, featuring clubs, cafes and workplaces. It is as a part of this wider community that De Ver is so important. I remember riding out with the Dulwich Paragon CC in the early 2000s, just on the cusp of the bike boom. Me and my friend Nick, two teachers, would ride with other white collar, White men, trundling around the lanes, me on my Condor Acciaio, Nick on his shiny blue Moser. Every now and then we'd come across other clubs in the lanes, the Addiscombe or Norwood Paragon, but the highlight would always be a glimpse of the yellow paceline of De Ver, the bold logo and stark V making them instantly recognisable. I felt at the time that somehow their group of ten or so reflected the London I lived in far more vividly than the thirty-strong group of Daves I was riding with. The same applied to Brixton Cycles, which somehow felt keyed into the community, through its co-operative roots, and evident through the coalition of different identities riding together. And yet the group of Daves were and still are the visible face of almost all aspects of cycling sport. These juxtapositions, for me, back in 2004, served to show the limitations of cycling clubs. No matter how supportive and kind they are, if they don't have diversity, they are doing something wrong. I think about Bristol South CC, the biggest club in Bristol, a diverse and complex core city, and yet defined by a membership that is overwhelmingly White. It's not an assault on the members, who have a tendency to feel like they are somehow in the wrong for being members, but it is reflective of wider factors in society; why the club is so singular, the message it sends to people of colour who are thinking of joining a community of cyclists when they see the beautiful jerseys worn only by middle-aged, middle-class White men. How can it demonstrate that this is a welcoming environment for people of colour when there are palpably no people of colour riding? In contrast, Maurice's presence at the heart of De Ver Cycles is a literal demonstration that cycling *is* for Black people.

24

Manchester

We're catching up over a video call, the book is all but done but there are a few loose ends to tie up. Maurice is hunkered down in Lanzarote, the Calima is breathing Saharan dust across the island and riding a bike is out of the question. It gets down in the lungs, fine particulates, it irritates, you don't want to be breathing hard through the haze. It gives us time to chat, to draw the threads together. We talk about the future, his pride in daughter Gracie's PhD and her plans to become more involved in the business. We talk about reading – Maurice threatens to read some of my other books, the one about Alf, to see what the conversation was like. He wants to do a degree in psychology, which makes perfect sense. 'It's a new challenge, Paul, the reading, all of that, I want to understand human beings more.'

We talk about the title. We've been working with 'Being Maurice Burton' but I don't think Maurice likes it, or it isn't what he thinks of when he imagines the book. I know that Maurice wants 'My Way' because he loves the song, it's his 'signature tune', but I don't want that as a title and I know the publisher won't want it because it will not feature in search engines and it hasn't got his name in it.

It's in my mind, Paul, I mentioned it last time. That's my tune. Yeah. And they named the cycling superhighway after me, that's the Maurice Burton Way! It's my way Paul!

241

I look back through the manuscript while we are talking, a quick control-F to find the bit, and there it is, and the other song, 'That's Life'. I mention it, and suddenly we are singing, 'I'm sure you knew… I bit off more than I could chew … but through it all …' and he is laughing, a joyful laugh, and so am I, and it's funny. Then he switches back to 'My Way', it's a proper megamix. We dissolve into laughter, it's infectious, two terrible singers singing a song terribly, but loving every word.

One significant thing has happened in the previous week. Maurice has been inducted into the British Cycling Hall of Fame, along with Emma Pooley, Rebecca Romero MBE and Paul Sherwen. He gave a speech via video link from his balcony in the Lanzarote evening sun. He mentioned Norman Sheil, who seemed to represent all of the people who believed in him and had faith in what he could achieve. Familiar insecurities come back to the surface as we talk about the induction.

It's amazing, Paul, but when I look at some of the names on that list, I question whether I am really good enough to be in the Hall of Fame. I didn't have the same results that others on there might have had, but then again, I didn't have the same opportunity to have the results, and they didn't have to do what I did, there is that. There are people out there, people at the dinner, people who saw me race, and they knew what I was capable of. People like Norman Sheil and Oscar Daemers, they saw what I could do, not what I looked like, and they believed in me. Back then, it's not like there was a film of you riding, you couldn't see your achievements, neither could anyone else, it was word of mouth. It was hard to know how good you were.

I'm not too bad for my age, but I'm not what I was, due to injuries, and everything else, age and time, but sometimes, when I am out here riding the bike, finding it hard, struggling, I find myself wondering, was I ever really able to get to that level? In 1974, I won the White Hope Sprint, then in 1975, the Golden Wheel, a points race, a sprint every lap, and I won it. There were world-class riders in that race and I beat them all. And I think of those races, riding and winning against the best track riders, and I find it hard to take in that I was able to do that. For a British rider, in those days, to go across to the Continent, and get into a team over there, as a foreigner, it wasn't easy. On top of that, for me, there was my colour, that's the thing. Everyone has to fight to get what they want, but they didn't have to fight the same fight as me.

The key to tackling the uncertainty is in Bob Howden's valediction, spoken that evening at the celebratory dinner: 'As Britain's first black cycling champion Maurice is one of our sport's true pioneers, whose inspiration and legacy continues to blaze a trail for others.' Howden is president of British Cycling, and his words recognise Maurice's ground-breaking achievements. When Maurice won his third national title at Leicester in 1975, his legacy was assured. At a time when Black football players were redefining what national sport looked like, how it could be played, Maurice transformed our view of cycling: what it was and who it was for. He was booed for it. Now we have gone full circle; the same federation that acted to stymie his selection for the Olympics and prevent him from taking up offers to ride, as a nineteen-year-old, in the Caribbean, is holding him up as a pioneer and a true champion. It is a belated step towards a recognition of Black sporting history, the reassertion of neglected narratives and a challenge to historic exclusion. The important part is using this legacy to construct a vision of the future where diversity is foregrounded. Instrumental to this process has been the work of Dr Marlon Moncrieffe, particularly via his exhibition, 'Made in Britain: Uncovering the life-histories of Black-British Champions in Cycling', and his book, *Desire, Discrimination, Determination – Black Champions in Cycling*. His work seeks to challenge accepted narratives, assert the significance of experiences in cycling for Black, minority and ethnic riders and establish visibility. This chimes with discussions I have had with the writer Jools Walker, that the lack of visible figures from the past, of inspirational narratives, is a limiting factor for riders of colour coming into the sport. The contrasts are sharp: for Ethan Hayter or Fred Wright, there is Bradley Wiggins, draped in the mod chic of mid-noughties Britain; Geraint Thomas, David Millar, fragile heroes and anti-heroes, celebrated media personalities, their books piled high in the sport section of Waterstones. Somewhere near the back, if you're lucky, is a copy of a book about Major Taylor. *Back in the Frame*, by Jools Walker, and Dr Moncrieffe's book set out to challenge this hegemony. Maurice recognises Dr Moncrieffe's role in the Hall of Fame induction: 'He pushed for this, for me to get this award, I feel that a lot of it is down to Marlon.' It is a vital step towards revising our sporting narratives, focusing on marginalised and neglected experiences.

We pause, think, talk about Maurice's business, his current order for what seems like an almost impossibly huge number of bikes, before going back around to British Cycling, because for all the intentions, the words, I have yet to see any tangible change in representation in cycling in the UK. I don't see young Black riders on the track or on the road.

No, that's true, but what I can say to you, there are some, but not a huge amount, but then, Paul, you can look at that from different ways. You get Black youngsters, gifted, athletic, and why would they choose to ride a bike? Football is a lot easier, in terms of accessibility. I mean it's hard to get to the highest level, but if you are good enough the money is crazy and you can't get that kind of money in cycling. As a young guy, you need to have a bike, this is a financial obstacle, not everyone can find one in a garden and do it up. Then you need to get to the event with the bike, and added to that, it's not always cool. Being a footballer is cool, and right enough, that's why being a role model is so important, but I'm not so sure that I am that role model. It's all well and good, me being there in the Hall of Fame, but if you take that to some kid of thirteen, and you're talking about somebody who was riding fifty years ago, maybe they can't relate to that person in the same way as someone who is only a few years older than them, someone they see on the television, like Marcus Rashford, and say, 'Wow, I could be that person, I could do that.' There is a way through with BMX, but where does it lead? From my perspective, does it lead to the track or the road? How far can you go with BMX? How much money can you make with that? If a young person is good at cycling, eventually they need to be able to move across into the British Cycling pathway, but it's not really financially viable, you have to find a way to get them on to the road. There has to be a progression. BMX is a great way to get them started, it's not so expensive, it gives skills and all this sort of thing, but eventually there has to be some sort of progression to the other end, the road, a proper team, making proper money. That's what has to happen.

BMX is cited, with good reason, as an example where grass-roots investment – from the community, Nigel White at Peckham BMX Club – leads to an elite pathway and Olympic success. The berms and tumps of Braintree, or Crewe, or Peckham pump tracks exist in stark contrast to the controlled environment of Manchester Velodrome, the home of British Cycling, the academy, the elite performance pathway. For many watching Tokyo 2020, the embrace by long-standing training partners Kye Whyte and Bethany Shriever – immediately following Bethany's gold medal – was an intense but momentary flash of emotion. However, the paradox is that in celebrating only the moment of the gold medal, we ignore the challenges faced by many in getting to that point in the first place. Peckham BMX Club is celebrated as a parochial success story, it can be vaguely patronising: 'Isn't it lovely how these people give up their time to support young people,' like a youth club in a troubled area, rather than a sophisticated, careful organisation that breaks down barriers and provides a diverse range of young people with the means to succeed. This is in contrast to the lack of engagement and investment from British Cycling, and evidence of a broken pathway at grass-roots level, a fundamental lack of representation and visibility, of role models. The simple question – How do we change this? – has a complicated and simple answer: it lies in systemic cultural change at all levels, in the organising bodies and institutions, commercially and ideologically. It isn't about grass-roots success, the numbers of cyclists, commuters, because in London nearly 20 per cent of cyclists come from ethnically diverse backgrounds: it is about transference – ethnic minority membership of British Cycling runs at just 5 per cent. Making it accessible to all requires concerted, long-lasting change and assertive action, like that seen at The Rapha Foundation, with a renewed 'commitment to dedicate at least 50 per cent of our athlete sponsorship to BAME, LGBTQ+ and female riders and their teams'. Kye Whyte identifies two clear but not exclusive long-term goals, of a sustained and successful future in the sport, but also the vital and equally life-changing goals of health and opportunity.

> We're in a position where we are going to break down a lot of barriers, and whether we make community champions or give the children a healthier lifestyle and something to do, that's what we're here for.[1]

The key is making that leap, from grass roots into elite competition; once this gap has been bridged, the pathway becomes secure and has the potential of a virtuous cycle. Without an increase in numbers, British Cycling's claim to be a diverse organisation lacks credibility: 'It's not that they're not accepting riders – they're not outwardly working to bring more diversity into the sport, which is what I think they need to do.'[2] As of 2020, Kadeena Cox was the only Black rider receiving top-level funding with British Cycling. The only one. Their response was one of 'deep concern', stating that: 'we are committed to learning from Maurice's and others' experiences to ensure that Black and minority ethnic riders feel welcomed and supported in the sport today… We still recognise that a lack of diverse ethnic representation

[1]https://www.bikeradar.com/advertising-feature/rapha-foundation-2/
[2]https://www.skysports.com/more-sports/cycling/news/15264/12101470/maurice-burton-the-unfulfilled-career-of-britains-first-black-cycling-champion

is a significant problem. This is a historical legacy that those of us who love cycling must tackle if we want to say with credibility that ours is a sport open to all.'[3]

With the Black Lives Matter movement, it can feel like institutions have fought over themselves to promote stories of diversity, to find a spokesperson who can help them to demonstrate their commitment to inclusion. In the bout of corporate soul-searching that followed the murder of George Floyd, Maurice was interviewed across a range of media. The risk is that the story of Maurice Burton's life, a celebratory, incredible story of an amazing bike rider, becomes defined by one thing only: 'the very bigotry and prejudice that tries to constrain us'.[4] It is a view echoed by Jools Walker when we met in 2022:

> It becomes exhausting to only be asked about the same thing over and over and only feel like you can talk about the same thing over and over, when you have so many other lived experiences that could tie into stories about race. Or maybe you have a completely different story or side of yourself that you haven't shared and you're not given that avenue to share it because this is your experience, this is the linear track of what you have done and we are going to talk about these things, and it's like, *no.*
>
> When George Floyd was murdered, all of sudden *lots* of people wanted to have conversations with me and they wanted to talk about it in relation to cycling and race and discrimination, and I was invited to do radio interviews, podcasts, to talk about it. And I had to stand my ground and very respectfully say, 'When you were talking about the joy of cycling, doing reviews about cycling kit, you didn't want to talk to me, I've been around for over a decade, and now that you need to tune into Black grief and Black trauma, I'm suddenly your go-to person. You knew of my existence, but

[3] https://www.skysports.com/more-sports/cycling/news/15264/12101470/maurice-burton-the -unfulfilled-career-of-britains-first-black-cycling-champion
[4] www.theguardian.com/culture/2021/nov/05/we-must-tell-our-stories-lenny-henry-introduces -a-black-british-culture-takeover

THE MAURICE BURTON WAY

now that you have something juicy, this is what you want to discuss with me. It feels insulting because it feels like that's your box that you needed to tick.'

In seeking out people of colour to assuage White guilt, we end up missing the things that make people matter, their narrative and life experience, in terms of joy and lived, quotidian experience as well as adversity, because these things are not mutually exclusive. If we valorise only racist experiences that happened, we broaden the diversity principle for ourselves and not the reality: White majority businesses garner worthy hits via search engine optimisation in a simulacra of diversity. Nothing changes. It falls back to the grass roots to carry on doing things that lead to actual change: to De Ver Cycles, to the Black Cyclist's Network, to some cycling clubs, to places like Herne Hill, who carry on raising participation, actively, as agents of change, with silent force. I think about this narrative, about Maurice Burton's life, about Maurice, as a friend, and I know that joy and adversity are not mutually exclusive.

One recent change was the informal renaming of Cycle Superhighway 7. It is now 'The Maurice Burton Way', and it was heralded in the press to much fanfare. Jack Barber made the nomination, 'It felt like one small way of giving Maurice Burton the positive public recognition he deserves as both a champion and as a pillar of the cycling community. It might encourage and inspire youngsters to get into the sport.'[5] I think it is a wondrous thing, a great idea, it raises the profile and narrative of Maurice Burton, someone who many people might not know about, outside of the cycling community, and even inside it. But equally, how is it symptomatic of actual change? There isn't any signage. There are no info-boards. It hasn't been renamed on the TfL website. Maurice even asks me if I know what's happening with it. I don't. I contacted TfL, they told me it was an 'unofficial' thing by a group called 'possible'. It remains abstract, a lovely sentiment. I

[5]https://www.standard.co.uk/news/transport/cycle-lane-maurice-burton-way-britain-first-black-cycling-champion-b246245.html

wonder if TfL will take it on, recognise the value in role models, in aspiration, see it as a chance for visibility. I don't hold my breath.

I think about Herne Hill and the London Schools cycling programme, about Bill Dodds, how these things led to success for Maurice, Joe Clovis and Russell Williams. Velo Club Londres keeps on going, De Ver cycles brings young people into the sport, reaching into the community. Both Maurice's sons, Robert and Germain, rode competitively as juniors. Robert made it through to the final of the National Schools Championship. Ultimately, for Robert, cycling wasn't the most important thing in his life whereas Germain carried on. He was just fifteen years old when he won the prestigious Bec Hill Climb as a junior, obliterating an elite field. He went on to ride for De Ver as part of a talented junior team. Through hard graft, he got on to the academy programme, rode with Tao Geoghegan Hart in the Junior Track World Championships, won the National Team Pursuit Championship two years running, the amateur six at Ghent. He left the sport a year or so later, a combination of a knee injury and a change in personal circumstances. Germain and Maurice were interviewed by the *Telegraph* in 2012, with the focus being Germain's potential and ambitions. Maurice was confident that 'there will be no racial barriers in Germain's sporting career', a feeling echoed by Germain. 'You have to work hard, but Dad had it much tougher, he got very little support and had to do everything the hard way.' There is truth in both assertions, but Maurice's experiences, his pioneering career, perhaps helped in that respect, both in terms of profile and in terms of influence. The key to future success, for most riders, and especially those from Black or minority ethnic backgrounds, is a pathway that supports those riders who have no connection to the sport. Looking at the experiences of Charlotte Cole-Hossain, Dave Clarke, Caelan Millar and Christian Lyte, among others, their compelling testimonies[6] indicate that being good enough is not good enough. I wonder what a concrete action looks or feels like. Maybe it's this:

[6]Moncrieffe, M. L., Black Champions in Cycling (2021). *Desire Discrimination Determination*. London: Blue Train.

Tony Hibbert

A big shoutout and huge thanks to the main man Maurice Burton De Ver Cycles Ltd for a hugely generous donation of 80-90 track frames to the Herne Hill fleet. #futurestars

#devercycles #sixdaystar

Maurice gave eighty track frames to Herne Hill. I'm staggered by this. I think about the maths of it; even if they were cost price, say, and very cheap, it's going to come in northwards of £20k. It's a huge amount of money. We talk it through.

Well, I had these during the pandemic, a lot of road frames and track frames. I sold the road frames, but the track frames were shifting slowly. They aren't drilled for the road, they are track machines. I just wanted to do it; they were taking up space. I was thinking about it while I was out on the bike; rather than go through the process, selling them slowly, over time, why not just donate the whole lot to Herne Hill? It just felt right, to be honest. I often think about these things when I'm out on the bike. I went down there, I didn't know if they had some other arrangement in place, I didn't want to step on toes, but it was fine, so I offered them, took some down, what I could. Later on, I found some more, because I've got so many bikes all over the place, and took those down as well. I introduced them to a couple of suppliers for wheels and stuff like that, they got rid of all the old ones, sold them off, £100 each, and now these are the best frames they've ever had. To be honest, it's a great honour and privilege to donate them to Herne Hill. It's where I started as a young rider, where I honed my craft. It's nice to think VC Londres youngsters might be riding on De Ver frames, it's going to be good. I'm hoping that it will help a lot of youngsters. It's bikes, but also it's De Ver and it's wonderful.

It is wonderful and it is a brilliant gesture, but I am unsettled that one of the key people being proactive in finding the next Maurice

Burton is … Maurice Burton. I think back to meeting Ethan and Fred at Ghent, both of whom came through the VC Londres ranks, started on hire bikes stored in rusty shipping containers. Ethan grew up just down the road and Maurice's bike shop was a crucial part of his formative years as a bike rider. Germain was also an important figure, his achievements mapping out the possibilities to all the riders in the club. It was one of the things we spoke about in Ghent, sitting in the stands, overlooking the track where both Germain and Maurice had ridden.

> Germain was an inspiration to all of us, we knew about him, what he had done, more so than his dad. I then met Maurice through De Ver Cycles. It was the nearest shop to me in Norbury, and he helped me out massively, right from the very start, and recently, building up team bikes, the Pinarello for INEOS. He was racing the six-days back with Merckx, and our swanny talks about it, those days, the madness of it. I mean, it's crazy now, but back then it was way more crazy, when Maurice was riding. And now he has my picture on his wall!

It goes full circle: riders inspire riders, meet their heroes, follow in their tyre tracks, inspire others. The role of VC Londres is vital, an emotional connection, a thread – Bill Dodds, Maurice, Russell Williams, Joe Clovis, Joanna Rowsell Shand, Germain Burton, Ethan Hayter and Fred Wright. For Fred, it's clear that VC Londres is more than simply a great community: 'It's a reinforcement of just enjoying riding your bike. I think we need to be careful that we don't lose that, because that's what it's all about.'[7] His comments are compelling, both Ethan and Fred were sitting in 't Kuipke, and they smiled, broadly, immersed in the joy of being paid to ride their bikes. 'We're getting round, we're enjoying it, that's the thing. Ghent is out there on its own, the style of racing, the crowd, everything, completely different

[7]www.cyclingweekly.com/news/britains-other-medal-factory-vc-londres

to anything else you'll ever do, but it's just great fun. We were doing the last chase at 1 a.m. yesterday and to be honest, we were just having a brilliant time.' I remember being suffused by their joy, the feeling of elation that bike racing can bring, the sense of all the stories from the past and present circulating in the air of the velodrome. Later, I felt a sense of melancholy, wondering where the next Black British track rider or road rider might come from, and when we might see them at Ghent. It would have been a neat ending.

We have one last chat about the title. Maurice relents, we go for 'The Maurice Burton Way'. By 'relent', he says, 'I can just about live with that.' I'll take it, it's classic Maurice. I hear Maurice get up and walk to the window, he is checking the wind, seeing if the dust is easing. An orange haze still hangs in the air above the island. There will be no bike rides for him today. I sense his disgruntlement at the weather gods. I have a couple more questions, then we are finished, bar the shouting. I will go away and finish this and he can read it and we can agree or disagree on things.

We agree on one thing: both before and after Covid-19, the sixes are struggling. The days we talk about are not coming back. One by one, the sixes fell into memory, tracks were removed, stadiums repurposed for mega-gigs. Only Ghent is left, sometimes Rotterdam, occasionally Berlin. That's it. He walks back into view, speaks.

It's not what it was. It was a circus back then; it wasn't an event. It's not like what we used to do. Things are different now, there is more going on, more distractions, different entertainment. You can see the riders on TV, in close-up all the time and the season is global, they're in Australia in January, or Oman, the UAE. Those races sit in the calendar where the sixes were. When we used to ride in Italy, it was full, people would stand there, they didn't have seating, they had a rail and they stood there for hours, fascinated, watching the race, on the track, off the track. There was a mystique about the riders, they were seen in glimpses, you couldn't follow their lives, listen to them talk online, get their unfiltered opinions or cat pictures, morning, noon and night.

Now, with social media, news, streaming, the riders are online, they are over-familiar to us. The mystique that drew people in to see them race has gone. Merckx, Gimondi, Moser, Maertens, De Vlaeminck, these guys rode the six-days, they were the big stars of the road, they were the stars of the Tour, of the World Championship. I rode in Antwerp with Rik Van Linden, he was the green jersey winner in the Tour; we were the taxi drivers, they were royalty. Who do you have like that now? Regularly? Where is the attraction, to the non-cyclist, the person who lives in the city in winter? Where is the crossover? You need riders like Alaphilippe, van der Poel, Pogačar, even the climbers – Bahamontes rode the sixes back in the 1950s, as did Coppi, Van Looy, Tom Simpson – that's what the event needs. But it can't happen because the teams don't want it, the sponsors don't want it, for one, and they can't take the risk of injury. Stephen Roche won the Tour, then did the Paris Six with Tony Doyle and crashed, he hurt his knee and he was never quite the same again. The teams are worried about their investment.

It's another paradox: we are closer than ever to the riders, yet somehow further away. They are in the bus, behind the curtain, in the start village, walled off from us. The analogue, tactile force of the six has gone. Melancholy returns, not for the lack of action, but the way the world has changed, and what has been lost. I'm trying desperately not to be a curmudgeon, to say that the old days were better, but sometimes in the constant wave of change we lose something important. Everything is digitised, people ride all winter indoors on smart trainers. They upload rides. They meet online. Music is curated, ads are served. In contrast, the six remains resolutely analogue, bill posters, smells, the sound and the fury, local heroes, cities in the cold rain of winter, different languages, different awful local food, and dreadful, exhilarating music. Ghent continues, it has a life force all of its own. Maurice does the same thing he does in every conversation we've had; he exhales – it is part sigh, part filler, a pause filled with reflection and memory and joy, is about the best way I can describe it.

Looking back on the whole thing, Paul, I don't have regrets, that I didn't do this or that. My cycling career could have been a lot better than what it was, and there's things that could have happened. I don't want to say *what if this* or *what if that*, because what's the point, you know? I don't have excuses. I could have done a lot better if circumstances had been different, but they weren't, so that's where we are. It is what it is, isn't it?

Cycling was an opportunity to have a better life, and I did the best with what I had, and I don't think I did too badly.

BIBLIOGRAPHY

Boakye, J. (2019). *Black, listed: black British culture explored*. London: Dialogue Books.

Cossins, P. (2023). *The Monuments*. Bloomsbury Publishing.

Friebe, D. (2022). *Jan Ullrich*. Pan Macmillan.

Grant, C. (2020). *HOMECOMING: voices of the windrush generation*. Vintage.

Grant, C. (2023). *I'm Black So You Don't Have to Be*. Jonathan Cape.

Hall, S. (2017). *Familiar Stranger*. Penguin UK.

Hemingway, E. (1996). *A Moveable Feast*. Simon and Schuster.

Hewson, T. (2006). *In Pursuit of Stardom*. Mousehold Press.

James, C.L.R. (2019). *Beyond a boundary*. London: Vintage.

Kynaston, D. (2013). *Modernity Britain. [Book one], Opening the box, 1957–59*. London: Bloomsbury.

Letts, D. and Peachey, M. (2021). *Don Letts: there and Black again*. London; New York: Omnibus Press.

Levy, A. (2009). *Small Island*. Tinder Press.

Maertelaere, Roger De (2000). *De Mannen van de Nacht*. Brussels: Uitgeverij de Eecloonaar.

Maertelaere, Roger De (1991). Zesdaagsen. Ghent: Uitgeverij Worldstrips.

Maertens, F. and Adriaens, A. (1993). *Fall from Grace*. Ronde Publication.

McGrath, A. (2022). *God is Dead*. Random House.

Moncrieffe, M. L., Black Champions in Cycling (2021) *Desire Discrimination Determination*. London: Blue Train.

Nicholson, G. (1992). *Tony Doyle*. London: Springfield Books Limited.

Olusoga, D. (2016). *Black and British*. London: Macmillan.

Pearson, H. (2019). *The Beast, the Emperor and the Milkman*. Bloomsbury Publishing.

Pitts, J. and Robinson, R. (2022). *Home Is Not a Place*. Harper Collins UK.

Selvon, S. (1956). *The lonely Londoners*. London: Hodder Education.

Two Fingas and Kirk, J. (2021). *Junglist*. Watkins Media Limited.

Walker, J. (2019). *Back in the Frame*. Hachette UK.

Wellings, M. (2016). *Ride! Ride! Ride!* London: Icon Books.

MAGAZINES

Archive issues of *Cycling Weekly* have formed a significant part of the research and inspiration for this book and have been quoted widely.

ACKNOWLEDGEMENTS

MAURICE:

My first duty of thanks goes to my mum and dad who in my early years installed in me the common sense, values and wisdom that I still use today.

Thank you to Bill Dodds who was my first coach and someone who would always give an answer to my questions. He was the one who showed me what could happen, where this thing could take me. Bill was one of the many brilliant coaches at Herne Hill Track, along with John Clarey, Bob Addy, and Mike Armstrong. Alongside the coaches were all of the professional and top amateur riders I trained with as a young man. They installed a toughness in me that enabled me to get to where I am today. These included Reg Smith, Reg Barnett, Ray Palin, Ron Keeble, Dave Rowe, Steve Heffernan, Murray Hall and Gary Wiggins. Thank you to Joe Clovis my schoolmate, training partner and close friend. Joe was there at the beginning and he came fourth when I won the Junior National Sprint Championship.

Thank you to Young's Cycles, Geoffrey Butler Cycles, and Charlie Roberts who supplied me with the bikes I rode when winning the British Championships. Former World Sprint Champion John Nicholson also supported me with equipment and advice (and taught me how to drive). Thank you to former World Champions Norman Sheil and Reg Harris who had confidence in me from the very start and passed on their valuable knowledge. It was Paul Medhurst and Danny Clark who persuaded me to make the leap into the professional ranks; they are an important part of this story.

There were many people in Belgium and Holland who supported me. Firstly, thanks to Oscar Dhaemers, the Director of the Ghent Sportpaleis. There were many others who offered advice, guidance and hospitality in those early days in Ghent. It is a long list of people who care passionately about cycling and wanted to see me succeed: Alain De Roo and family, Bernard Stoops, Raf Dierickx and family, Marleen Bakkers and family, Etienne Bauwens, Staf Boone, Marcel Rijckaert, Frau Oelen and family. At the races I was supported by soigneurs and mechanics, including Gust Nassens, Angus Fraser, and others.

When I first took over De Ver Cycles I was helped by Monty and Grant Young from Condor Cycles, along with Peter Murphy and Nico Sport Clothing. A big thank you to John Estick who built my first website over 20 years ago and started me selling online. There are many people who have supported me in the shop over the years: Paul Searle, Jason Wheeler, Mark Turner, Pauline Stokoe, Ian Harmon, Steve Simpson, Troy Fraser, Julian Morgan, 'Maverick', Charlie Allen, Eric Whitmarsh, Junior Black, Dexter Stewart and customers Terry King, David Phillips, Eddie Hughes, Steve and Sally Avery, Dr Rob George, Nathan Morris, Johan Thisanayagam, Delroy Riely, Wayne Hoilett, Justin Carpenter, Martin Wiles, Mark Dibblin, Gareth Hughes, Leo Curtin, Karla Winter, Andy Prosser, Ethan, Leo and the Hayter family, Caroline Wilson, Ed Benton, Roger Murray, and many more, so please forgive me if I haven't mentioned you.

Thank you to the key members in our Team De Ver Cycling Club, Giles Barnard, Mike Gibbons, Simon Godfrey, Patricia Umunna, Fran Bourne, Everard White, Hugh Scott, Justas Stanisauskas, Helga Rahim, Drew Hyde. Thank you to Paul Jones, James Spackman, and the team at Bloomsbury for making this happen.

Finally, last but not least, thank you to my devoted wife Mia, and my children Germain, Robert and Grace for their support over the years.

PAUL:
I'd like to thank Maurice for sharing his story with me, for his time and kindness. Writing someone's story with them is a privilege and a joy. Mia has been a constant support throughout this process. Thanks also to Gracie for reading the book and giving brilliant feedback, as

well as sorting out images and scans. Eddie Hughes was also kind enough to read an early draft and offer sage advice.

Thanks to Jon Hughes and Andy Cook for advice and support at key moments. Thank you to Jools Walker for her time, openness and advice at the outset. Simon Smythe is a hero, constantly supportive and encouraging and I'm particularly grateful for his help with access to the image archive. Thank you to Simon Richardson and all the staff at *Cycling Weekly*, past and present; Keith Bingham especially. This magazine is a big part of my life and research.

There are people to thank in Ghent, firstly Guy Vermeiren for the press pass. Thanks also to the unendingly charming and brilliant Fred Wright and Ethan Hayter. Thanks to everyone who was there and had a great time and got really drunk with me, including anyone from Brixton Cycles, Olly and Chris, Fred Wright's parents. Thank you Dee for the time off so I could go in the first place (and for being brilliant). The staff and students at Nailsea School have been kind/bemused and supportive of this thing I do. It is a lovely, heart-warming place to work. The Bristol cycling community have been great; people like Jack Luke, Joe Norledge, Kieran Ellis, Adam Ferris, Steve Green, Richard Spink and anyone in Bristol South CC.

On a personal level, deep and heartfelt thanks to the amazing Helen, for being supportive and brilliant throughout this process and in my life. Thank you to Elliot and Penny for supporting my trips to Ghent in return for copious amounts of Belgian chocolate. They love Maurice and talk about him all the time, especially the time he took us all out for a lovely dinner in Bristol. Elliot would like it noted that he still wants a ride in Maurice's car.

Lastly, thank you to Charlotte Croft, Sarah Skipper and everyone at Bloomsbury who believed in and supported this book from the outset. Sarah has been instrumental in bringing this to the page, she is brilliant. Thank you to James Spackman, someone who loves cycling and loves books, and when he finds a project that combines these does everything he can to get it into the hands of the reader.

INDEX

Page numbers in italics are photographs.